Sociological Theory: Uses and Unities

for Barbara

Sociological Theory
Uses and Unities

Stephen Mennell

Nelson

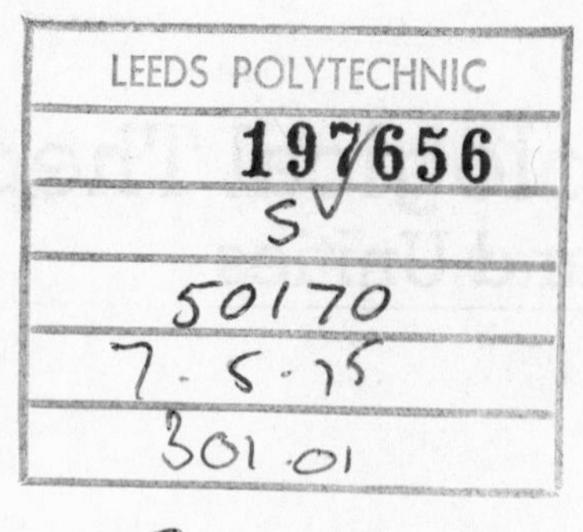

Thomas Nelson and Sons Ltd.
36 Park Street London W1Y 4DE

Nelson (Africa) Ltd.
PO Box 18123 Nairobi Kenya

Thomas Nelson (Australia) Ltd.
597 Little Collins Street Melbourne Victoria 3000

Thomas Nelson and Sons (Canada) Ltd.
81 Curlew Drive, Don Mills Ontario

Thomas Nelson (Nigeria) Ltd.
PO Box 336, Apapa Lagos

First published in Great Britain by Thomas Nelson and Sons Ltd., 1974

ISBN (hardback) 0 17 711121 6
ISBN (paperback) 0 17 712121 1

Printed in Great Britain by
Willmer Brothers Limited, Birkenhead

Contents

Preface vii

Introduction 1
On the meanings of 'Sociological Theory'
Notes **6**

1. Action 7
Skinner *versus* Chomsky **9**
George Herbert Mead, Social Behaviourism and Symbolic Interactionism **13**
Durkheim and 'Social Facts' **18**
Weber and Social Action **22**
Talcott Parsons and the 'Voluntaristic Theory of Action' **27**
The Action Perspective in Sociological Research **30**
Conclusions **34**
Notes **36**

2. Knowledge 39
Language and Cognition **40**
Alfred Schutz and Sociological Phenomenology **45**
Berger and the Sociology of Religion **50**
The Ethnomethodologists **51**
Lévi-Strauss and Structuralism **61**
Conclusions **67**
Notes **68**

3. Interaction 70
Roles **72**
The Inadequacy of the Dyad **78**
Games, Numbers and Social Complexity **81**
Conclusions **89**
Notes **89**

4. Power 91
Social Exchange Theory **93**
Resources for Power **102**
The Creation and Distribution of Power **107**
The Elusiveness of Power: A Case-Study **112**
Notes **114**

5. Social Integration 116
Specialization, Interdependence and the Division of Labour **117**
Collective Action **119**
Interdependence and Constraint **121**
On Consensus **123**
On Conflict **128**
Group Interests, Group Consciousness and the Structure of Conflict **131**
Changes since Marx **135**
Conclusions **138**
Notes **139**

6. System Integration 141
Systems Analysis **143**
The Biological Analogy **147**
Merton's Critique of Functionalism **154**
The Problem of Teleology **156**
Three Escapes from Teleology **158**
Functionalism: The Indispensable Second-Best **164**
Notes **165**

Conclusion 168
Irony and Sociology

Bibliography 173

Index 185

Preface

This book has grown out of lectures I have given at the University of Exeter since 1967. I hope it will prove useful as a guide to some of sociology's more general theoretical problems and their relationship to social research. In a book of this size, it was obviously not possible to cover every topic which might be described as one of 'sociological theory'. Nor could all the subjects included be discussed in equal depth. So at several points I have included rather more references than strictly necessary, in lieu of formal 'suggestions for further reading'.

I should like to express my gratitude to the following colleagues and friends who read parts of earlier drafts of the book and made most helpful comments and suggestions: Michael and Joy Cooper, Robert Dowse, Margaret Hewitt and Fred Lewes, all of Exeter; David Thorns, now at the University of Auckland; Martin Harris, University of Salford; and Eric Dunning, University of Leicester. Earl Hopper of the London School of Economics read the entire book in draft and discussed its central arguments with me in detail. Between them, they greatly improved the final product; but I must, of course, accept responsibility for all the remaining imperfections.

Dr Norbert Elias very kindly gave me permission to quote from forthcoming translations of his books by Eric Dunning and by Grace Morrissey and myself. I am also indebted to the following for permission to quote passages and use diagrams: Oxford University Press, New York, for passages from Max Weber's *Economy and Society* originally published in *From Max Weber* (translated by H. H. Gerth and C. Wright Mills, 1946) and in *The Theory of Social and Economic Organisation* (translated by A. M. Henderson and Talcott Parsons, 1947).

The Linguistic Society of America, for the quotation on page 11 from Noam Chomsky's review of B. F. Skinner's *Verbal Behaviour*, in *Language*, 1959.

Claude Lévi-Strauss and the American Folklore Society, for Figure 2, which first appeared in Lévi-Strauss's article 'The Structural Study of Myth', *Journal of American Folklore*, 78, No. 270, 1955.

Juventa Verlag for Figure 3, which is based on a table in Norbert Elias's *Was ist Soziologie*? (1970).

Dr Elizabeth Bott and the Editor of *Human Relations* for Figure 4, which is taken from Dr Bott's article 'Urban Families: Conjugal Roles and Social Networks', in *Human Relations,* 1955.

The Editor of the *American Journal of Sociology* for Figure 7, which is taken from James S. Coleman's article 'Foundations for a Theory of Collective Decisions', in that Journal (1966).

Appleton-Century-Crofts for Figure 8, taken from Hubert M. Blalock's article 'The Formalization of Sociological Theory', in *Theoretical Sociology: Perspectives and Developments* (J. C. McKinney and E. A. Tiryakian, eds.).

I should also like to thank Professor G. Duncan Mitchell for arranging reduced teaching duties for me during Spring 1973, and Rosalind Webber and Jenny Maher for typing the manuscript. Most of all, however, I have to thank my wife Barbara for her encouragement, for intercepting split infinitives, and for making me stay at home and write the book.

S.J. MENNELL

Exeter, September 1973

Introduction

On the meanings of Sociological Theory

'Sociological theory' is not sociological theory. At least, it should not be imagined that the body of ideas to which that label is usually attached is the only part of sociological knowledge which can be dignified as 'theory'. The real business of sociology is empirical research and explaining why society is as it is. Theories are formalized and ultimately testable explanations, and they are accumulated in large measure in the ordinary process of sociological research—in urban sociology, political sociology, industrial sociology, sociology of religion, and all the other specialized fields of sociological investigation. Theories are attempts to explain limited and specified properties of social reality. That reality is so immense and complex that no theory, however well authenticated, ever represents more than a drop in the ocean. Some theories are broader in scope than others, but no theory can ever explain everything. Many sociologists might therefore be inclined to argue that, to get on with their research, all they need is a knowledge of previous research, of statistics and research methods, and perhaps a little logic and philosophy of science. Yet most courses in sociology contain a component which does not entirely fall under any of these headings, and which is by convention known as 'sociological theory'. This book is about 'sociological theory' as thus conventionally understood.

What, then, is 'sociological theory' in this customary sense? It is a rather amorphous collection of topics. On the one hand, it certainly tends to include the discussion of some epistemological issues, such as the never-ending disputes as to whether 'sociology is a science', and how it is possible for the sociologist to be at once involved in the social world and its detached interpreter. These questions hinge as much on our understanding of the social process called natural science as of that called social science. They are matters of 'metatheory'—theories about the nature of theories—which properly belong to the philosophy of science and theory of knowledge. They will not be especially prominent in this book, for in the end the proof of the pudding is in the eating—does sociology yield reliable and cumulative knowledge, or does it not? On the other hand, 'sociological theory' also tends to cover matters very much closer to empirical research—discussion of theories about social roles, relative deprivation and reference groups, for example. These seem to be included because they are of wide relevance but do not belong to any one of the conventional problem areas—religion, industry, politics and the rest—which are traditional in sociology departments. Merton (1968) calls these 'theories of the middle range', but they are in fact real, empirically rooted, theories.

Much of 'sociological theory', however, is best described neither as metatheory nor as theory *tout court*. It is what Dahrendorf (1967 :30) terms 'para-theory'.

> 'Para-theory' describes all statements before, around and after sociological theory which are incapable of empirical test themselves, but are definitely geared towards testable theories.

Philosophers of science of various shades of opinion have increasingly recognized the importance of 'pre-theoretic elements in theory'. These include taxonomies, conceptual schemes, and the general assumptions—conscious, semiconscious and unconscious—which scientists make about their subjects. They are not directly testable themselves, but enter into or point towards more limited and specific propositions. The value of concepts especially is not to be assessed in terms of truth or falsity, but in terms of clarity and usefulness when employed in theories.

Sociologists have given a great deal of time and attention to the merits of rival concepts and rival approaches. Yet not surprisingly they have achieved little unanimity, for they have often discussed issues of 'theory' in a vacuum, failing to relate them adequately to practical problems of empirical research. Too often, systems of 'sociological theory' in the traditional sense have appeared to attempt to explain everything at once. They expressed an emotional need to map out and label everything observed in the social world, but did not *explain* very much. Social order and social change were two problems typically approached in this way. Of course it is absurd to look for *a* theory to explain why societies are stable or *a* theory to explain why they change. But it is not absurd to develop theories which explain how particular features of society originated or why they persist. And any theory which successfully explains that something is static because certain specific conditions are met, also necessarily explains that it would change were these conditions no longer to be met. That is why, though social change is of central interest to sociologists, there is no separate chapter on social change in this book. Though there can be studies of particular processes of change, there is no separate and distinct 'theory of social change'. Andreski (1972:63) put the point well:

> As Heraclitus said, everything changes all the time; and, therefore, a work offering a theory of social change without specifying any restrictions should in strict logic amount to a comprehensive treatise on general theory.

Theories about all aspects of social organization implicitly have something to say about the conditions of social change. This should be apparent in every chapter; if it is not, I hope at least to have avoided implying any general tendency to social stasis.

In his widely read book, *The Structure of Scientific Revolutions* (1962), Thomas Kuhn suggests that competing schools of basic theory are characteristic of an immature science in the stage before the establishment of its first generally accepted 'paradigm', or framework of fundamental assumptions. It is often said that sociology has not yet acquired such a paradigm. Yet fruitful traditions of research have been established in many branches of empirical sociology. In the higher realms of sociological theory, however, not only is there no recognizable paradigm, but sociologists often seem not to aspire to acquiring one. In textbooks on the history of sociological thought, the great thinkers of the past are divided up into schools and played off against each other. Their different concerns are seen as contradictory rather than complementary,[1] and there seems little expectation that things will ever be different. Alan Dawe (1970) speaks of 'The Two Sociologies', one individual-centred, the other system-centred, with small confidence either that one or the other will triumph, or that the two will ever be synthesized. To the present day, new sociological sects arise from time to time, loudly proclaiming their own final solution to the sociology problem, denying any merit in rival approaches, yet remaining minority sects.

With so little agreement in the higher reaches of sociology, it is not surprising that some have gone so far as to propound a *chacun à son goût* view of social reality. Dahrendorf (1959:159) suggested that reality is in some sense Janus-faced (integration and conflict being the two unpropitious faces) and, despairing of ever encompassing both aspects in one theoretical framework, appeared to leave the choice of reality to the whim of each sociologist. This is at odds with Macaulay's wise remark:

> *Experience* can never be divided or even appear to be divided, except with reference to some hypothesis. When we say that one fact is inconsistent with another fact, we mean only that it is inconsistent with *the theory* which we have founded on that fact. But if the fact be certain, the unavoidable conclusion is that our theory is false . . . [1889:162, his italics]

The remarkable thing is that supposedly profound disagreements at the level of 'grand theory' are often more apparent than real. Merton (1968:43) asserts that many generally accepted theories 'of the middle range' are consistent not only with a wide range of empirical findings, but with several competing systems of grand theory. It is easy to see why. Such hoary debates as that between 'consensus' and 'conflict' views of society are entirely misconceived. That issue can never be settled in realms of disembodied 'theory', for it is essentially an empirical question whether a society, or group within a society, of a particular type, at a particular time and in a particular situation, will show a high level of conflict or consensus. We might as well argue whether a glass of water is better described as half full or half empty. Problems of measurement are here more profound than problems of conceptualization. Not all 'theoretical' disputes, of course, can be dismissed in this way; many are rooted in ancient and unresolved philosophical issues. Yet even recognizing this to be so, the disjunction between sociological theory and sociological research often seems to be unnecessarily wide. So, in this book, I have attempted in every chapter to illustrate the relevance of 'theory' to research.

The viewpoint put forward in this book may be too eclectic for some tastes. My position is nevertheless consistently (I hope) one of methodological individualism.[2] George Homans's celebrated plea (1964) to 'bring men back in' to sociological explanations was pertinent and timely. I agree with Homans that the highest order propositions in sociological theories are generalizations about how typical people behave in typical social situations. That does not mean that such generalizations can be arrived at without considering the influence of the social context in shaping the individual. Nor does it imply that I share Homans's predilection for behaviourist psychology, though in fact the generalizations about people's behaviour needed for many sociological purposes are so simple that they are compatible with several different schools of psychology, and are often so obvious that they are not explicitly stated. Still less does this mean that I am a psychological reductionist (nor is Homans, though he once thought that he was). Propositions about the behaviour of individuals may be an essential ingredient of any social scientific explanation, but they are not the only ingredient. Statements about the structure of groups, situations and systems also enter into explanation. A social norm, for instance, can only be a property of several people. It is true that it can be *defined* and observed in the activities of individuals, but it cannot be *reduced* to a psychological characteristic of any of them.[3] Another illustration is macroeconomic theory, which is very clearly methodologically individualist. Its propositions about consumption, saving and investment functions are based firmly on the behaviour of individuals taking their own economic decisions, and so are, in a sense, psychological. But its predictions about the dynamics of the economic system stem also from the observation that decisions to save and to invest are taken by two not entirely coinciding sets of people. That statement can in no sense be reduced to psychology.

This general point of view is reflected in the sequence of the following chapters. Each deals with an analytic problem rather than historically with a school of thought. Though the 'founding fathers' are frequently mentioned where their work is still a living influence, I have tried to avoid simple ancestor worship. Starting with a discussion of the assumptions sociologists need to make about the nature of human action and knowledge, the chapters gradually become more concerned with the structural properties of social systems. Chapter 1 skirts the old philosophical problem of free will and determinism, recasting it for sociologists' purposes as a problem of method. Chapter 2 explores the relationship between the mind and society, covering in particular phenomenological approaches in sociology and Lévi-Strauss's structural analyses of myth. Then Chapter 3 discusses how individuals' actions intermesh to form patterns of progressively greater complexity. The next two chapters review the patterns of power and control, of co-operation, competition and conflict which emerge in complex social structures, while Chapter 6 discusses the difficulties of analysing such structures as 'systems', raising the old issue of functionalism. Men having been brought back in, however, they do not gradually disappear again as the book proceeds. On the contrary, it is argued that causal or systemic analysis (purged of functionalist fallacies) and analysis in terms of individuals' actions are both essential. For people's imperfect knowledge of and control over the structures of systems in which they are enmeshed is crucial to our understanding of social processes.

Notes

1. Of course there are exceptions to this remark—such as Fletcher (1971).
2. For a collection of papers on the issue of methodological individualism *versus* holism, see O'Neill (1973).
3. May Brodbeck (1958) elaborates the position of which this is intended to be a very brief statement.

1. Action

'The central problem of social science,' writes George Homans, 'remains the one posed in his own language and in his own era by Hobbes: How does the behaviour of individuals create the characteristics of groups?' (Homans 1967:106). The fundamental explanatory principles of sociology, Homans argues, are psychological. The highest-level generalizations a sociologist can make concern the behaviour of human beings. Homans is confident that we already know these broad principles of psychology. Sociology's central problem, therefore, 'is not analysis but synthesis, not the discovery of fundamental principles, for they are already known, but the demonstration of how the general principles, exemplified in the behaviour of many men and groups, combine over time to generate, maintain and eventually change the more enduring social phenomena.'

The majority of sociologists probably feel uneasy with Homans's bold assertion of the logical relationship between psychology and sociology. Certainly the actions and interactions of individuals do intermesh to produce and change many kinds of social groups. Yet is the individual's behaviour, mind and personality not equally shaped by society? For mankind has never existed other than in societies. Society precedes any particular human organism; everyone is born into society, grows up within it and experiences it, in broad outline, as fixed and given. So is it not equally true that psychology must be explained by reference to the social?

Such reflections have led to repeated arguments about the primacy of the 'individual' or 'society' as a starting-point for sociology. In the way it is usually presented, this is a chicken-and-egg problem. Norbert Elias (1970, ch. 4) has suggested reasons for its persistence as a dilemma among sociologists. It is not a substantive, empirical problem, but a conceptual one. Our very terminology encourages us to conceive of 'individual' and 'society' as separate and static entities, rather than as inseparable aspects of one complex and constantly changing set of interrelationships. It is fairly easy to see that 'society' is an abstraction and that it is composed of innumerable human beings, thinking, feeling and behaving. It is a less familiar thought that 'the individual', too, is something of an abstraction; for by 'individual' is meant something more than a human organism. We mean an organism that has already learned much in social relationships, and has absorbed ways of thinking, feeling and behaving from other people who constitute 'society'. There is therefore no sharp break between the subject matter of sociology and that of psychology, though the two subjects differ in focus. Psychologists may be more interested in differences between particular individuals, but sociology cannot avoid being concerned with the general process by which human organisms are turned into human beings by the process of 'socialization', as well as with how their actions intermesh to form and change social patterns. So although Homans is correct in asserting that the logically prior propositions in sociological explanations concern how real people behave, this by no means establishes the *causal* priority of the 'individual' over 'society'.

What *kind* of psychological propositions are necessary for sociological purposes? Homans himself believes that the general principles needed are those readily available in behavioural psychology. (See especially Homans 1961, ch. 2.) By that is meant the school of psychology which, on the basis of experimental work, largely with animals, formulates propositions about how behaviour is shaped by learning or 'operant conditioning'. It is sometimes called learning or S-R (stimulus-response) theory. Behaviourists take a very clear stand on two philosophical issues which have long plagued social scientists. One is the ancient question of 'free will *versus* determinism'. Are people's actions determined by social or other forces, so that any appearance of freedom of choice is illusory, or can they really follow their own purposes and make choices? The second problem is whether we can know anything of other people's 'inner mental states' and particularly whether such knowledge can be used as scientific data. Behaviourists assume, rightly I think, that if behaviour is to be explained scientifically, it must be possible to give a causal account of it and to predict it. But they further assume something more dubious, that if behaviour is predictable, it must be inevitable and determined. 'I myself believe that what each of us does is absolutely determined,' writes Homans.[1] If behaviour is inevitable, then our subjective impressions that we are choosing what we do must be illusory, for our choices cannot be predetermined. So it is not surprising that behaviourists also hold subjective purposes, intentions and mental states to be irrelevant to the explanation of behaviour. A number of sociologists (see, for example, those represented in Burgess and Bushell, 1969) would agree with Homans in accepting behavioural psychology as a basis for sociological theory. Many more, variously described as social action theorists, symbolic interactionists and phenomenologists, join in rejecting behaviourism. The issues at stake can best be seen in the famous controversy between B.F. Skinner, Homans's 'favourite experimental psychologist' (Homans 1961:18), and the linguist Noam Chomsky.

Skinner versus Chomsky

Skinner has been the most celebrated recent exponent of behaviourism, expounding his views in a series of elegant books (1953, 1957, 1972). Skinner seeks to give a 'functional' or causal explanation of behaviour patterns; for this scientific purpose the human organism is to be regarded with detachment as differing in no fundamental way from lower organisms. Man, if necessary, must be seen as a machine. To explain behaviour as caused by inner mental states is, in Skinner's view, to walk up a blind alley. 'The objection to inner states is not that they do not exist, but that they are not relevant in functional analysis' (1953:35). Skinner sees any psychology whose primary causes are internal and mental as akin to astrology and alchemy.

> The practice of looking inside an organism for an explanation of behaviour has tended to obscure the variables which are immediately available for scientific analysis. These variables lie outside the organism, in its immediate environment and in its environmental history. They have a physical status to which the usual techniques of science are adapted, and they make it possible to explain behaviour as other subjects are explained in science. [1953:31]

The kind of explanation acceptable to Skinner can best be illustrated by one of his own experiments in 'operant conditioning' the behaviour of pigeons. A pigeon in a 'Skinner box' is fed by means of an electrically operated retractable tray. Once the pigeon is accustomed to this source of food, its behaviour can be shaped by the scientist. As it moves around the box, the pigeon occasionally and randomly raises its head above the usual height. Whenever its head reaches a predetermined level, the scientist operates the tray and feeds the pigeon. The bird is soon observed to emit the behaviour much more frequently. By manipulating external stimuli, the experimenter changes the bird's normal posture. The change is brought about by the selective reinforcement of one element in an originally random repertoire of behaviour, and can be explained without any reference to the pigeon's mental processes. Skinner soon extends this argument to human behaviour. For instance, by depriving a man of water for a period, or by administering a uretic drug, we can increase the probability that he will drink a glass of water. His action can then be explained without reference to his internal state of thirst, which we cannot directly observe. The causal chain consists of three links: (a) an operation performed on the organism from without (deprivation of water); (b) an inner condition (thirst); and (c) a kind of behaviour (drinking). For the behaviourist, any reference to the middle link is redundant to parsimonious theory building.

It may be objected that quenching a thirst is a very simple example of human behaviour, directly related to physiological need. Our behaviour is typically far more complex and much more remotely linked to biological necessity. Skinner is quite right in replying that complexity in itself is not an adequate objection to his views—complex phenomena merely require a more elaborate theory, which may in practice, it is true, be difficult to construct.

> Self-determination does not follow from complexity. Difficulty in calculating the orbit of a fly does not prove capriciousness, though it may make it impossible to prove anything else. [1953:20]

But the sources of that complexity are relevant. *Control* is essential to Skinner's theory; he predicts and therefore explains behaviour from known and controlled stimuli. He could not explain the behaviour of even a pigeon in the wild, a pigeon whose history is unknown. And human beings in the wild are, of course, capable of much more complex learning. Sociologists are typically interested in very complex kinds of behaviour resulting from the past history and biography of individuals and groups, which is generally unknown and unknowable to the determinedly 'external' observer. Nor is much of human behaviour susceptible to transfer to the controlled situation of the laboratory without being hopelessly distorted.

Where the external stimuli to which the organism has been exposed are unknown, even Skinner admits the desirability of information about inner states.

> Independent information about the second link [inner conditions] would obviously permit us to predict the third [behaviour] without recourse to the first [external stimuli]. It would be a preferable type of variable because it would be non-historic; the first link may be in the past history of the organism, but the second is a current condition. *Direct information about the second link is, however, seldom, if ever, available.* [1953:34, my italics]

What a curious assertion the last sentence contains! Certainly, we are unable to talk to pigeons, but we can ask human beings what is going on inside them. They *can* give us an account of their thoughts and internal states. Their accounts may not be entirely accurate but they are likely to be more so—and more valid—than behavioural explanations based on 'speculative history'. And explanations in terms of external stimuli must be speculative in uncontrolled, non-experimental conditions. (Of course, we could ask them to give an account of their past 'stimulus history', but the logical contradiction there is too obvious to dwell upon.)

A more profound issue still arose when Skinner sought to extend his theories to that most human kind of behaviour—verbal behaviour (Skinner 1957). It was this book which was subjected to a devastating critique by Noam Chomsky (1959). The gist of Chomsky's case can be captured in one extended quotation:

> A typical example of 'stimulus control' for Skinner would be the response to a piece of music with the utterance *Mozart* or to a painting with the response *Dutch*. These responses are asserted to be 'under the control of extremely subtle properties' of the physical object or event. Suppose instead of saying *Dutch* we had said *Clashes with the wallpaper*, *I thought you liked abstract work*, *Never saw it before*, *Tilted*, *Hanging too low*, *Beautiful*, *Hideous*, *Remember our camping trip last summer?*, or whatever else came into our minds when looking at a picture (in Skinnerian translation, whatever other responses exist in sufficient strength). Skinner could only say that each of these responses is under the control of some other stimulus property of the physical object. If we look at a red chair and say *red*, the stimulus is under the control of the stimulus 'redness'; if we say *chair*, it is under the control of the collection of properties (for Skinner, the object) 'chairness', and similarly for any other response. The device is as simple as it is empty. Since properties are free for the asking . . . we can account for a wide class of responses in terms of Skinnerian functional analysis by identifying the 'controlling stimuli'. But the word 'stimulus' has lost all objectivity in this usage. Stimuli are no longer part of the outside physical world; they are driven back into the organism. We identify the stimulus when we hear the response. [Chomsky 1959:31–2, his italics]

Human language is far more flexible and elaborate than any means of communication used by other animals. Behaviourism according to Chomsky, is quite unable to explain one of the most striking of all features of language. Why is it that all normal people have the capacity to utter new sentences which have never before been spoken by themselves, nor very likely by anyone else? Why is the listener able to understand sentences never heard before, and why is he able to determine whether they are grammatical and 'make sense'?

> The idea that a person has a 'verbal repertoire' — a stock of utterances that he produces by 'habit' on an appropriate occasion — is a myth, totally at variance with the observed use of language. [Chomsky 1967:400]

Innovation, not repetition, is the rule.

Chomsky's own proposed solution to this problem is too involved to be adequately explored here.[2] He points out that the language actually used by parents gives the child who is learning to talk only a relatively limited amount of evidence from which to acquire the normal flexible use of vocabulary and, more relevantly, grammar. Furthermore, in the formative years, the child's use of language is simply too different from that of adults to be regarded as a direct mirroring of what he hears.[3] Chomsky's answer is that the child has to 'infer' the 'generative grammar' of his language from the evidence available to him, and can then use this to generate grammatical but *new* utterances. Children are obviously not born with a propensity to speak one language rather than another, and superficially this might seem to lend support to the learning theorists' view. But probably the 'deep structure' of every language is much the same. Certainly there is evidence that the human mind processes data in orderly fashion according to rules of 'transformational grammars'.

It will be seen that Chomsky's arguments have a bearing on the question of internal mental processes and, to a lesser extent, on 'free will *versus* determinism'. The latter is ultimately a metaphysical issue incapable of empirical proof either way. Chomsky's work does, however, suggest that it is far simpler to assume that people are capable of a degree of choice in their use of language, and, by extension, in their social behaviour, than it is to speculate about unidentifiable stimuli determining every apparent choice. Obviously everyone is born into some specific niche of society, and much of his behaviour can be accounted for by simple mechanisms of learning and habituation. It may be that, in some fundamental sense, behaviour at one moment is determined by the total history of the organism up to that moment. But, for all practical purposes, much behaviour of interest to the sociologist is sufficiently complex that it appears *as if* people pursue purposes and make choices. It is most important to recognize that to adopt the working hypothesis that people are, to some extent, capable of reflecting upon and choosing between the courses of action possible in their social situation by no means precludes a causal account of these actions. As John Stuart Mill argued (1843, Book VI; Fletcher 1971 :I, 201-5), our past choices themselves become the causes of our future actions. We may to some extent be able to choose our career but the choice we make becomes a potent influence on the future course of our life. Moreover people's characters and ways of life become settled and established; therefore they are predictable, not as certainties but as probabilities. Even if people are in a position to behave in other than the predicted manner, they usually have no reason to do so. So, fortunately, for purposes of social science it is not necessary to meet the 'free will' issue at the metaphysical level.

What Chomsky does show more conclusively is that linguistic behaviour is beyond the reach of the behaviourists' present methods, and that they are implicitly 'driven back into the organism'. Again by extension, this appears to be true of much social behaviour, in which language plays so important a part. At any rate, if we accept strictly 'external' behaviourist methods as the only 'scientific' way to study human behaviour, we must necessarily exclude from study great areas of social life of great interest to sociologists. What is needed is a psychological and methodological basis for sociology which recognizes that human behaviour, beliefs and knowledge are learned in society, and yet at the same time does justice to the human capacity to reflect upon and modify behaviour, and makes people's intentions, feelings and purposes available for investigation.

George Herbert Mead, Social Behaviourism and Symbolic Interactionism

Many different schools of sociology have rejected the behaviourist position. Much as they differ among themselves, they share the basic tenet of 'subjective realism' (Tiryakian 1965), which is best captured in W.I. Thomas's dictum 'if men define situations as real, they are real in their consequences'. In America, one such school of thought grew out of the pragmatist philosophy and psychology of William James (1842–1910) and John Dewey (1859–1952). Pragmatist ideas were first carried into sociology by Charles Horton Cooley

(1864–1928), famous for his concepts of 'primary group' and the 'looking-glass self', and by Thomas.

George Herbert Mead (1863–1931) is, however, the theoretically central figure in the development of the school of thought which he called 'social behaviourism', but which is known more familiarly as 'symbolic interactionism', a label first applied to it in 1937 by Herbert Blumer, one of Mead's chief disciples (Blumer 1969:1). Mead was professor of philosophy and social psychology at the University of Chicago, where he had great influence during the golden years of 'Chicago sociology'.[4] Yet his thought made its main impact on sociology beyond Chicago only after his death, for he published little and the books on which his fame rests were posthumously salvaged from students' notes (Mead 1932, 1934, 1936, 1938).

Mead says his social psychology is behaviouristic in the sense of starting from the observable activity of the ongoing social process.

> But it is not behaviouristic in the ense of ignoring the inner experience of the individual — the inner phase of that process or activity. On the contrary, it is particularly concerned with the rise of such experience within the process as a whole. It simply works from the outside to the inside instead of from the inside to the outside, so to speak, in its endeavour to determine how such experience does arise within the process. [Mead 1934:7–8]

The lower animals interact and communicate with each other, but their communication is limited to the *conversation of gestures.* A gesture is part of the social act which acts directly as a stimulus to the other animal. A dog attacks by biting. The initial gesture is the baring of its teeth. This stimulates the other dog to respond by adopting a defensive posture and perhaps bearing its teeth too; which in turn acts as a stimulus to the first dog. So the dog-fight begins. But there is no need to assume deliberation and conscious interpretation by the dogs of the other's actions. Skinner could well explain the process as consisting of learned responses. The interaction is non-symbolic. Gestures of this kind remain important in human behaviour. Mead points to boxing and fencing. The boxer or fencer, who has trained and practised, parries a punch or thrust without conscious deliberation. And just as the involuntary tensing of the animal which has sensed danger communicates danger to the rest of the herd, so, in human crowds, panic can be communicated by signs expressed involuntarily.

Man's unique ability, however, is the use of symbols. The difference between a gesture and a symbol for Mead is the difference between punching someone and shaking a fist at him. Shaking a fist normally communicates not the possibility of attack, but the *idea* of anger in the shaker's mind. The person at whom the fist is shaken is able to interpret it as meaning hostility; it is the *idea* of anger which has been communicated from one mind to another. Rather than calling forth an appropriate physical, observable response, the *significant symbol* answers to a *meaning* in the second person's experience. But by far the most important category of significant symbols are those made vocally, called language.

Sounds, obviously, do not have intrinsic meaning. Their significance, the connection between a sound and its object (whether a physical or 'abstract' object) is learned in social groups: this is how symbols come to have the same (or much the same) meaning for all members of a group. We have to learn the connection between the sounds produced on uttering the word 'chair', and that class of objects sharing the minimum characteristics such as are listed under that word in a dictionary. Yet this may be slightly misleading. It should not be taken to imply that words merely serve to express pre-existent inner meanings. In Mead's words:

> Language does not simply symbolize a situation or object which is already there in advance; it makes possible the existence or appearance of that situation or object, for it is part of the mechanism whereby that situation or object is created. [1934:78]

Mead could not have anticipated the recent work on language associated with Chomsky, but he appreciated that the millions of meanings which can be processed in the human brain make possible integrated, precise, differentiated, yet plastic social behaviour far beyond that possible in sub-human animals.

Mead argued that it is only by means of language that thinking can take place. Thought is made possible by the internalization of the symbolic communication of society. Man's unique use of language is the outward manifestation of his unique ability to think about himself as an object. Man is the only self-reflexive animal; the 'I' is able to regard the 'Me' as object. In consequence we are able to anticipate our future actions, to examine the likely outcome of a number of alternative courses of action, and to determine which of them to implement. From this stems the possibility of purposive action.[5] Mead's social behaviourism is thus seen to be very much at odds with behaviourism as conventionally understood.

Language, thought and reflection thus make possible highly complex behaviour. Verbal communication also makes it possible to learn a vast amount indirectly from other people. At the same time, Mead emphasized that the origins of these capacities in any individual can only be understood by looking at his social experience. The very young child does not have the self-reflexive ability, cannot take himself as the object of his thoughts. The genesis of the self is to be found in the social process.

The child's acquisition of language begins quite early, when cognitive development first permits the discrimination of others' responses.

> The world of the infant is at first a motley confusion of sights, sounds, and smells. He becomes able to differentiate a portion of this world only when he is able to designate it to himself by means of a symbol. Initially the infant acts in random fashion, and a socialized other responds to random gestures in a meaningful way, thus giving a social definition to the random gesture of the infant. Once the infant understands the meaning of the gesture (e.g. a cry, a wave of the arm) . . . that gesture has become a symbol for him. [Rose 1962:15]

The development of self-consciousness is, however, not seen clearly until the child begins to understand the set of relationships expressed by the personal pronouns, 'I', 'we', 'you', 'he', 'she', and 'they'. As Elias notes,

> the individual positions in this set of relationships cannot be treated separately . . . The function of the pronoun 'I' in human communication can only be understood in the context of all the other positions to which the other terms in the series refer. [Elias 1970:133]

When the child demonstrates its understanding of these relationships by using 'I' to refer to that which others address as 'you', it is exhibiting the beginnings of self-consciousness, its ability to think of itself as objects, the origins of its 'self'. Close observation of children at play shows that at first they do not really 'play with' each other, but merely in each other's company. Each child's activity is repetitive and solitary, unco-ordinated with that of the other child. Analysis of their 'conversation' reveals it to be not a dialogue but two monologues. A crucial development takes place when the child begins in play to act out the role of 'mother' to its dolls, or 'cowboy' and 'indian'. Mead calls this *taking the role of the other*. It marks a stage in the growth of reflexive self-awareness, but cowboys-and-indians requires minimal co-ordination. The rules can be varied at whim, the role abandoned or changed at will. Only much later does the child become capable of taking part in more elaborate games like football with established rules. In order to play his own part in such a game, the individual has to be able to put himself in place of all the other participants. His role only exists in relation to the roles of others. Each player has to take the role of the *generalized other*; he has to see his own moves as they appear from the perspective of the other participants before carrying them out. The game is a microcosm of social life. Taking the role of the other is involved in all symbolic communication, because, to communicate, we have to anticipate the interpretation the hearer will put on our words. And only thus is organized, co-operative activity possible.

The concept of the generalized other is central to Mead's view of how society shapes the individual's personality and his actions.

> It is in the form of the generalized other that the social process influences the behaviour of the individuals involved in it and carrying it on, that is, that the community exercises control over the conduct of its individual members; for it is in this form that the social process or community enters as a determining factor into the individual's thinking. [Mead 1934: 155]

Sociologists have in the past tended to pay a great deal of attention to Mead's discussion of the generalized other and neglect other aspects of his work. Anselm Strauss has suggested that 'sociologists, who tend to be social determinists, read Mead as if he too were a social determinist' (Strauss 1964:xii-xiii). They have tended to transform Mead's 'generalized other' into the concept of 'culture', by which they mean 'an elaborate set of meanings and values, shared by members of a society, which guides much of [man's] behaviour' (Rose 1962:9), and which the individual learns during socialization. But, for all his awareness of social control and the place of the 'generalized other' within it, Mead certainly did not see dominant patterns of behaviour and social attitudes as mere external stimuli which the individual passively absorbed and replicated. This can be seen in two quotations from the less popular parts of his writings. From that on 'Society':

> A member of a community is not necessarily like other individuals because he is able to identify himself with them. There can be common content, common experience, without there being identity of function. A difference of functions does not preclude a common experience: it is possible for the individual to put himself in the place of the other although his function is different from the other . . . [T]hat sort of functionally differentiated personality [is quite different] to that which is simply common to all members of a community. [1934: 325]

And on the nature of attention:

> The human animal is an attentive animal . . . Our whole intelligent

process seems to lie in the attention which is selective of certain types of stimuli . . . Not only do we open the door to certain stimuli and close it to others, but our attention is an organizing as well as a selective process . . . Our attention enables us to organize the field in which we are going to act . . . One organism picks out one thing and another picks out a different one, since each is going to act in a different way. [1934: 25]

Durkheim and 'Social Facts'

Emile Durkheim (1858–1917) might at first appear to be entirely out of sympathy with Mead's approach to the study of society. It is a commonplace that one of the central themes of his work was his concern to establish the independence of sociology from psychology. His study of suicide (1951; orig. 1897), seemingly the most individual and 'psychological' of acts, was undertaken for that reason. He sought to demonstrate that individual psychology could not explain why some societies and social groups had higher rates of suicide than others. Suicide rates were an instance of a 'social fact', and social facts were to be explained by reference to other social facts. 'The determining cause of a social fact should be sought among the social facts preceding it and not among the states of the individual consciousness' (1938:110; orig 1895). Moreover, social facts were to be recognized by their *externality* to the individual and the *constraint* which they exercised over him (1938 :2). Even the *conscience collective,* the common orientation or outlook shared by members of a society, and its constituent *représentations collectives* were properties of the group, not of individual minds. This side of Durkheim's thought is summed up in his dictum 'Consider social facts as things' (1938:14).

This is, however, only one side of his thought, and highly misleading if considered alone. Durkheim was, in fact, struggling with exactly the same problem as Mead; unfortunately his mode of expression (and, perhaps, poor English translations) often seems to obscure the fact. What Durkheim consistently rejected was any attempt to explain diverse social patterns in terms of psychological constants. Individualistic psychology in the nineteenth century had tended to posit a universal 'human nature' apparently antecedent to society. Durkheim attacked introspectionism, which described the contents of the mind without accounting for how they got there (1953:32), but reserved his greatest scorn for those theories which explained behaviour in terms of biology or innate instincts. Many rival lists of 'basic instincts' have been advanced in the past; they are a very cheap form of explanation. Any item of behaviour, from sexual activity to butterfly collecting, can be 'explained' by attributing it to an instinct. If butterfly collecting is considered too specific to merit an instinct of its own, doubt arises as to which other instinct it is to be subsumed under, and how many separate instincts really exist. Durkheim readily saw that any theory involving constants of human nature was an inadequate explanation of the immense variety of human behaviour and social organization. Individualistic psychology could not explain why societies had different kinds of family patterns, or why one social group had higher suicide rates than another: 'the psychological factor is too general to predetermine the course of social phenomena' (1938:108).

Durkheim's less charitable remarks on the relationship of psychology to sociology need to be interpreted in the light of his perfectly valid criticisms of a good deal of psychology in, or immediately prior to, his day. They largely explain why he failed to recognize consistently that if individual psychology could not explain differing suicide *rates*, it could help to explain the *incidence* of suicide—why one particular person should commit suicide while others in a very similar social situation did not. Durkheim's problem was that he saw very clearly that individual psychology needed to be explained largely by reference to the individual's experience in society rather than by innate mental properties or innate biological drives. Sometimes this led him to write as if psychological processes were an irrelevant intervening variable between antecedent and succeeding social facts, and that no reference need be made to them. If that were so, individual organisms would be seen as passively absorbing and reproducing social patterns as automata, and it would be difficult to account for social change. Yet it is important to recognize that Durkheim was never opposed to consideration of inner mental processes as such. He recognized that man must be seen as a reflecting and reasoning creature, not as a puppet whose actions were utterly predetermined by the social and cultural environment.

> The more this faculty for understanding what happens within ourselves is developed, the more the subject's movements lose that automatism which is characteristic of physical life. The agent endowed with reason does not behave like a thing of which the activity can be reduced to a system of reflexes. He hesitates, feels his way, deliberates, and by that distinguishing mark he is recognized. External stimulation, instead of resulting immediately in movements, is halted in its progress and is subjected to *sui generis* elaboration; a more or less long period of time elapses before the expression in movement appears. This relative indetermination does not

> occur where there is no thinking mind, and with thought it increases. [1953: 3]

The pivot of Durkheim's work is his effort to reconcile this 'relative indetermination' with the undoubted power of society over the individual consciousness. In his first major book (1933, orig. 1893), he pointed out that, in primitive societies, to which he attributed 'mechanical solidarity', individuality was less developed than in complex societies with 'organic solidarity'. Individualism develops progressively with the division of labour. Mechanical solidarity is the consequence of people sharing very similar activities; they share not only a common way of life but very specific common beliefs and sentiments, the *conscience collective*. In complex societies with an advanced division of labour, people pursue different occupations and have different training and education; the *conscience collective* 'comes increasingly to be made up of highly generalized and indeterminate modes of thought and sentiment which leave room open for an increasing multitude of individual differences' (1933:172).[6] Even so, Durkheim recognized that there is and can be no total conformity even in societies with mechanical solidarity. 'Crime is present ... in all societies of all types,' he remarked (1938:65).

What, then, did Durkheim mean when he defined 'social facts' as externally constraining the individual? *Externality* means something obvious, familiar and uncontroversial. It means that everyone is born into a pre-existent and organized society, and that he is only one element in a larger pattern. Language, religious beliefs, money —none of these are individual creations (1938:2). As Giddens (1971:87) comments:

> Durkheim's point here, in other words, is a conceptual one. It is true that this is to some extent obscured by Durkheim's insistence upon talking of social 'facts'; but it should be obvious that the criterion of 'exteriority' is not an empirical one. If it were, it would lead directly to the ludicrous conclusion that society exists externally to *all* individuals . . .

The presence of moral *constraint*, on the other hand, is an empirical question. In all societies there are conventions concerning the individual's obligations as father to his children, employer to his employees, priest to congregation, or whatever. If these are supported with legal or informal social sanctions against transgressors, their constraining power is obvious. They can be broken, but at a cost. Durkheim emphasizes, however, that constraint is equally real when the individual accepts them unquestioningly as right and legitimate.

Nevertheless, Durkheim did not find it easy to define exactly the balance between society's undoubted influence in shaping the individual's actions and the individual's scope for autonomous or innovative behaviour. For instance, in a footnote to his preface to the second edition of the *Rules of Sociological Method* (1938: lvi-lvii), he wrote:

> Because beliefs and social practices come to us from without, it does not follow that we receive them passively or without modification. In reflecting on collective institutions and assimilating them for ourselves, we individualize them and impart to them more or less personal characteristics . . . It is for this reason that each of us creates, in a measure, his own morality, religion and mode of life. There is no conformity to social convention that does not comprise an entire range of individual shades.

But he then appeared to equivocate:

> It is nevertheless true that this field of variations is a limited one. It verges on nonexistence or is very restricted in that circle of religious and moral affairs where deviation easily becomes a crime. It is wide in all that concerns economic life. But, sooner or later, even in the latter instance, one encounters the limit that cannot be crossed.

If this is equivocation, Durkheim was right to equivocate, for the scope of 'variation' cannot be established conceptually; it is a matter for empirical investigation in every society, institutional area, and social group.

Numerous interpretations have been put on Durkheim's thought. Parsons (1937) considered that he had swung right over from a position of 'radical positivism' to one of philosophical idealism. Harris (1968; ch. 18) contends, on the contrary, that he was never anything else but an idealist. Neither is entirely correct. Durkheim began his work within the intellectual tradition stemming from St Simon and Comte (Lukes 1973 :66ff.), and, in this sense, Parsons is right to use the label 'positivist'.[7] But Harris is right when he points out that positivism is not 'the opposite' of idealism as Parsons implies. Parsons uses 'radical positivism' to mean a crude empiricism or even a behaviourism of the Skinnerian type. Durkheim unwaveringly rejected explanations in terms of any innate, universal psychology, of any 'human nature' prior to society. However, neither Durkheim nor, for that matter, Comte ever had any epistemological objection to the consideration of 'inner mental states'. Though Durkheim never developed as sophisticated a social psychology as Mead's, that he was grappling with the same problem as Mead is especially clear in his last major work, *The Elementary Forms of Religious Life* (1965, orig. 1912). Indeed, Stone and Farberman (1967) have argued that, at the end of his life, Durkheim was on the verge of adopting a 'symbolic interactionist' stance. In lectures on 'Pragmatism and Sociology' (in Wolff, 1960:386–436) he examined the work of James and Dewey, but, of course, he knew nothing of Mead's work. The purpose of *Elementary Forms* had been to investigate the social sources of shared concepts and conceptions of the world, and their part in facilitating in turn the functioning of society. *Représentations collectives* by then fairly clearly resembled Mead's significant symbols.[8] James seemed to Durkheim to leave too much scope for subjectivity; James's individual seemed to construct his own social reality. But it is likely that Mead's approach would have been much more acceptable to Durkheim. For what Mead contributed was a sociologically plausible psychology and an account of how concepts, symbols or *représentations* have their origins in social communication and interaction.

Weber and Social Action

'Social action theory' is more readily associated with the name of Max Weber (1864–1920) than with either Mead or Durkheim. Like Durkheim, but unlike Mead, Weber declared it 'erroneous . . . to regard any kind of psychology as the ultimate foundation of the sociological interpretation of action' (1968:I, 19), though the context of this remark makes it plain that, by 'psychology', he understood explanation in terms of inherent characteristics independent of the social environment. A major aspect of his work, as of Mead's, is a justification of the relevance and indispensability of information about 'inner mental states' to social scientific explanation. That Weber produced no analysis comparable to Mead's account of the social genesis of self-reflexive thought and how thinking makes possible purposive action was, no doubt, a consequence of purposive action being relatively unproblematic within the German intellectual tradition to which Weber was heir. But, in the end, Weber and Mead are epistemologically very close.

Weber's position was the very antithesis of behaviourism as can be seen from his definition of social action.

> In action is included all human behaviour when and in so far as the acting individual attaches a subjective meaning to it. Action in this sense may be either overt or purely inward and subjective; it may consist of positive

> intervention in a situation, or of deliberately refraining from such intervention or passively acquiescing in the situation. Action is social in so far as, by virtue of the subjective meaning attached to it by the acting individual . . . it takes account of the behaviour of others and is thereby oriented in its course. [1968:I, 4][9]

So not all human behaviour is action; the accidental collision of two cyclists is akin to a natural event, though their attempt to avoid it and any subsequent exchange of insults or friendly concern are social action. Nor is all action social action; the response of many members of a crowd in putting up their umbrellas is normally a response to rain, not to each other. Action may also be orientated not to a single known individual, but to 'collective' concepts like the State, church, class and so on.

Weber insists that in order to explain an action, we must interpret it in terms of its *subjectively intended meaning*, something quite distinct from its objectively valid meaning. That is to say, a person's action is to be explained in terms of the consequences he intended it to have—his *purpose*—rather than in terms of its actual effects; the two are sometimes at variance. We have to grasp what *ends* he is pursuing and how *he* perceives that he can achieve them. This is obviously very close to Thomas's emphasis on understanding 'the definition of the situation'. Cohen (1968:81) gives a good example: how do we explain why a man is touching his toes by his bedside early in the morning? Does the action have religious or physiotherapeutic significance? We find out by asking him his purpose, or alternatively infer it by generalizing from our previous knowledge of behaviour in his society. This process of *Verstehen* certainly has nothing to do with introspection or any *special* ability of the sociologist to 'emphasize' with his subjects. It is the same process of interpretation of other people's meanings which is essential to normal social intercourse and even to natural science, and it is no more arbitrary (cf. Schutz 1962:56). Verification of such an explanation is achieved by statistical or comparative analysis of many cases, or very occasionally by laboratory experiment (Weber 1968:I, 10).

Having established the 'subjectively intended meaning', however, we have a *causal* explanation of the action (of Fletcher 1971:II, 419–20). This is true not only in Mill's sense that choices once made take their place among the causes of later actions, but in the sense that the end in view is a cause of present actions. Of course, an essential feature of a cause is that it precedes the effect; but the 'cause' of an action is not exactly its intended outcome but the 'mental experiment' of anticipating its consequences in advance before implementing the action. As Alfred Schutz pointed out (1972:61), the actor pictures the projected act as completed. He sees the situation in the future perfect tense, as it *will have become* if the action has the consequences he expects. Schutz (1972:86–96) described this as the 'in-order-to motive' of the action, distinguishing it (as Weber did not) from the 'genuine because-motive'. The latter refers to some event or experience in the actor's *past* which he views in the pluperfect tense as the cause of his action. We put up an umbrella *in order to* keep dry and *because* we had got unpleasantly wet in the past. In both cases it can be seen that the notion of the self as object, explicit in Mead, is also implicit in Weber.

The simplest actions to explain in terms of subjectively intended meaning are those which involve the fully conscious and rational adaptation of available means to ends in view. Weber had very much in mind the achievements of the British and Austrian economists in analysing economic actions in terms of 'economic rationality'. In building a typology of action, therefore, he thought it best to treat non-rational and emotionally governed action as a deviation from ideal rationality. He distinguished four types of action beginning with two varieties of rationality, *Zweckrationalität* and *Wertrationalität*.[10]

Zweckrational action is 'determined by expectations as to the behaviour of objects in the environment and of other human beings; these expectations are used as "conditions" or "means" for the attainment of the actor's own rationally pursued and calculated ends' (1968:I, 24). What this means is that the actor weighs, one against the other, not only the means available for attaining a given end but also the costs and benefits of using those means for one end or another and finally various ends themselves. Weber has in mind, of course, the models of rational economic action developed in classical economics, involving concepts such as marginal utility, marginal revenue and opportunity cost.

Wertrational action is 'determined by a conscious belief in the value for its own sake of some ethical, aesthetic, religious or other form of behaviour, independently of its prospects of success' (1968:I, 24–5). The various means towards ends may be weighed against each other, but the end itself is not questioned: it is accepted as a binding and absolute good.

The two non-rational (*not* irrational) types of action are *affectual* and *traditional*. Action is affectual when it is directly under the control of the emotions; it may be an uncontrolled response—anger, for instance—but it is meaningful only if orientated towards some social object. Last is a residual category; traditional action is 'determined by ingrained habituation' (1968 :I, 25).

Many criticisms have been made of this typology, and Weber anticipated several of them. It may be objected that the actions we actually observe in society are very frequently a mixture of the pure types. For instance, the economic activities and attitudes of Protestant entrepreneurs (as illustrated by Benjamin Franklin's view of time as money—Weber 1930, ch. 2) are prototypically *zweckrational*, and yet, in so far as they are an expression of rigid religious and ethical principles, are also *wertrational.* Weber himself was very conscious of this, and emphasized that the four modes of orientation of action were ideal-types. Ideal patterns of action were seen to be embodied in ideal-types of institutions, such as *Zweckrationalität* in rational-legal bureaucracy. Yet any concrete institution might contain characteristics both of, say, rational-legal and patrimonial bureaucracy, and comprise elements of all four patterns of action. Weber was most careful not to reify his ideal-types, and consistently spoke in terms of *probabilities* of features being found in concrete examples. And he emphasized that the four-fold typology was only tentative and to be judged in terms of its usefulness.

It has proved useful, and the distinctions between *Zweck-* and *Wertrationalität* is often particularly illuminating. Yet there are real difficulties. Even conceptually the boundaries between the four categories become blurred. The emotions are not easily cordoned off in a separate compartment from other actions. This is especially true when the conscious intention conceals even from the actor himself his true subconscious motives, a possibility of which Weber was fully aware (1968:I, 9–10, 25). Nor is the category of traditional action satisfactory. For one who had an encyclopaedic knowledge of other civilizations, Weber was surprisingly and ethnocentrically sceptical about the possibility of understanding action in primitive societies in rational terms (1968 :I, 16). Since then, anthropologists have succeeded, by extended fieldwork, in explaining many superficially 'irrational' customs as rational in terms of native cognitive systems. Nor is traditional action necessarily 'habitual'; as Weber himself pointed out (1968:I, 25), when action is more or less consciously justified by the claim 'we have always done it this way', the tradition becomes an absolute value, and the action shades over into *Wertrationalität.*

At this point it becomes apparent that Weber too was confronted with the problem which Mead and Durkheim approached from different angles: how much of human behaviour can be explained as self-directed purposive action, and how much as determined by established social patterns. Weber's real difficulty is interpreting any *institutionalized*, stable and long established social pattern as consciously rational action. Habit is not associated only with traditional action. We may, for instance, habitually shop at one supermarket, but our action is in no sense traditional; if its prices moved far above those of other shops, we should no doubt bestir ourselves to break the habit. As Germani (1968:149) notes, 'An elective action that has been repeated many times becomes almost habitual, and the whole elective and deliberative process becomes permanently implicit.' To complicate the matter further, original motives for the promulgation of a rule or arrangement may be lost sight of, or the motives may change.

In this connection, it is significant that although Weber was fully aware that, in real life, action takes place in situations of uncertainty, he followed the economists in leaving uncertainty out of his ideal-types of rational action. His actor plans his actions in a situation of complete subjective certainty. His knowledge of the situation may objectively be incomplete; there may be a discrepancy between subjectively intended and objectively valid meaning. But the ideal-typical actor is not uncertain of his subjective knowledge. Now, economists have long known that, if uncertainty is introduced, their models of rational economic action are robbed of much of their parsimonious elegance. The same applies to models of social action generally. Under uncertainty, each possible action has a *distribution* of potential outcomes, only one of which will materialize if the action is taken, and that one outcome cannot be foreseen.[11] And, implicitly, the distributions of outcomes associated with different actions overlap. In such situations, notions like 'optimal' profit or utility maximizing strategies and their social equivalents become meaningless. Under extreme uncertainty, the course of action which, objectively, would produce the most desirable outcome would be hit upon, if at all, by random chance. Introducing a Darwinian analogy, the course of action would appear by random mutation and might then be 'naturally selected' by market or social forces.[12] To suggest that this is typical of all social action would, of course, be to minimize purposeful rationality and swing back towards Skinner's rejection of the relevance of inner mental processes, and that is not my intention. Nonetheless, rational action in new situations is possible only by learning and generalizing from the results of one's own and other's actions. This does not contradict Weber's emphasis on the relevance of subjectively intended meanings to explanations. But it introduces the qualification that even *zweckrational* patterns of action may have been hit upon initially by the unconscious social selection of a pattern within a particular social situation.

The ideas of uncertainty and evolutionary theory seem to me to introduce a useful perspective on the question of how typical patterns of action become embodied in concrete institutions. After all, no one ever said 'I am a rational person and am now going to set up the world's first rational-legal bureaucracy'. An element of trial and error is clearly involved, and imperfections in the processes socially analogous to natural selection *help* to account for the persistence of non-rational elements in even the most 'rational' institutions.

Talcott Parsons and the 'Voluntaristic Theory of Action'

Another author whose writings centre on the nature of social action is Talcott Parsons (b. 1903). His first book, *The Structure of Social Action* (1937), is still generally considered his finest. It had a twofold importance. First, more than any other single book, it introduced the work of Weber and Durkheim[13] to the sociologists of the English-speaking world. Secondly, its substantive thesis was that those writers had been converging towards the 'voluntaristic theory of action' which Parsons himself advocated as a general sociological perspective. The 'voluntaristic theory' was not, in outline, so original as Parsons himself seems to have thought. In slightly differing forms, it can be traced back not only to Weber and Durkheim, but also to numerous American writers prior to Parsons, including James, Mead, Cooley and Thomas (see Hinkle 1963), none of whom Parsons mentioned.

What, then, was the voluntaristic theory of action? It can be very briefly summarized in the following axioms:

(1) People's actions are directed towards the achievement of *ends*, goals, objectives. (We have already mentioned more than once the relevance of Mead's discussion of how purposive behaviour is possible.)

(2) People select appropriate *means* and procedures from those available, to attain their ends.

(3) Courses of action are constrained by the *conditions* of the physical and social environment.

(4) Individuals have emotions and make moral judgements which influence the selection of ends and means, as well as their order of priority.

(5) Actions are to be explained by the subjectively intended meaning given them by the actor, or, roughly, by his perception and definition of the ends, means and conditions of his situation.

There is nothing very new in this. The real interest of Parsons's work is not in the 'means-ends schema', but in his treatment of the other side of the equation: how 'society' influences the ends the actor will pursue and the means he will use in attaining them. In *The Structure of Social Action,* he did not himself probe deeply into the psychology of socialization. But he did praise Durkheim and Weber, and the English economist Alfred Marshall, for realizing that the ends of action were neither innate nor random, but deeply influenced by social experience and moral values. The difficulties of Parsons's later work revolve around his efforts to formulate this influence more precisely.

Whatever else it was, *The Structure of Social Action* was a polemic against behaviourism's refusal to consider evidence of inner mental processes as essential data. Yet *Toward a General Theory of Action* and other writings in the 1950s show Parsons flirting with behaviourism, under the particular influence of the behaviourist E.C. Tolman.

> The organization of observational data in terms of the theory of action is quite possible and fruitful in modified behaviouristic terms, and such formulation avoids many of the difficult questions of introspection or empathy. In Tolman's psychology, it is postulated that the rat is orientated to the goal of hunger gratification and that he cognizes the situation in which he pursues the goal. Tolman's concepts of orientation and cognition are ways of generalizing the facts of observation about the rat's behaviour. Ellision . . . What the actor thinks or feels can be treated as a system of *intervening variables.* [Parsons and Shils 1951:64, their italics]

This is one example of the series of 'crucial equivocations' vividly traced by Scott (1963), by which Parsons maintained superficial continuity with his pre-war work. Apart from revealing a misapprehension about the nature of *Verstehen,* it shows that once again Parsons ignored Mead's social behaviourism.

In spite of his equivocations, the salient feature of Parsons's post-war writings is a rather mechanical conception of social norms and their place in the determination of action. Norms and values were increasingly seen as rigid and unambiguous standards. They form patterns of 'institutionalized normative culture' which the individual takes as given and 'internalizes', 'introjects', or just plain learns, thereafter behaving in obedient conformity to them. Once internalized, normative culture seems to have the status of a repertoire of behavioural computer programmes, the appropriate one being called up not by the self-reflexive, thinking individual, but by external stimuli in each situation.

After 1937, Parsons also paid a lot of attention to Freudian psychology, and particularly to the concept of the 'super-ego'.[14] Again, it is interesting that Parsons paid little attention to Mead, though parallels have often been noted between the super-ego and the generalized other. Freud saw the super-ego as the voice within the individual conscience of the demands of social life, struggling to control the impulses of the ego and id. Socialization was never perfect (see especially Freud 1962). Parsons, however, argued that not only the super-ego but the ego and the id too were products of social experience. In consequence, Dennis Wrong (1961) attacked Parsons for developing an 'oversocialized conception of man'. 'Sociologists,' he alleged, 'have appropriated the super-ego concept, but have separated it from any equivalent of the Freudian id.' Yet, in 'socializing' the ego and the id, Parsons was not out of line with the trend of neo-Freudian thinking, nor with Mead's discussion of the social origins of thought and self-conceptions. Certainly the social influences on the psyche run very deep indeed. This emerges very clearly in Norbert Elias's *Über den Prozess der Zivilisation* (1969). Elias shows that though we react deeply and almost 'instinctively' to such matters as habits of personal hygiene, table manners, physical cruelty to animals and fellow humans, the expression of our feelings is nevertheless socially patterned. And the patterning has varied greatly.

> The expression of affect by people in the Middle Ages was altogether freer and more spontaneous than in the subsequent period. But it certainly did not lack social patterning and control in any absolute sense. There is, in this sense, no zeropoint. The man without restraints is a phantom. But the type, the strength and the elaboration of taboos, controls and interdependencies can certainly change a hundredfold. And as these change, so does the tension-balance of the emotional structure and, with it, the degree and type of gratification which the individual seeks and finds.

Yet Wrong's underlying criticism of Parsons is valid: he sometimes seems to use Freudian terminology to express behaviourist ideas. In his hands, 'internalization' or 'introjection' of moral norms often seems to mean little more than simple learning or habit formation.

Parsons's post-war decline into something remarkably like

behaviourism is, of course, conditioned by his desire to relate the voluntaristic theory of action to a view of social order dominated by consensus and harmony rather than by coercion and conflict. In still later writings he distinguishes between three levels of organization—the personality, the social and the cultural—which are 'cybernetically' interdependent and capable of a degree of independent variation.[15] In practice, however, he tends to talk about the same thing at each level: approved patterns of behaviour are institutionalized in patterns of culture and internalized into personalities. There seems, in fact, to be a general tendency for sociologists adopting an action perspective to simplify greatly the process of cultural conditioning, especially in the context of empirical research.

The Action Perspective in Sociological Research

The action perspective has, in its various forms, been very widespread in sociological and social psychological research. Mead's theories in particular invite empirical test by studies of the growth of cognitive processes and moral judgements during the socialization process. Indeed, the broad outlines of his ideas have received substantial support from the work of the great Swiss child psychologist Jean Piaget (b. 1896). Piaget was influenced by Durkheim, and though his ideas first took shape before Mead's work was much known beyond Chicago, they are in many respects remarkably close to Mead's. Sociologists of the Chicago school, and others more directly influenced by Mead, have also emphasized that socialization continues far beyond childhood. Almost every social process—social mobility, emigration, incarceration or just ageing—involves new social milieux and has its impact on the self-conceptions, the personal identity of participants.[16]

The strengths and weaknesses of the action perspective in sociological research can, however, best be illustrated with reference to sociological explanations of crime and 'deviant' behaviour. Merton's theory of deviant behaviour (1968:185–248, orig. 1938), although directly inspired by Durkheim, is, with its emphasis on ends and means, also redolent of Weber and Parsons. Merton argued that 'culture' defines certain legitimate objectives for members of society, things 'worth striving for'. Success in the United States and other industrial societies is largely defined in terms of money and wealth. Commonly accepted rules and norms also define the means which may legitimately be employed to attain these goals. But, Merton pointed out, though in contemporary societies the goals tend to be held out equally as objectives for all members of society, opportunities for pursuing them legitimately are not equally distributed. People receive very different starts in life; educational and career opportunities, for example, are markedly worse towards the bottom of the social scale. There is always widespread disappointment. Merton identified various ways in which people could adapt to frustrating situations. They could reject conventional goals but continue to accept the conventional means, as in the case of the 'ritualist' clerk at the bottom of some bureaucracy. They could reject ends *and* means, becoming 'retreatist' drop-outs. They could rebel, seeking to change society. Or, most interestingly, they could continue to accept conventional goals such as wealth, but pursue them by illegitimate means such as theft. Merton recognized, however, that most people, even in unencouraging situations, do none of these things, and continue to conform.

Merton's theory points to some kinds of social pressure which may be conducive to deviance. But why do some people conform and others deviate, though they are equally subject to these pressures? And why does deviance take so many different forms in response to the same pressures? Edwin Sutherland (1947:7–8) expressed his doubts as follows:

> Thieves generally steal in order to secure money, but likewise honest labourers work in order to secure money. The attempts by many scholars to explain criminal behaviour by general drives and values, such as . . . striving for social status, the money motive, or frustration, have been and must continue to be futile since they explain lawful behaviour as completely as they explain criminal behaviour.

To explain criminal behaviour, it is clearly necessary to examine the individual in his immediate social context as well as in relation to the general conventional values. For, as Cloward and Ohlin (1960) argued, it is not only opportunities generally considered legitimate which are socially structured and unequally distributed. Opportunities for illegitimate activities are also unequally distributed in society. This aspect of crime was always emphasized by the Chicago school of sociologists, and it was epitomized in the idea of 'subcultures'.

People are socialized not only into one culture common to a whole society, but into the innumerable subcultures found in complex societies. Chicago between the wars was a teeming diversity of sub-cultures, providing a laboratory on the doorstep for its sociologists.[17] They not only depicted the many ways of life they found, but studied their location within the urban structure. One of the by-products of the study of urban ecology, developed under the leadership of Ernest Burgess and Roderick McKenzie, was the analysis of the geographical distribution of crime in Chicago reported in *Delinquency Areas* (1929) by Shaw and his collaborators. And Thrasher (1927) located 1,313 gangs among juvenile delinquents in the city. These studies demonstrated that delinquency was concentrated in limited areas of the city. Most acts of delinquency were committed in the company of other delinquents, and gangs and associates gave social support to delinquency. It was a reasonable conclusion that the likelihood of a person becoming delinquent was related to opportunities for learning criminal techniques and patterns of behaviour, and for receiving encouragement from associates. Shaw therefore spoke of the 'cultural transmission' of crime and delinquency. Yet not everyone in even the most crime-ridden area is a criminal. Inner-city Chicago in the 1920s must have been one of the most crime-ridden districts on earth, but nothing like a majority even of its inhabitants were criminals.

How is this to be explained? Rose (1962:13–15) set out some of the conventional answers. First, it is argued, many cultural expectations neither prescribe nor proscribe specific behaviour, but permit a *range* of actions. Moreover, many of them are specific to certain roles such as occupations, and the individual has a certain degree of choice in the roles he adopts. Secondly, cultures and subcultures contain internal contradictions; in some situations the cultural signposts may, so to speak, point in opposite directions. Thirdly, people move from subculture to subculture, and their contradictory standards present further opportunities for choice and innovation. This last point, though, might rather be taken to suggest the difficulties of defining the boundaries of a subculture. The term may have appeared reasonably unambiguous in studies of ethnic groups in Chicago with their own territory and even languages. However, Suttles (1972:21–43) has suggested that the neighbourhoods never were factually so homogeneous as they were depicted, and their boundaries were gradients rather than clear-cut lines. The clear-cut lines, he argues, were imposed by the *simplified* cognitive maps of residents, and accepted as factual by sociologists.

To resolve this difficulty in the notions of subculture and cultural transmission, Sutherland (1947, ch. 1) advanced his 'differential association' theory. Though applied to crime, it was intended as a general explanation of how patterns of behaviour are acquired.[18] Such factors known to be associated with crime as poverty, bad homes and personal quirks have, according to Sutherland, 'a causal relation to crime only as they affect the person's associations'. The techniques, motives and rationalizations required for criminal behaviour are learned like other behaviour in immediate face-to-face encounters. But we all experience 'culture conflict in relation to legal codes'. We all encounter situations in which laws are defined as not to be broken and some in which they (or some of them) are defined as breakable. For most of us, the former exceed the latter. The principle of differential association states that 'a person becomes delinquent because of an excess of definitions favourable to violation of law over definitions unfavourable to violation of law'. This sounds remarkably behaviourist, and runs into the same difficulties as Skinner's explanation of verbal behaviour. As Sutherland admits, an 'excess of definitions favourable to violation of law' is not easily quantified. There is a risk of *post hoc* explanation: only when we see the crime can we decide whether favourable or unfavourable definitions were in excess. The difficulty is that, in the last resort, every man is his own subculture: he has his own unique past experience, and though it may resemble that of his associates closely enough to make generalization possible, it is not identical. *If* we aspire to explain why a particular person becomes criminal and others similarly placed do not, we need to study him in detail, which in practice means talking to him and interpreting what he says. That is why many of the most convincing accounts of deviant behaviour have been participant observation studies focusing on small groups of people. An early example was Shaw's *The Jack-roller* (1930), and a more recent one Howard Becker's account (1963) of how people learn to be marijuana users. This is by no means to suggest that 'ecological' and 'action' studies are in any way incompatible or contradictory. They are complementary. Ecological studies, whether by Durkheim, the Chicago school, or by means of contemporary survey methods, can certainly throw light on crime rates. But close-up participant observation studies also give a basis for generalization and help in the interpretation of ecological correlations. The difference is one of focus and generality, and the depth of focus can vary continuously from one person to millions of people. There is no point along the scale at which it can meaningfully be said that we have passed from psychology to sociology.

Conclusions

Sociology has been plagued by misconceptions—in the strict sense of the word – about the 'individual' and 'society', and by consequent attempts to draw hard-and-fast boundaries between psychology and sociology. This often leads to needless confusion. For instance, the authors of the famous *Authoritarian Personality* study (Adorno, *et al.* 1950) certainly thought they were studying personality characteristics. But, it has been argued, the picture produced from interviewing a large sample of people was, in fact, a description of certain common characteristics of lower-class culture (Brown 1965 :550–53; Lipset 1960 :97–130). One way of thinking about this issue is to see the personality as 'sampling the culture'.[19] Let us suppose, in line with Mead, that the whole cultural or subcultural pattern of meanings, values and behaviour is not simply internalized *en bloc*, but that some selective mechanism is at work. *For purely heuristic purposes*, personality development could be thought of as a series of binary decisions between courses of development, each decision being made by the toss of a coin (Figure 1). Whether or not the decision at each stage is determined or not (a metaphysical matter), whether the individual's attention selects stimuli (as Mead suggested), or whether stimuli are subject to '*sui generis* elaboration' inside the mind (as Durkheim put it), it influences where the person will be, as it were, in the next round. In other words, what is sampled at one point strongly influences what is sampled next. Yet Figure 1 is drawn so as to show many convergent courses of development as well as divergent ones, so that after only five stages the probability of attaining a position towards the middle of the cultural stream is ten times that of ending up at one of the 'deviant' poles. (In fact, Figure 1 shows the genesis of a binomial distribution, tending towards a normal curve.) It cannot be too strongly stressed that this is a purely heuristic device, not to be interpreted too literally. Nevertheless, it makes it obvious why it is that if the social scientist collects 'subjective' or attitudinal data from a cross-section of people, the composite picture will be more one of what we speak of as 'the culture' than of individual personalities. If they have 'sampled' from the same population of cultural patterns, their individual samples will differ, but their common features will represent the culture rather adequately and individual personality quirks will tend to be averaged out. Therefore when sociologists present findings in terms of central tendencies, paying less attention to the

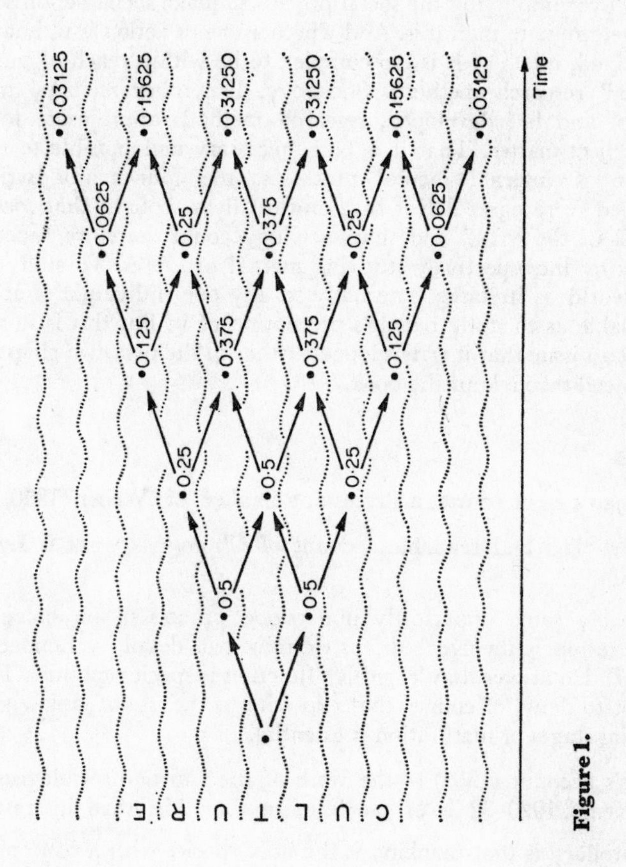
C
U
L
T
U
R
E
0·5
0·5
0·25
0·5
0·25
0·125
0·375
0·375
0·125
0·0625
0·25
0·375
0·25
0·0625
0·03125
0·15625
0·31250
0·31250
0·15625
0·03125
Time

Figure 1.

variance, they make people's actions appear more rigidly socially determined than they are.

Ultimately, as we have remarked earlier, the 'free will *versus* determinism' issue neither can be resolved nor needs to be resolved for purposes of sociology. Sociologists should, however, be on guard against oversimplifying the social process to make social action seem more determinate than it is. And whether or not action is ultimately determined, much of it is too complex to be within reach of purely 'external' research methods. Sociology, like other sciences, must develop, and has developed, research methods appropriate to its own subject-matter. That it is both necessary and possible to take account of internal mental processes, the four major writers examined were agreed. Not that any of them thought that society was 'all in the mind' and that sociology could therefore function entirely by introspectively studying mental processes. To study the social world as it stands externally to any one individual is as indispensable as to study people's perception of it. But this is so substantial an issue that it is developed further in the next two chapters, and indeed throughout the book.

Notes

1. Homan's is, of course, a Protestant Yankee. cf; Weber (1930)!
2. A first-class and readable account of Chomsky's work is Lyons (1970).
3. Probably some imperfectly understood process of physiological maturation is involved; this is examined in detail by Lenneberg (1967). He argues that 'cognitive function is species-specific'. That is not to deny, of course, that exposure to the use of language at crucial stages of maturation is essential.
4. Faris's account (1967) of the work of the Chicago sociologists in the years 1920–32 is of much more than historical interest.
5. A corollary is that mankind is the only species with a conception of time. See esp. Mead (1932).
6. The standard translation is clumsy at this point, and I have taken the improved wording from Giddens (1971:79).
7. So ambiguous is the term that it is, in my view, best avoided. Comte is usually considered the main founder of positivism, so a follower of Comte might reasonably be called a positivist. But

'positivist' has also come to mean 'crude empiricist'—one who emphasizes observation at the expense of the equally necessary intellectual processes of induction and deduction—and this Comte certainly was not (see Elias 1970 : ch. 1). From this second sense has been derived a third, almost synonymous with behaviourism (see Murphy 1972). And fourthly, the sense is at other times much weaker, indicating merely someone who agrees with philosophers like Popper that there are no substantial *logical* differences between the natural and the social sciences.

8. See R.C. Hinkle's essay 'Durkheim in American Sociology', in Wolff, 1960: 267–95.
9. References in this book to *Wirtschaft und Gesellschaft* are to the 3-vol. complete translation of 1968. In this one case, however, I have quoted Talcott Parsons's original translation, which conveys the meaning slightly more fully.
10. These two terms pose such problems of translation that they are generally used in the German. Literally they mean 'purpose-rationality' and 'value-rationality' respectively. *Zweckrationalität* is sometimes rendered as 'instrumental rationality' or even 'economic rationality'. The best rendering of *Wertrationalität* I have come across is Fletcher's (1971 : II, 443) 'Social Action employing Rational Means in the service of an Accepted End.'
11. Here I am drawing heavily on the argument of the economist A.A. Alchian (1950). See also G.S. Becker (1962).
12. cf. the discussion of evolutionary theory below, pp. 161–164.
13. It also discusses Pareto and, to a lesser extent, the classical economists, especially Alfred Marshall. For reasons of space I cannot discuss these authors. In any case, greater lip service is paid to Pareto than I believe his real influence on contemporary sociology justifies.
14. See esp. Parsons's 'The Super-ego and the Theory of Social Systems' (Parsons, Bales and Shils 1953 : ch.1)
15. Parsons normally mentions the organism as a fourth level of organization. Though sociologists rarely need to refer to biological processes, Parsons is right to mention them, as it is known that hormonal disturbances or drugs, for instance, can have temporary or even permanent effects on behaviour. More generally, the body is among the conditions which physically limit action. For a discussion of cybernetics, see below, pp. 159–161.

16. One of the earliest classics of Chicago sociology, Thomas and Znaniecki's *The Polish Peasant in Europe and America* (1918–20), studied the Pole's experience of emigration, the disruption of his stable and traditional way of life, and his struggle to come to terms with his new situation in the U.S.A. More recently, the same concern with 'transformations of identity' can be seen in much of Anselm Strauss's work (e.g. 1959), as well as in Erving Goffman's discussion of 'total institutions', which he described as 'forcing-houses for changing persons; each is a natural experiment on what can be done to the self' (1961:12).

17. They made such use of their laboratory that the 'Chicago tradition' is often thought of as a school of urban sociology; but, as Rose notes (1962:viii), urban sociology as such was never considered more than a minor sub-field by the Chicago interactionists themselves. Among the classic texts of Chicago sociology which depicted many of the groups and their subcultures to be found in the city may be mentioned Nels Anderson's *The Hobo* (1923), H.W. Zorbaugh's *The Gold Coast and the Slum* (1929), E. Franklin Frazier's *The Negro Family in Chicago* (1932), and Louis Wirth's *The Ghetto* (1938).

18. This is emphasized by Daniel Glaser (in Rose 1962:425–42), on whose article I have drawn here.

19. I am indebted for this phrase to an article (1971) by my colleague Robert Witkin.

2. Knowledge

'The basic problem with empiricism is not whether we trust the evidence of our senses but whether we accept their transmutations into the constructs of the mind'.—*Robert F. Murphy* (1971: 206)

How is it possible to interpret the meanings, intentions and purposes which lie behind people's actions? This question has usually seemed of little practical moment to sociologists studying people in their own society, with whom they share a similar cultural background and language. Misunderstandings occur, but are often apparent and easily resolved by further questioning. Anthropologists studying exotic societies very different from their own have, however, long been unable to avoid confronting serious problems of interpretation. Among the hundreds of past and present societies known to us, there is a diversity to challenge their most ethnocentric assumptions. Multifarious patterns of family and kinship, modes of government and economic and technological organization are relatively familiar. But the variety extends much further: to morals, to beliefs—religious, mythological and cosmological—and, of course, to language. Societies have not only divergent ways of organizing their practical activities, but vastly different ways of expressing their thoughts about themselves and their world. Anthropologists have therefore had to grapple with the problem of understanding modes of thought and conceptions of reality very different from their own. No matter how strange to our eyes are primitive societies' conceptions of reality—their explanations of natural processes and the supernatural for example—they apparently organize their lives successfully on these assumptions. So, how different are they from the assumptions on which Western industrial man bases his way of life? This question has inevitably led to closer examination of the cognitive foundations of all societies. It has also led to the disturbing question of whether Western science, and social science in particular, is not just another way of organizing a conception of reality, no more and no less valid than any other socially accepted construction of reality.

Language and Cognition

A particularly strong version of the hypothesis of cultural relativity was put forward by the anthropologist Edward Sapir (1884–1939) and his student, the linguist Benjamin Lee Whorf (1897–1941). They argued that differences in the world-views of different cultures were grounded in different linguistic structures. They went beyond Mead's view that language made possible complex and self-reflexive thought, suggesting that the vocabulary and grammatical structures of the languages people learn actually determine the way they perceive the world.

Now, it is certainly true that languages differ greatly both in the vocabulary they apply to similar sets of phenomena and in their (surface) structure and grammar. Words frequently do not have exact equivalents in other languages, because cultures 'group' phenomena in different ways. For example, in English we use the one word 'uncle' to designate mother's brother, father's brother, mother's sister's husband and father's sister's husband. Other societies have a distinct word for each of these four relations, while others group them differently under two or three words. Nor is this confined only to social categories of which kinship terms are a most prominent manifestation. The taxonomies used for natural phenomena such as flora, fauna and even colours vary widely indeed. Distinctions which find expression in one language fail to do so in another; similarities apparently significant in one culture seem not to be so in another. Why? The problem was brilliantly stated, though not solved, by Durkheim and Mauss in a pioneering study (1963:7–8, orig. 1903).

> A class is a group of things; and things do not present themselves to observation grouped in such a way. We may well perceive, more or less vaguely, their resemblances. But the simple fact of these resemblances is not enough to explain how we are led to group things which thus resemble each other, to bring them together in a sort of ideal sphere, enclosed by definite limits, which we call a class, a species, etc. We have no justification for supposing that our mind bears within it at birth, completely formed, the prototype of this elementary framework of all classification. Certainly, the word can help to give a greater unity and consistency to the assemblage thus formed; but though the word is a means of realizing this grouping the better once its possibility has been conceived, it could not by itself suggest the idea of it.

The sheer variety of cultures justifies Durkheim and Mauss in their assumption that categories of thought must be learned, not innate. If concepts are learned, however, there still remain three ways in which this might take place. These are, in Roger Brown's words, that

> (1) Concepts are learned from direct commerce with the physical world without any social mediation;
> (2) concepts are socially mediated but the mediation is non-linguistic;
> (3) concepts are socially mediated and the mediation is linguistic. [Brown 1965: 314]

If either the first hypothesis or the second (that favoured by Durkheim and Mauss) were true, then language would be merely a 'cloak' covering what is, in some sense, 'essentially' the same underlying patterns of thought and perception of reality in all cultures. If the third were correct, then language would rather be a 'mould' which shaped the way in which those who speak a given language perceived and thought about the world.

Probably all three kinds of learning do occur. Some of Piaget's studies give support to hypothesis (1). In the first eighteen months of life, the child learns to conceive of the existence of objects in space and time, independent of himself and his own volition, and this learning seems to be achieved by manipulating the objects and observing the results. Later on, the child learns the principles of 'conservation' of quantity, number, area and volume—that, for example, milk poured from a short fat glass into a tall thin glass remains the same in volume. Speech is needed to express the understanding that it is 'the same', but, in this case, words seem only to label an extra-linguistic conception. But then it is unlikely that there are any societies in which the principle of conservation is not recognized. What of domains of meaning less likely to be cultural universals—kinship, moral codes, botanical and colour terminology? These are 'mapped out' by languages in many different ways; even the colour spectrum, which in physical terms is a continuum, is 'cut' at different points by different languages.

Now it is fairly obvious why the Eskimos should have words for many different kinds of snow (Whorf 1956:216), where the one word 'snow' suffices for most purposes in English, or why rice-eating tribes are reported to be able to distinguish by name several dozen forms of rice. But it is not so obvious that this abundance of vocabulary indicates anything more profound than that their ways of life make fine distinctions necessary and give opportunities for practice in making them. An English speaker who takes to skiing or Indian cookery is also likely to become able to identify at least a few different kinds of snow or rice. Likewise, English may have only one word for four kinds of uncle, but the distinctions can be drawn, albeit clumsily, if need arises. A great deal of the evidence with which Whorf supported his hypothesis is of this kind of superficial lexical variation, and is therefore inconclusive. There is some evidence that the ability to distinguish colours is related to the 'codability' of particular colours in one's native language; but though this suggests that words play a part in the process of memorizing, it scarcely proves that people are led by their vocabulary to quite different views of the world.

Of much greater interest to the sociologist is Whorf's assertion that 'users of markedly different *grammars* are pointed by their grammars towards different types of observations and different evaluations of externally similar acts of observation, and *hence are not equivalent as observers* but must arrive at some different views of the world' (1956:221, my italics).[1] Whorf thought that Western science had been markedly coloured by European languages (1956:221–2), the characteristics of which were perhaps a necessary though certainly not a sufficient condition for the development of science. The languages which Whorf grouped together as 'Standard Average European' (SAE) tended to represent even abstract ideas as a series of distinct entities and events. Similarly, SAE objectifies time, representing it as a linear scale marked off in equal units, a conception alien to many other languages, such as that of the Hopi which Whorf studied:

> Newtonian space, time and matter are no intuitions. They are recepts from culture and language. That is where Newton got them. [1956: 153]

This is a point of some significance for sociology; Norbert Elias (1970:118ff.) for one has argued that language has misled sociology into representing social happenings as falsely static, as 'things doing' rather than as processes or as orderly sequences of change.

Interesting and plausible as it may be that language flavours the way members of different societies think about the world, there is no substantial reason to suppose that there are insuperable linguistic barriers to making the world view of one society intelligible to another. The fact of successful translation shows that languages do not define incommensurable cultural universes. As Lewis Feuer (1953) pointed out, Aristotle's philosophy was translated from Greek into Arabic and Hebrew, and reached Western Europe by retranslation from the Semitic languages. Though there were obstacles to the expression of certain key ideas of Aristotelian metaphysics in Arabic and Hebrew, the misrepresentations resulting from the double translation were relatively minor. More generally, Feuer argued that

> how the relativist has escaped his own linguistic *a priori* to know, for example, the details of the Hopi *a priori* is incomprehensible. For he does manage to state the Hopi perspective in English, and this, if his doctrine were true, he should be unable to do.

This is not to deny that the 'translation' of another culture's world view is a considerable intellectual achievement, and only possible by prolonged study of fieldwork. In the past, the effect of poor 'translation' has often been to make natives of other societies seem illogical or even childish. Yet, in the end, it is inevitable that such translations are made, no matter how circuitously, for the subject-matter of exotic societies only becomes social scientific data when it is made communicable to fellow scholars.

These problems led one school of anthropologists in the 1950s and 1960s to draw a sharp distinction between two kinds of data, which they called 'emic' and 'etic'. These terms are derived from the linguistic distinction between the studies of phon*emics* and phon*etics*. Phonetics is the study of the consonantal and vowel sounds produced by those who speak a language; languages are transcribed for comparison using the standard phonetic alphabet. The accuracy of the transcription is tested by whether *other phoneticists* achieve the same results; the transcription is almost certainly unintelligible to the speaker whose sounds are being studied. By contrast, phonemes are the minimal units of *meaningful* sound, roughly equivalent to words, and no language uses more than a fraction of the total number of phonemes which could exist, given the range of perceptually different speech sounds. The test of whether a sound is a phoneme in a particular language is whether it is recognized as such by one who speaks the language. After establishing the phonemes of a language, the linguist can establish structural relationships in the use of phonemes within the language. The test of grammaticality and meaningfulness is always the native speaker's intuitive knowledge of the rules. Yet it should be remembered that if the rules were abstractly formulated and put to him, he might once more not recognize or comprehend the rules which he used intuitively.

The anthropological school variously known as 'ethnoscience', 'ethnolinguistics' and 'ethnosemantics' (Harris 1968 :568) sought to extend the emic/etic distinction to all anthropological data.[2] Whenever we need to 'crack the code' or to understand the native's purpose or meaning underlying his behaviour, we are collecting emic data. Apart from language itself, this is true of all forms of non-linguistic communication, such as systems of gestures, and particularly of ritual, magic and religion. Nonetheless, though the 'new ethnographers' expressed a preference for emic data, the importance of 'etic' data, such as information about population, food supplies, technology and so on, should not be underestimated.

It is a mistake to think of emic information as any less 'empirical' than etic data (Harris 1968:576). It can still be rigorously inter-subjective and replicable, because different anthropologists ought to be able to seek information from the same informants, or from different informants in the same society if informants are reasonably typical, and come up with similar results and interpretations. It is also a mistake to think that emic data cannot be compared cross-culturally. Colour classifications, botanical categories and kinship terminology in many societies can be and have been compared by plotting them on a 'standard grid'. Kinship terms can be plotted on a 'family tree', plant names located in the Linnaean classification, and colour terms located on the spectrum according to strict physical definitions. In fields such as religion, ritual and beliefs, the absence of a well-defined standard grid means that the anthropologist has to rely on less precise comparisons with 'Western' modes of thought in order to make himself intelligible to his readers. Yet, even when a standard grid is available, this does not change emic into etic information. Native kin terms which we identify with a distinction between, say, father's brother and mother's brother, still derive from the usage of the native speaker. As Harris puts it, 'Identification of similar emic categories merely establishes such categories as cross-culturally valid logico-empirical abstractions; it does not transform them into etically derived phenomena'. (1968:577) So long as this is remembered, it poses no real problem. The real source of difficulty is otherwise: all ethnographies written before the significance of the emic/etic distinction was fully recognized frequently confound the two types of data. This is especially true of kinship, one of the anthropologists' favourite fields of study. Kinship is a 'mixed domain'. Mating, reproduction and genealogy are etic categories with a precise biological reference. But anthropologists are usually concerned to trace genealogy only through *socially approved* matings, the equivalent of what is called 'marriage' in English. As soon as social approval enters the situation, emic tests of validity apply.

But what is the relationship between, on the one hand, etic data and social scientists' standard grids, and, on the other, the emic categories and everyday knowledge available to ordinary members of society? This is one of the preoccupations of phenomenological sociology, of which several variants became prominent during the 1960s and to consideration of which we now turn.

Alfred Schutz and Sociological Phenomenology

Phenomenological philosophy, as propounded especially by Edmund Husserl (1859–1938), is so called because it tells us to concern ourselves only with what is directly apprehended by our senses, with things as they appear to our consciousness—in short, with *phenomena*. We cannot determine anything about the *noumenon,* the thing-in-itself which lies, or does not lie, behind the phenomenon, for this remains unknowable. Kant said so much; Husserl went further, and said there was no purpose in speculating about noumena. All knowledge derives from phenomena, and so the programme he proposed consisted of the precise description of phenomena. All experience could be reduced to sense data. Sociologists influenced by Husserl have carried this programme over from philosophy as a methodological precept for the social sciences.

To describe phenomena precisely as they appear to our consciousness: put as simply as this, phenomenological programme may seem naïve. Descriptions, whether of conscious experience or anything else conceivable, employ language; and, as we have seen, the relation between language and cognition is not a simple one. Nevertheless, phenomenologists have produced subtle analyses of how reality is constructed within the social process and how the individual acquires his categories of thought—and that is the central problem of this chapter.

Phenomenology has had its main impact on sociology through the work of Alfred Schutz (1899–1959). Schutz was principally a philosopher of social science, whose early work, *Der sinnhafte Aufbau der sozialen Welt* (1972, orig. 1932), was a synthesis of Weber's approach to the methodology of the social sciences with Husserl's phenomenology. Subsequently, after emigrating to the United States, Schutz incorporated into his later writings (1962, 1964, 1966) many of the main ideas of James, Mead and other American writers. Schutz's views have been popularized by Peter

Berger and Thomas Luckmann in their widely read book *The Social Construction of Reality* (1967).[3]

The focus of Schutz's analysis is *intersubjectivity*—how we understand each other and how we come to have similar perceptions and conceptions of the world. Out of his analysis emerge the foundations of a sociology of everyday knowledge. Schutz begins with the Life-World (*Lebenswelt*), also variously referred to as the 'commonsense world', the 'world of daily life' and the 'everyday world'. This is the sphere of physical and social objects within which men live and work, meet each other, and pursue their routine activities. Towards it we adopt, in Husserl's term, 'the natural attitude'—we take it for granted, and suspend doubt that things might be otherwise. Our attitude to it is pragmatic—we are concerned not so much to interpret it as to change it, to make our way within it. In short, it is experienced as already organized, for it was there before we were born. Most knowledge of it is handed down to us, and is therefore experienced as being detached from us, as having objective truth and being the same for everyone. Above all, we do not question that we have a being in the world, that there are others like us, and that they make similar assumptions.

Each of us is born into a unique *biographical situation*. We are brought up by adults, usually our parents, from whom we acquire a fundamental part of our knowledge of the world. They, their unique qualities and their location in society, leave their imprint upon us. Our biographical situation carries with it a *stock of knowledge* at hand. No two people have precisely the same biographical situation, so they do not have identical stocks of knowledge. Knowledge is socially distributed; no one knows everything about everything. Therefore, they see the world from perspectives to some degree different. Yet the very objectivity and externality which knowledge has for the individual depends on it being to a large extent shared by others. This requirement is met in the case of those whom one is likely to meet within one's everyday world, and so interaction within this sphere proceeds on the assumption of the *reciprocity of perspectives*. Though our perspectives are not precisely the same, we assume that, if we changed places, we should perceive as the other does now. In interaction, we assume different points of view are irrelevant and that we each interpret the situation in a similar manner. The assumption of the reciprocity of perspectives is therefore very close to Mead's idea of taking the role of the other. The assumption is only challenged when interaction fails to proceed smoothly, when we fail to anticipate the other's reactions, when perspectives prove not to be reciprocal.

But what is the nature of the knowledge of which everyone has a unique stock? Schutz argues that we experience the external world of things, people and events as *typifications*. Typifications are classifications and categorizations. As Durkheim, Whorf and others recognized in their various ways, Schutz too appreciates that we have to classify and group in order to organize reality, and that most of these typifications are socially learned and handed down to us. Trees and colours as much as people and events have to be typed and organized. Any unique qualities are seen against a background of typification. And as Schutz remarks:

> The typifying medium *par excellence* by which socially derived knowledge is transmitted is the vocabulary and syntax of everyday language. The vernacular of everyday life is primarily a language of named things and events, and any name includes a typification and generalization referring to the relevance system prevailing in the linguistic in-group which found the named thing significant enough to provide a separate term for it. [1964: 14]

Typifications can be thought of as ideal-types; one consequence of Schutz's view of knowledge is that ideal-types no longer appear to be a methodological device peculiar to social science, as Max Weber implied, but an inherent feature of everyday knowledge. Weber's famous ideal-types, among them those of bureaucracy, of rational bourgeois capitalism and of religious prophecy, then appear merely as highly formalized and unusually coherent typifications consciously created for sociological purposes.

People, too, are typified. Only our own experience is immediate and directly accessible to us, though even that is typified and interpreted in our reflections about ourself. Other people's experience is inferred indirectly. R.D. Laing, a psychiatrist deeply influenced by phenomenology, puts the point vividly:

> . . . how can one ever study the experience *of the other*? For the experience *of the other* is not evident to me, as it is not and never can be an experience of mine.
>
> I cannot avoid trying to understand your experience, because although I do not experience your experience, which is invisible to me (and non-tasteable, non-touchable, non-smellable and inaudible), yet I experience you *as experiencing*.
>
> I do not experience your experience. But I experience you as experiencing. I experience myself as experienced by you. And I experience you as

> experiencing yourself as experienced by me. And so on. [1967: 16, his italics][4]

But we experience others in varying degress of anonymity. Fundamental to our understanding of the social world are our 'consociates' with whom we have 'We-relationships'. In other words, we interact frequently with them face-to-face and they share our social world. We know a great deal, though never everything, of their biography, and more than any others they are seen as unique individuals. Other contemporaries, the countless people we meet fleetingly and impersonally or not at all, are seen as functional ideal-types: shop assistants, bus conductors, bureaucrats. We also typify our predecessors and successors. The dead can be known only through the reports of others, and those yet to be born have an even more shadowy existence in our thoughts.

The corpus of everyday knowledge handed down to us also includes an armoury of practical actions, 'efficient recipes for the use of typical means for bringing about typical ends in typical situations' (Schutz 1964:14). Not that they always work. For some purposes, the stock of knowledge at hand is quite adequate, while in other situations, the individual has to improvise. As the individual's unique biography unfolds, his experience is accumulated. This process is called *sedimentation*; layer upon layer of new knowledge is assimilated into old typifications or forms the nucleus of new typifications.

The everyday, commonsense world is, in Schutz's view, the *paramount reality*, fundamental to our understanding. Within it, by means of what Schutz calls the *epoché of the natural attitude*, we suspend any doubts that things might be other than they seem, that the outer world and other people exist, that they have a past, present and future. This commonsense attitude constantly reasserts itself. However, there do exist *finite provinces of meaning* within the paramount reality, in which we may allow ourselves to doubt, in which our commonsense beliefs about the real world may be suspended. Among the most important of these provinces are those of magic, religion and science. Each of these 'multiple realities', Schutz contends, is experienced as 'real' while it has our attention. But we cannot pass smoothly from one province of meaning to another; they are discontinuous, and we must progress from one to another by a 'leap of consciousness'.

For the sociologist, the most interesting of the finite provinces of meaning is that of social science in which he himself works in his professional capacity. He must work on a plane of reality which offers a sharp contrast to the everyday world. Any individual's stock of everyday knowledge taken as a whole is to a greater or lesser degree incoherent, inconsistent and fragmentary. Perfect clarity is neither attainable nor necessary, for it serves essentially practical purposes. The sheer diversity of practical actions is an obstacle to coherence and, moreover, while the practical recipes 'work', producing the desired and expected results, there is little incentive for conscious pursuit of clarity. Scientific knowledge, on the contrary, serves purely intellectual interests, and clarity, consistency and coherence are a positive requirement of activity in the scientific world. For the social scientist, this poses a paradox. He has to give clear and consistent explanations of a subject-matter which itself is often unclear and inconsistent. In order to do so, he has to construct typifications, for his own scientific purposes, of the typifications his subjects make for their practical purposes. He builds ideal-types of ideal-types, 'constructs of the second degree'.

Much of Schutz's exploration of the grounds of everyday knowledge seems to have been widely accepted as a contribution to a basic but hitherto neglected question in sociology. More controversial are his views on the relationship of social science to commonsense reality. Many would at least say that, in his theory of multiple realities connected by 'leaps of consciousness', the metaphysical aspects of phenomenological philosophy show through. Can 'everyday reality' and 'commonsense', no matter how incoherent, be considered something quite discontinuous with, or even antithetical to, scientific understanding?

More generally, to speak of multiple realities conveys an impression of the relativity and even the subjectivity of truth, that all perspectives on reality are equally valid. What is truth on one side of the Pyrenees may, as Pascal observed, be error on the other, but this does not establish whether the French or Spanish conceptions of truth are to be accepted as equally valid by social scientists. Of course, all scientific knowledge remains provisional, and much that was once believed to be true even in the natural sciences is now known to have been in error. Relativists, however, usually have in mind mythological, religious, political or ethical systems which are not open to empirical refutation in quite the same way as are beliefs about natural phenomena. This should be no great worry to the sociologist, for he is not concerned with whether these systems of thought are 'true'. It is enough for sociological purposes that such phenomena can be compared cross-culturally, can be related to the societies and historical situations in which they were formed, and be shown to have consequences and 'work' more or less effectively for the people who created and transmitted them.

Berger and the Sociology of Religion

Two strangely contrasting groups of sociologists have made prominent use of Schutz's ideas. The writings of Berger and Luckmann and their followers are macroscopic and even speculative, stating broad generalizations about society; while the ethnomethodologists have preferred to focus a microscope on everyday interaction, eschewing generalization, and producing studies which many sociologists have thought trivial.

To give a full account of Berger and Luckmann's *The Social Construction of Reality* (1967) would be to go over much of the ground just covered; it is essentially Schutz's synthesis with large dollops of Durkheim. What distinguishes Berger and Luckmann from Schutz is their preoccupation with the 'legitimation' of overarching symbolic universes in society. From a discussion of man's biological nature, his lack of relatively specific instincts and a specific habitat, they conclude that 'the inherent instability of the human organism makes it imperative that man himself provide a stable environment for his conduct' (1967:70). This they suggest is created by the habitualization, 'objectivation' (awful word) and institutionalization of meanings and patterns of action. Where they differ from Schutz is in focusing on the *common* stock of knowledge in society. Even in complex societies they find it possible to speak of a central reality common to all members.

> It is important to bear in mind that most modern societies are pluralistic. This means that they have a shared core universe taken for granted as such, and different partial universes coexisting in a state of mutual accommodation. [Berger and Luckmann 1967: 142]

Superficially, this sounds like Schutz. But it is not. For him, the everyday world was experienced by the individual as the paramount reality, but he did not say that everyone shared the same experience. Rather he emphasized the unique biographical situation carrying with it a unique stock of knowledge at hand, and the social distribution of knowledge; precisely the same commonsense reality was not common to everyone. Certainly, people in similar biographical and social situations share much of their everyday knowledge and perspective on everyday reality, making it possible to assume reciprocity of perspectives. If their perspectives and knowledge at hand had nothing in common, members of different subcultures would scarcely be able to interact and communicate with each other. But if the many subcultures of complex societies (no matter how their boundaries are drawn) have to be seen as a series of overlapping circles, Schutz does not go so far as to assert that each one must overlap with *every* other one, so that there is some 'core universe' common to *every* member of society. *Perhaps* in many societies nearly everyone shares a common language—but there are great differences in language use, and there are also multilingual societies. *Perhaps*, too, there may be values and beliefs common to almost everyone in a particular society—but that is usually just asserted, not empirically demonstrated. It cannot be established, as Berger and Luckmann seem to attempt, by fiat.

Much is explained by the fact that both Luckmann and Berger are sociologists of religion (Luckmann 1967; Berger 1973). Berger in particular has been concerned to establish the centrality of religion as an institution even in modern society. Using a very broad definition of religion, he argues that religion is the means by which a 'sacred cosmos', a 'sacred canopy', is established. This is co-extensive with the 'nomos', the meaningful order and core values of a society, and religion thus provides man with an ultimate shield against anomie. In short, religion always plays an important part in world building, and is 'the audacious attempt to conceive of the entire universe as being humanly significant' (1973:37). Having started with such a broad definition of religion, he gets himself in some confusion when discussing 'secularization' (1973:111ff.), which surely acquires its meaning from a rather narrow, institutional definition of religion. The important point, however, is that Berger's and Luckmann's emphasis on the common stock of knowledge and on institutionalization can be seen to represent a form of consensus theory of social order. The not inconsiderable problems which all such theories raise are discussed in Chapter 5 below.

The Ethnomethodologists[5]

Ethnomethodology was the name given by Harold Garfinkel to the school of thought and type of research of which he is usually counted the founder. Others sharing similar interests include Aaron Cicourel, Jack D. Douglas, Peter McHugh and Harvey Sacks, although they have disagreements amongst themselves.

At first glance, ethnomethodology appears to be just one more variety of microsociological study of interaction. Its methods, particularly its reliance on participant observation, do not appear so very new (Gidlow 1972). However, ethnomethodologists themselves reject comparisons with the work of Goffman (made by Gouldner, 1971:390–5) or with the symbolic interactionist perspective (made by Denzin, 1969). They see their challenge to 'conventional' sociology as much more profound than such comparisons suggest. For ethnomethodologists, the very process of communication and interaction—how we understand each other—remains extremely problematic, as it does for other phenomenological sociologists. The ethnomethodologists, however, take a much more radical view of this. They place immense stress on the apparently infinite ambiguity of actions and statements. They seem reluctant to admit even a minimal degree of trans-situational constancy of meaning—or at least to admit that it can be proven—and therefore hesitate to make any generalizations. Thus they move away from Schutz in the opposite direction to Berger.

Douglas (1971:32) loosely distinguishes two kinds of ethnomethodologist: the 'situational' and 'linguistic' varieties, of which the latter is the more radical. The central concern of the situational ethnomethodologists is the 'negotiation of social order'. People entering a situation have to explore it, striving to discern consistency and, if possible, gradually establishing agreement as to its definition. One of the finest demonstrations of this process is the 'counselling' experiment described by Garfinkel (1967, ch. 3) and more fully by McHugh (1968, ch. 6 and 7). Subjects were told that the purpose of the experiment was to test the feasibility of counselling students on their personal problems entirely by means of yes/no answers. The answers they were given, no matter what each of them asked, were in fact a fixed sequence of yes's and no's predetermined by a table of random numbers. Most of the subjects flounderingly attempted to make sense of the nonsensical pattern of answers by imposing on it their own interpretation of the 'counsellor's' thought and intentions.

Laboratory experiments are not, however, the hallmark of ethnomethodology. One of Garfinkel's basic research strategies is purposely to disrupt real, everyday situations to expose the background assumptions underlying them.

> Procedurally it is my preference to start with familiar scenes and ask what can be done to make trouble. The operations that one would have to perform in order to multiply the senseless features of perceived environments; to produce and sustain bewilderment, consternation and confusion; to produce the socially structured affects of anxiety, shame, guilt and indignation; and to produce disorganized interaction should tell us

something about how the structures of everyday activities are ordinarily and routinely produced and maintained.

...[M]y studies are not properly speaking experimental. They are demonstrations, designed ... as 'aids to a sluggish imagination'. I have found that they produce reflections through which the strangeness of an obstinately familiar world can be detected. [Garfinkel 1967: 37–8]

In one such 'demonstration', students were asked to act the part of a lodger in their own homes, to the confusion and consternation of their families (Garfinkel 1967:41–4). Disruption of implicit, taken-for-granted assumptions are used to emphasize the endless flux and pervasive ambiguity of social life.

Some ethnomethodologists, especially Sacks and his followers, have turned their attention directly to linguistic phenomena, studying tape-recorded conversations. Despite a fascination with Chomsky's work (see Cicourel 1973), and a professed desire to establish some sort of 'socio-semantics', they discover no 'deep structure' in social life generally comparable to that which Chomsky postulates in language. Chomsky works with 'an ideal speaker-listener, in a completely homogeneous speech-community . . .' (Chomsky 1965:3), while the ethnomethodologists emphasize the ephemerality and variability of meanings in every situation. Like Chomsky, they emphasize the human ability constantly to generate 'new' sentences, but use this only to bolster their belief that meanings cannot be generalized from one situation to another. The key term they use is *indexicality* (see Garfinkel and Sacks 1970; Cicourel 1973). Conversations, they stress, always convey more than actually is, or can be, said. All conversations contain countless terms which are not explicitly defined in the particular situation. Sentences cannot be understood merely from the dictionary definitions of the words comprising them. The participants have to achieve 'operational' or working definitions of all such 'indexical expressions', drawing not only on their stock of knowledge, including linguistic knowledge, but also on their exploration of the situation at hand. This process is called 'glossing' and the working definitions 'glosses'. Garfinkel (1967:25–6, 38ff.) gives as an example a highly elliptical conversation between a husband and wife, with their much longer expansion making it intelligible to an outsider. It is a commonplace that, with those to whom we are close, each of us assumes a large stock of relevant knowledge on the part of the other, making possible elliptical conversation. Most sociologists also assume, however, that participants could *explain* their conversation to an outsider like a sociologist if asked to do so, and that this provides sufficient understanding for sociological purposes. If ethnomethodologists do not regard people's explanations as acceptable evidence of their meanings and intentions (and if they do, there seems little point in elevating the fact of indexicality—trivial for most sociological purposes—into a major criticism of conventional sociology), then they come surprisingly close to the behaviourist position.

The Ethnomethodological Critique of Conventional Sociology

This brings us to the ethnomethodologists' objections to what they variously call 'positivism', 'absolutist sociology' and 'constructive analysis'. They have found much fault in the practices of their fellow sociologists. Let us look at some of their criticisms.

(1) Conventional sociology is accused of conceptual reification, of committing the 'fallacy of misplaced concreteness' (see, for instance, Filmer, *et al.* 1972:62–6 *et passim*). Thus, having abstracted a concept like 'role', sociologists frequently proceed to treat roles a little too literally as things, as if they were bits of Meccano which make up a static social structure. This criticism has been made by many others, including anti-phenomenologists like Norbert Elias (1970 :118ff.). It was made by Parsons in *The Structure of Social Action*, though in his later work he is seen as one of the chief offenders.

Related to this is the allegation that social scientists have a tendency to portray their subjects as 'judgmental dopes', or more narrowly as 'cultural dopes'. A 'cultural dope' is a man who produces 'the stable features of the society by acting in compliance with pre-established and legitimate alternatives of action that the common culture provides' (Garfinkel 1967:68). This is reminiscent of Wrong's argument (see above, p. 29). Garfinkel puts it like this :

> A favoured solution is to portray what the member's actions will have come to by using the stable structures – i.e. what they *came* to – as a point of departure from which to portray the necessary character of the pathways whereby the end result is assembled. [1967: 68, his italics]

(2) Yet, at the same time, the ethnomethodologists accuse conventional sociology of the opposite fallacy, the fallacy of misplaced abstraction or 'abstractionism', 'the fallacy of believing that you can know in a more abstract form what you do not know in the particular form' (Douglas 1971 :11). Or, as Phillipson puts it, 'the linguistic architects of sociology have constructed vast edifices which bear unknown relationships to the world which they purport to describe'

(in Filmer, *et al.* 1972:77). Parsons has frequently been the target for such accusations. But in the hands of the ethnomethodologists, the drift of the argument is increasingly towards a mistrust of all abstraction. Thus, says Douglas, 'we must stop treating macro-analyses *as if* they were scientific arguments, that is, based on carefully done, systematic observations of concrete phenomena' (1971:11, his italics). It is worth remembering that natural scientists (especially in quantum mechanics) and statisticians in general repeatedly assume that one *can* know in a more general form what cannot be known in the particular.

(3) On the first page of his *Method and Measurement in Sociology*, Cicourel wrote:

> My basic assumption is that the clarification of sociological language is important because linguistic structure and use affects the way people interpret and describe their world. Since sociologists have evolved their own theoretical terminologies and frequently discuss, on the one hand, in these varying terms the language and substance of each other's theories and on the other hand the language of persons in everyday life whose behaviour they are interested in explaining and predicting, it is quite likely that the syntax and meaning of these languages will become entangled. [1964: 1]

This argument is much more distinctive of ethnomethodologists. Adopting what is close to an orthodox Sapir–Whorf point of view, Cicourel used it to launch a thoroughgoing critique of the whole paraphernalia of sociological research, from participant observation to questionnaires and attitude scaling. It has not deterred conventional sociologists from using traditional methods, though it may have made them slightly more cautious. For ethnomethodologists themselves, Cicourel's book served to reinforce an incipient tendency to rely heavily on participant observation, and to emphasize the value of simple description as a source of sociological knowledge.

The far more basic issue raised by Cicourel, however, was again exactly that which is at stake in the 'emics' *versus* 'etics' controversy. What Cicourel and others since him (e.g. Filmer, *et al.* 1972:19ff.) have alleged is that sociologists work with a muddle of first- and second-degree constructs (derived from the 'native' and 'sociological' worlds respectively), and that the two need sorting out. This is certainly true. The ethnomethodologists argue that to the extent that it draws on first-order or 'everyday' explanations, sociology is just another life-world, a 'folk' sociology created by its members, with no less, but no greater, validity than any other socially constructed reality. Unconscious appeals to everyday, taken-for-granted knowledge certainly have their dangers for sociology. Douglas points out, for example, that in *Suicide* Durkheim explains away discordant facts by the use of such *ad hoc* propositions as 'Jews place a high value on education', which he could have derived only from 'commonsense' knowledge available to him as a member of his society but neither confirmed nor disconfirmed by him as sociologist (Douglas 1967:3–78; 1971:5–6).

In *The Social Meanings of Suicide* (1967), Douglas also pioneered the ethnomethodologists' distrust of official statistics. He cast doubt on the facticity of suicide rates, pointing out that they relied upon coroners making an inference about the suicide's *intentions.* Suicide rates reflect the operations, purposes and categorizations of an official bureaucracy.[6] This is true and cautionary. But the real question is not whether coroners make interpretations, but whether they do so inconsistently. If they consistently used the same criteria, the suicide statistics would acquire a certain facticity, even if they did not mean quite what Durkheim took them to mean. And coroners *may* be subject to the same kind of social controls guiding them towards the consistent use of criteria as are sociologists and other social scientists.

This problem of consistency of meanings both in social science and in everyday life, is at the roots of the ethnomethodologists' critique of conventional sociology. Schutz contended, notably in his paper 'The Problem of Rationality in the Social World' (1964:64–88), that while scientific knowledge could attain coherence and consistency, the corpus of everyday knowledge *taken as a whole* remained inconsistent and unclear. This was restated more dogmatically by Garfinkel (1967, ch. 8); but Schutz did not rule out *parts of* the corpus of everyday knowledge being consistent and clear, especially in areas of expertise—such as a coroner might be expected to have acquired. In fact, some ethnomethodologists have gone far beyond Garfinkel, casting doubt on the possibilities of clarity even in the finite province of social science. Their argument is finally a linguistic one:

> . . . the linguistic expression of sociological theory follows the ordinary rules of grammar and syntax so that those words which are specifically regarded as sociological concepts, such as 'role', 'status', 'norm' are always embedded in sentences composed of other words. . . . If we can make sense of sociological concepts only when they are embedded in a context of meaning that relies on our commonsense understanding of grammar and ordinary language, it becomes clear that we cannot regard

> concepts as . . . different from, or separable from commonsense reasoning. [Phillipson, in Filmer, *et al.* 1972: 106]

Here we have the *reductio ad absurdum* of any rigid distinction between scientific and everyday knowledge, for these remarks would apply equally to the concepts of natural science. In taking up this curious position, the ethnomethodologists owe more to Wittgensteinian philosophy than to Schutz.

Ethnomethodology and Schutz

When Schultz said that social scientists must create 'constructs of the second degree', typifications of the typifications employed in everyday life, he said that these must conform to the 'postulate of adequacy'. By this he meant

> that each term in such a scientific model of human action must be constructed in such a way that a human act performed within the real world by an individual actor as indicated by the typical construct would be understandable to the actor himself as well as to his fellow men in terms of commonsense interpretation of everyday life. [1962: 64]

Now the key to the ethnomethodologists' relation to Schutz is their interpretation of the postulate of adequacy which, as it is stated here, Emmet and MacIntyre point out, is deeply ambiguous.

> If Schutz means no more than that there are certain truths which we all in our everyday lives learn about the character of those lives and that any theory inconsistent with those truths would necessarily be false, then what he says is true and obviously true. But if what he means entails that the commonsense view of the social world must be immune from correction and modification by the discoveries of social science, then what he asserts is not only false but deprives the social sciences of part of their genuine importance. Our commonsense beliefs about society are not only often false, but are also sometimes incorrigible at the level of commonsense. [Emmet and MacIntyre 1970: xiv]

The ethnomethodologists opt for the second of these two interpretations, for one corollary of their criticism that conventional sociology is merely a first-degree or 'folk' sociology is their frequent complaint that its vocabulary and theories seek to 'remedy' the commonsense world (see Garfinkel 1967:11; Filmer, *et al.* 1972, *passim*). Schutz, on the other hand, I believe to have intended his remarks in the contrary sense, the sense which is 'true and obviously true'. He accepted such concepts as roles and goals, often criticized by the ethnomethodologists, and spoke appreciatively of the progress of economic theory (1962:64–5; 1972:244–6) which claims great generality and is poles apart from the ethnomethodologists' style of investigation.[7] He admitted that a great part of social science can be performed 'at a level which legitimately abstracts from all that happens in the individual actor' (1964:84–5), though he regards it as a kind of intellectual shorthand. Where 'real scientific work' is done, however, the scientist will always have the option of shifting to the level of the individual actor. This condition is met even in so apparently 'abstract' a branch of social science as macroeconomic theory, and it is all that is required to meet the postulate of adequacy—nothing so sweeping as the ethnomethodologists seem to require.

Ethnomethodology and Wittgenstein

The consequences for the ethnomethodologists of their chosen interpretation of Schutz are far-reaching. For it leads them towards the philosophical position of the later Wittgenstein (1953), as developed by the Oxford linguistic philosophers. Of these, the writings of Austin (1961), Louch (1966) and Winch (1958, 1964) bear most closely on sociology and, after Wittgenstein himself, are most frequently cited by ethnomethodologists. I believe it is their debt to linguistic philosophy rather than to Schutz which marks off ethnomethodology both from sociology in general and from other varieties of phenomenological sociology.

Put extremely succinctly, the idea of Wittgenstein's which has implications for sociology is that the meaning of a word is to be understood through its use. Winch extends this into a form of the Sapir—Whorf hypothesis : 'Our idea of what belongs to the realm of reality is given for us in the language that we use' (1958:15). We can only grasp the meaning of a word, and by extension can only grasp the speaker's reality, if we know the rule which governs its use. To deny that a word means what it is customarily meant to mean, we must either be ignorant of the language or bent on reforming or correcting it. To ethnomethodologists, the vocabulary used by sociologists imposes their reality on that of their subjects. Subjects' meanings become ephemeral and can only be grasped in particular situations.

It is interesting to note that Cicourel and Douglas, the main thrust of whose work has been the clarification of conventional sociology, both handle Wittgenstein with greater caution than do many of their colleagues. Cicourel comes down against 'the view that meaning is a situational fiction because use changes continuously' (1964:179), but elsewhere (1973) comes close to that view. Douglas notes that the linguistic ethnomethodologists 'have a strong tendency to agree with the Wittgensteinian edict that "language is its use", which leads them to try to get at "meanings" by analysing the uses of language in everyday life' (1971:33). He goes on to point out that they are led, in turn, to try to get at meanings entirely by what is externally observable—so that paradoxically they end up in a behaviourist position.[8]

What is really at stake is the ethnomethodologists' reluctance to allow sociology to discuss its problems according to different rules, within a distinct province of meaning—and this is precisely one of the criticisms made by Ernest Gellner (1968) of Oxford linguistic philosophy. This is odd, for the ethnomethodologists are always accusing conventional sociology of *not* using second-degree constructs. In practice, they seem sceptical about second-degree constructs of any generality, because they consider what Gellner calls 'polymorphism' to be inevitable and universal both in the concepts and meanings of everyday life *and* within the sociological realm.

What does Gellner mean by polymorphism? This is most easily explained by means of the distinction between a concept and a homonym. An example of a very obvious homonym is the word 'racket', which can refer either to the activities of Al Capone, to an artifact used in the game of tennis, or to a medieval musical instrument, there being no connection between these three meanings. As Gellner points out, pre-Wittgensteinian philosophy assumed that

> a concept if clear, has one criterion (which may of course contain a number of conditions in conjunction or even as alternatives), and that if on the other hand there is a multiplicity of sets of criteria, we are already dealing with homonyms. [1968: 50–51]

But this clarity in the use of language is precisely what is denied by linguistic philosophers (and ethnomethodologists). They see homonyms or, more generally, polymorphism everywhere. They strenuously emphasize complexity, variegation, blurred boundaries and transitions between concepts; therefore generalizations *as such* tend to be suspect.

Now, am I right in contending that polymorphism is a key part of the ethnomethodologists' case? Certainly even Jack Douglas, who has certain reservations about ethnomethodology, states it quite clearly—and not only in his insinuations about coroners! The general principle underlying all phenomenological sociologies, writes Douglas, is 'the principle of the integrity of the situation'. While it is true that most sociologists would accept that 'concrete human events are always to some degree dependent on the situational context in which they occur and can be adequately explained only by taking into consideration the situational context' (1971:37), the principle of the integrity of the situation is something more radical than that. It can alternatively be called 'the principle of the contextual determination of meaning', namely that 'the context within which a given statement or action occurs is of fundamental importance in determining meanings imputed to it by the members of society'. Actually, it is probably impossible to produce a coherent theory of meaning wholly independent of context—linguistic and extra-linguistic—and yet people do seem to interpret meanings also in a more general and relatively context-free manner. The question is one of degree. If the dogma of the contextual determination of meaning is pushed to extremes, as it is by ethnomethodologists much more than other social phenomenologists (Garfinkel 1967:31; Filmer, *et al.* 1972:108ff.), it leads implicitly to the supposition that an ideographic, a purely descriptive, social science is possible. As Gellner remarked of the linguistic philosophers, 'they implicitly claim to know or describe an individual thing, or a use of language, *without* having to employ some general concept' (1968:57).

Just how pervasive is polymorphism? Certainly it is fairly extensive in everyday language. Probably no complex language could ever attain perfect consistency. Ambiguity may, indeed, be essential to its working. In his paper 'Concepts and Society' (1970), Gellner gave several examples of ambiguous terms—'nobility' (the people and the quality) in English, and others from the Berbers of North Africa. Yet he was able to expose the polymorphism and explain the usage using clear words, unambiguous to his sociological readers. More fundamentally, he demonstrated the final inevitability of translating 'native' or 'member' meanings into terms with common currency in the sociological 'province of meaning'. So, finally, we return to the realization that emic terms, though not translatable into etic ones, have to be laid out on a standard grid, whether that be truly etic or merely 'standardized sociological emic'.

The main positive contribution of the ethnomethodologists has been to make sociologists think again about their procedures, even if not to accept all the criticisms as valid. And it is a useful reminder that many conventional sociological concepts—like those in the field of social stratification, or roles, which will be discussed in Chapter 4—are not perfectly unambiguous. Most sociologists, however, believe they can be improved, and are justified by their usefulness and intelligibility *to sociologists.*

Lévi-Strauss and Structuralism

Ethnomethodologists, adopting a very emic approach, are led to a particularistic reluctance to generalize about cultural phenomena. Claude Lévi-Strauss's brand of structuralism offers a contrast. Though his raw data are no less emic, the structures Lévi-Strauss seeks are not mere phenomena of social life, but are inferred by him, as anthropologist, to be behind the phenomena. And his theories, intended to have universal scope, often involve the wildest generalizations. Lévi-Strauss's explanations, whether of myths or of kinship systems, would fail by a mile to satisfy Schutz's 'postulate of adequacy', being entirely incomprehensible to the native and far from perfectly clear to many of his social scientific readers. Andreski says of Lévi-Strauss:

> . . . he began to spin out speculations sufficiently vague to be safe from the danger of confrontation with awkward facts, where undigested bits of mathematics and linguistics are juxtaposed with an unordered array of bits of ethnography, seasoned with Marxism *à la mode* and served with that coffee-house philosophy known as existentialism. [Andreski 1972: 84]

If this does not explain why Lévi-Strauss has excited so much attention among professional social scientists, it at least expresses Andreski's emotions quite well. Murphy (1963) speaks more tersely of 'Zen Marxism'.

Unlike most anthropologists, Lévi-Strauss's ultimate concern is not the explanation of the organization of particular societies, but with the discovery of fundamental structures of the human mind. For him,

> Ethnographic analysis tries to arrive at invariants beyond the empirical diversity of human societies. . . . Rousseau foresaw this with his usual acumen: 'One needs to look near at hand if one wants to study men; but to study man one must learn to look from afar. . . .' [1968a: 247]

Ethnographic evidence, of which Lévi-Strauss makes abundant use, is in the end of interest to him only in so far as it can be used as evidence of mental processes valid for all human minds.

> The recurrence of a detail of custom in two different parts of the map is not a matter to which Lévi-Strauss attaches any particular importance. In his view, the universals of human culture exist only at the level of structure, never at the level of manifest fact. [Leach 1970: 27]

Lévi-Strauss, like Durkheim and Mauss before him, sees it as a universal requirement of the human mind to divide, to categorize and to classify phenomena. Even the colour spectrum, which physicists know to be a continuum, is universally divided up, though by different cultures in different ways. Lévi-Strauss argues that the fundamental form of our categorization is binary. Our minds process what we observe in the form Red/not-Red, Tree/not-Tree, most generally X/not-X. His inspiration for this assumption is drawn from the world of computers, which carry out complex operations entirely on the basis of binary logic, and particularly from Roman Jakobsen and the Prague school of linguistics. Jakobsen and his colleagues showed that the recognizable phonemes which constitute any language are constructed by the binary opposition of contrasting phonetic sounds. We discriminate between phonemes in terms of opposed 'distinctive features' of consonant and vowel sounds, such as compact/diffuse, grave/acute, nasal/oral. Lévi-Strauss seems merely to assume that, if our minds process sounds in this fashion, they must process everything else that way too (1963, ch. 2–4); his debt to linguistics is limited to an analogy, and analogies are always suspect. Moreover, the Prague school is not the latest thing in linguistics. Chomsky's work makes it appear

> not necessarily false but . . . certainly inadequate. Where speech is concerned, the ultimate objective of research is to discover not merely how children learn to distinguish noise contrasts as significant but how they acquire the generative rules which allow them to formulate meaningful patterns of sound in the first place and what sort of rules these may be. By comparison, the manifest cultural data with which Levi-Strauss is playing are very superficial. [Leach, 1970: 113]

But let us now look at what Lévi-Strauss does with his cultural data. Primitive man, as much as civilized man, says Lévi-Strauss, thinks about his society, seeking to understand himself and his environment, and mentally manipulating what he perceives. Men everywhere develop semi-coherent schemes by which they give meaning to their activities. Thus far, neither Schutz nor the ethnomethodologists would demur. But these 'conscious models' or 'informants' models' are incomplete, contradictory and distorted. Lévi-Strauss believes it possible for the anthropologist to discern an underlying structural truth, which native explanations reflect but do not expose.

Now discrepancies between native accounts and observable social realities have been exposed by other than structuralist methods.

Both Redfield (1930) and Lewis (1951) studied the village of Tepoztlán in Mexico, and the anthropological world was disturbed by the radical disagreement between their two accounts. Redfield painted a picture of a close-knit, harmonious community and went so far as to base an ideal-type of peasant or 'folk' society on his findings (1947). Lewis, however, discovered conflict, distrust and social isolation in the same society. A great controversy raged, but the most plausible reconciliation seems to be that each portrayed part of the truth, each equally essential to the other (Murphy 1972:104). Redfield recorded the accepted 'conscious model' of the society—the ideology by which the natives represent the situation to themselves and others; Lewis recorded the action—the way things worked in practice. Lévi-Strauss has pointed to a number of similar, if superficially less dramatic, contradictions. For instance, the Sherente, Bororo and other Brazilian Indians depict their own societies as organized in two exogamous moities. But do such 'dual organizations' actually exist? Lévi-Strauss contends that the conscious model simply cannot explain the actual pattern of marriages which takes place: 'this image amounts to a theory, or rather a transmutation of reality, itself of an entirely different nature' (1963:121). The conscious model is an essential clue to reality but does not itself explain it. To explain it, it is necessary for the anthropologist to construct by inference the 'unconscious model', which is often obscured both for him and for his informant by the conscious model. In the case of the Sherente, the latent reality seems to involve three, not two descent groups, and in practice they seem to prefer to marry their patrilineal cross-cousin, while expressing preference for the matrilineal one (1963, ch. 7).[9]

None of this, however, does more than hint at the use Lévi-Strauss makes of his assumptions about the binary organization of the mind. For this it is best to turn to his more recent works on myths. These include *The Savage Mind* (1968a) and the four-volume *Mythologiques* (1968c, 1969, 1971, 1973). The latter title is significant—'mytho-logic'. Lévi-Strauss is not concerned, as earlier writers like Sir James Frazer were, with the manifest meaning of myths. Rather he is concerned with their 'logic' and transmutations.

> Mythological analysis has not, and cannot have, as its aim to show how men think. ... I therefore claim to show, not how men think in myths, but how myths operate in men's minds without their being aware of the fact. [1969b: 12][10]

The manifest meaning of myths is often obscure, even to those who tell them and hear them. And as they are passed on, they are changed and transformed. There are many variations on similar themes, and in different versions some elements are omitted or inverted. Contradiction abounds.

Lévi-Strauss believes that the structure can best be discovered by considering a whole complex of myths together and rearranging the elements. He compares a complex of myths to a musical score, which can be read simultaneously for the melodic sequence (horizontally) and for the harmonic structure (vertically). The counterparts to melody and harmony in the study of myth he calls the syntagmatic and paradigmatic dimensions. (These terms are, again, borrowed from linguistics, where *syntagmatic* refers to the sequence of words in a sentence, while the *paradigmatic dimension* is the stock of alternative nouns, verbs and so on which might alternatively have been used in the sentence.) The syntagmatic chain refers to the actual sequence of elements in a particular myth, while the paradigmatic dimension links the similar elements in alternative and related versions of the myth. Lévi-Strauss does not ask which is the earliest or 'true' version of a myth—never an easy question to answer, especially in pre-literate societies. 'On the contrary, we define the myth as consisting of all its versions; or to put it otherwise, a myth remains the same as long as it is felt as such' (1963:216–17). So the different versions are arranged along the paradigmatic axis.

How this works out can be seen in reference to one of the most famous of all complexes of myths, that centring on Oedipus. In Figure 2 (derived from Lévi-Strauss 1963:214) these themes are set out. Normally the story would be read from left to right and top to bottom. But, apart from the syntagmatic chains (the stories, left to right), it can be seen that certain similarities emerge in the elements as arranged in the vertical (paradigmatic) columns. Now, where do binary oppositions come in? This hinges on the interpretation of the four paradigmatic themes. To explain Lévi-Strauss's interpretation would involve following him through a long argument. But, briefly, the theme of Column I is blood relations which are more intimate than they should be—'the overrating of blood relations'. Column II expresses the opposite—fratricide and patricide are 'the underrating of blood relations'. Column III relates to the slaying of monsters, and Column IV to difficulties in walking straight and standing upright. By a spectacularly speculative route, Lévi-Strauss then reasons that the third and fourth columns symbolize, respectively, the *denial* and the *persistence of* the autocthonous origin of man

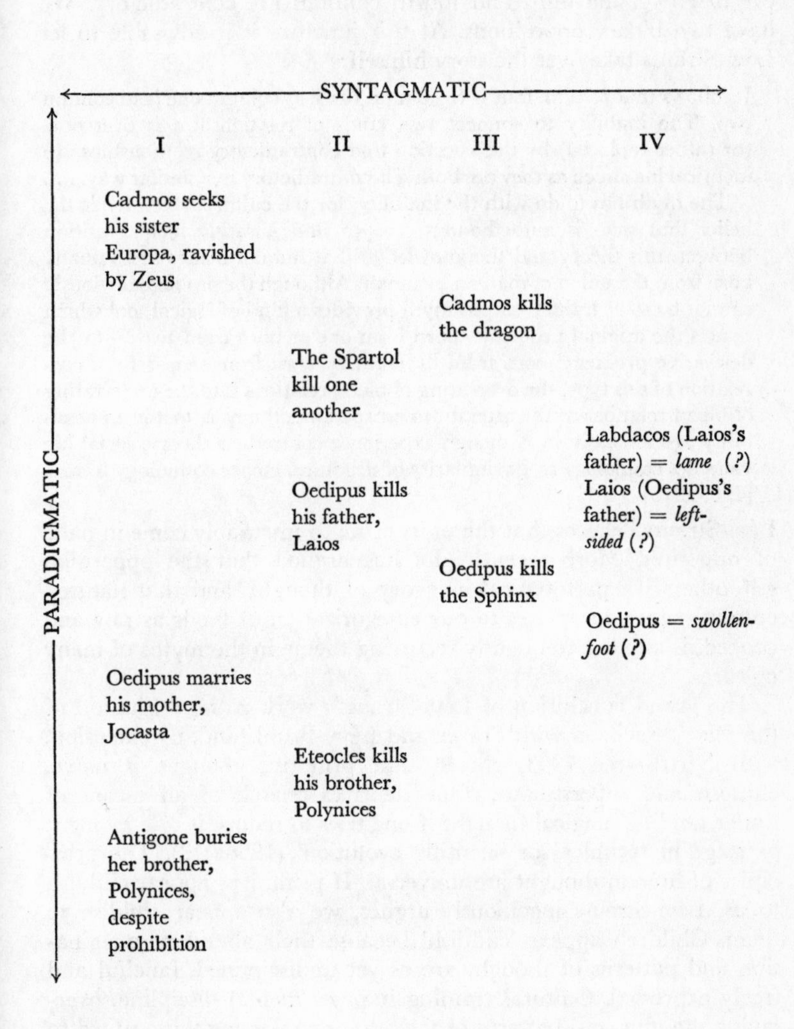

Figure 2 (from Lévi-Strauss 1963:214)

(1963:215–16). (*Autocthonous* means 'sprung from the soil', incidentally—the Greeks claimed to have originated in this way.) Like the first two, the third and fourth columns are contradictory. We have two binary oppositions. At this juncture it is advisable to let Lévi-Strauss take over the story himself:

> It follows that column four is to column three as column one is to column two. The inability to connect two kinds of relationships is overcome (or rather replaced) by the assertion that contradictory relationships are identical inasmuch as they are both self-contradictory in a similar way....
>
> The myth has to do with the inability, for the culture which holds the belief that man is autocthonous, ... to find a satisfactory transition between this theory and the knowledge that human beings are actually born from the union of man and woman. Although the problem obviously cannot be solved, the Oedipus myth provides a kind of logical tool which relates the original problem—born from one or born from two?—to the derivative problem: born from different or born from same? By a correlation of this type, the overrating of blood relations is to the underrating of blood relations as the attempt to escape autocthony is to the impossibility to succeed in it. Although experience contradicts theory, social life validates cosmology by its similarity of structure. Hence cosmology is true. [1963:216]

Lévi-Strauss believes that the units of myth invariably come in pairs of opposites. More recently, he has argued that the opposition self/other is a prototypical category of thought, and that nature/culture, which he relates to our categorization of foods as raw and cooked, is another frequently recurring theme in the myths of many cultures.

The grand conclusion of Lévi-Strauss's work is the refutation of the view associated with Frazer and Lévy-Bruhl (and, by extension, with Sartre—see 1963, ch. 9) that primitive thought is naïve, childish and superstitious. 'One deprives oneself of all means of understanding magical thought if one tries to reduce it to a moment or stage in technical or scientific evolution' (1968a:13). The principles of human thought are universal. If primitives appear childish to us, Lévi-Strauss ingeniously argues, we also appear childish to them. Children appear 'childish' because their abundant imagination and patterns of thought are as yet undisciplined, fanciful and freely expressed. Cultural training imposes mental discipline, overlaying the universal patterns of thought and selecting those suited to a particular social environment. Primitives appear childish to us because their thought is ill-suited to our technological society; but we also appear childish to them, for *our* logics are ill-adapted to *their* environment.

This outline, however bald it is, should suffice to suggest the fascination of Lévi-Strauss's ideas, and a fundamental doubt: is this social science? Tracing paradigmatic themes seems often to rest on a poetic sensibility rather than on anything reducible to logic. Are Lévi-Strauss's analyses replicable—could any two anthropologists hope to come up with the same interpretation of the same raw myths, even if they were familiar with structuralist methods? Furthermore, Lévi-Strauss has often been accused of selecting data to illustrate his theories rather than to test them. Are they, indeed, testable? Since any contradiction seems to be grist to Lévi-Strauss's mill, perhaps they are irrefutable and therefore mean little. Yet, while making all these points, Edmund Leach still feels able to conclude:

> And even if his argument eventually has to be repudiated in certain details, we simply must accept certain fundamental parts of it. Any knowledge that the individual has about the external world is derived from structured messages which are received through the senses . . . patterned sound through the ears, patterned light through the eyes, patterned smell through the nose, and so on. But since we are aware of a *single* total experience . . . *not* a sound world plus a light world plus a smell world . . . it must be because the coding of the various sensory signal systems can be made consistent—so that hearing *and* sight *and* smell *and* taste *and* touch etc. seem all to be giving the *same* message. The problem then is simply to devise a means of breaking the code. Lévi-Strauss thinks he has solved this problem; even those who have doubts can hardly fail to be astonished by the ingenuity of the exercise. [Leach 1970: 93, italics and ellision marks in original]

Conclusions

Lévi-Strauss may well take speculation too far, spinning out his theories well beyond the point of testability. Yet it *is* an essential part of the social scientist's task to *generalize* about what he observes and to produce theories which can be tested by fellow scholars. This is true even when the subject under scrutiny is ordinary people's cognition and interpretations in everyday life. The ethnomethodologists' particularistic focus on microscopic social situations is a prison of their own choosing; there is nothing in the work of Alfred Schutz to confine sociology to this level. The cognitive foundations of society cannot now be neglected, but it is also possible to study the structure and dynamics of social processes at a more general and macroscopic level. This we shall now proceed to do.

Notes

1. If Chomsky's view is accepted that languages have a common 'deep structure', then the Sapir–Whorf hypothesis must rely upon differences in the surface structure of different grammars.

2. For a much fuller discussion of this school of thought, see Harris (1968), ch. 18, 'Emics, Etics and the New Ethnography'.

3. Schutz represents a rather 'positivistic' form of phenomenology. A few sociologists have been directly influenced by the more romantic phenomenology of Maurice Merleau-Ponty. See Filmer, *et al.* (1972:123ff.) and esp. John O'Neill's *Perception, Expression and History: The Social Phenomenology of Maurice Merleau-Ponty* (1970), as well as O'Neill's volume of essays (1972). For an interpretation of earlier sociologists in the light of 'existential-phenomenology', see Tiryakian (1965).

4. The resemblance to Cooley's idea of 'the looking-glass self' is striking; indeed, Laing conjures up a whole hall of mirrors.

5. Since writing this section, I have had access to the pre-publication typescript of John Goldthorpe's review essay (1973), in which he makes some of the same points.

6. Cicourel (1968) extended similar reasoning to the field of delinquency.

7. Schutz did say (1964:83) that we should not speak of an 'ideal-type' *tout court*, but must specify the problem for which it had been constructed. Here Schutz was, essentially, criticizing what Helmut Wagner (1964) was later to call the 'fallacy of the displacement of scope' (of concepts and theories from their micro- or macro-sociological level of origin to the other), but rather broadened the issue. Somewhat Delphically he said, 'To be sure, it must be admitted that the term "level" applies strictly only to whole systems of problems; nevertheless, the consequences are, in principle, the same.' However, I do not take even this as warranty for the ethnomethodologists' extreme distrust of generalities.

8. Some surprising common elements in behaviourism, phenomenology and Wittgenstein's philosophy are indicated by Day (1969a, 1969b).

9. These remarks touch upon the controversy surrounding Lévi-Strauss's *Elementary Structures of Kinship* (1968b), but there is

no space to discuss that here. A very clear (brutally clear) account of this involved debate can be found in Harris (1968:487–513); alternatively, see Leach (1970:95–111), or (briefer and more sympathetic) Murphy (1972 :197–205).

10. The last sentence is obscure in the French: '*Nous ne prétendons donc pas montrer comment les hommes pensent dans les mythes mais comment les mythes se pensent dans les hommes et à leur insu.*' Two published English translations are somewhat at odds.

3. Interaction

In discussing the nature of social action and the knowledge people employ in their actions, a great deal has been implied about social *inter*action. Now something more explicit must be said about it, for interaction is the key to understanding what sociologists mean by 'social structure'. So far we have spoken rather indiscriminately of actors defining 'situations'. Yet individual definitions and even collectively 'negotiated' meanings, though an essential starting-point, do not exhaust the observations the sociologist can make about the social process. The interaction of several people produces structure and structured processes of change within situations which cannot easily be deduced from knowledge of individual definitions of the situation. Let us examine why this is so.

Obviously, the interpretation and anticipation of others' actions—or of one's own for that matter—are unlikely to be a fully conscious process. Indeed, the only situations in which we are fully conscious of this are likely to be ones of some strain and difficulty. It is only when we interact with someone else whose actions are not predictable or do not 'make sense' that we become acutely aware of the usually unconscious or semiconscious skills required for smooth interaction. The existence and importance of these skills can be demonstrated, as we have seen, by intentionally disrupting familiar situations, and they are the ethnomethodologists' chief interest in society.

Conscious or unconscious interpretation of other people's actions and intentions is inevitable within interaction. As Erving Goffman argued in a brilliant early paper (1955), in social encounters every person tends to act out a 'line'. A 'line' is

> a pattern of verbal and non-verbal acts by which he expresses his view of the situation, and by this, his evaluation of the participants, especially

> himself. *Regardless of whether a person has consciously taken a line, he does so in effect, because the other people assume he is doing so*, that he is taking a stand. So if he is to cope with their responses to him, he has to allow for the impression he has made on them. And so on. [1955: 213, my italics]

'Lines' can express many qualities: equality, subordination, superiority, friendliness, social distance. But many encounters are of a stylized, conventional nature, giving little scope for choice of line. In such situations, we assume a great deal on the basis of only a few known attributes of the other person. The course of action is then particularly easy to predict because many similar situations have been observed before. The cursory encounter between customer and shop assistant is an illustration. Frequently repeated between people usually otherwise unknown to each other, it ordinarily comprises little more than an exchange of goods and money accompanied by the common courtesies. Another kind of fairly superficial encounter is conversation at a cocktail party. The main expectation in such a situation, as Georg Simmel noted in his discussion of the 'sociology of sociability' (1950 :part 1, ch. 3), is that smooth, pleasant interaction will be an end in itself. The situation is more egalitarian; people are not expected to go beyond certain limits in scoring points off one another. The encounter is somewhat stylized and predictable, but much less so than the anonymous transaction between customer and assistant, and the actor has rather more choice of 'lines'. The main requirement is that once a line is taken, it is taken consistently, so that it gradually becomes reasonably predictable. If a person has not previously met the others, and particularly if he is unlikely to meet them again, he has more choice of 'line', for the necessity to say and do nothing inconsistent with his past and future actions is diminished.

The idea of consistency is a key one. It is essential to our interpretation and anticipation of others' actions, and equally essential to our anticipation of their interpretations of our actions. What we interpret is not the 'unit act' (Parsons's term) in isolation, but the act as part of a pattern of action. We group acts together into meaningful configurations or *Gestalten*. These configurations have a consistency which may not be in any testable sense logical, but which is, or comes to be, recognized as consistent by the participants in a given situation, and often more widely than that. This is the essence of the idea of *roles*. Placing an action in the context of a role is what makes it possible not only to interpret its meaning and anticipate what will happen next, but also to evaluate it. Ralph Turner notes that

> the lie which is an expression of the role of friend is an altogether different thing from the same lie taken as a manifestation of the role of confidence man. Different actions may be viewed as the same or equivalent; identical actions may be viewed as quite different; placement of the actions in a role context determines such judgements. [1962: 24]

Roles

The term role has become universal in sociological parlance. Unfortunately, agreement on what the concept denotes has been less than universal. Underlying many rival definitions have been disagreements about the origins of the standards by which a pattern of action is recognized as consistent role-playing. For Mead, a role was a vantage-point, and his followers have tended to emphasize that interaction is a tentative process, in which consistent roles are gradually established (see especially Turner 1962). In contrast, for the anthropologist Ralph Linton (1936 : ch. 8), a role designated a pattern of behaviour 'defined by the culture' and merely enacted by the individual. Linton distinguished between role and status, though recognizing that empirically they were inseparable.

> A status, as distinct from the individual who may occupy it, is simply a collection of rights and duties. . . . The relation between any individual and any status he holds is somewhat like that between the driver of an automobile and the driver's place in the machine. . . .
>
> A *role* represents the dynamic aspect of a status. The individual is socially assigned to a status and occupies it with relation to other statuses. When he puts the rights and duties which constitute the status into effect, he is performing a role. [1936: 113–14]

It can be seen that Linton's view of roles is somewhat mechanistic. As an anthropologist, he seems to have been so impressed by the diversity of human cultures that he came to see roles as pre-existent slots into which the plastic individual could be inserted and trained. Roles were models by which the individual's attitudes and behaviour were made congruent with those of others involved in the pattern of interaction. And the more congruent they were, the more smoothly would the social group or society run. Even in modern societies, most roles were ascribed rather than achieved; Linton placed most emphasis on how people were reared, trained and moulded for given roles, learning to conform to their requirements, rather than on competition for and choice among roles, let alone on the creation of new roles. Obviously this view sheds relatively little light on how roles come to be made, especially within informal and newly forming groups, the process of innovation in roles, nor on the conditions in which roles become *or do not become* adjusted to each other. Yet it was the Lintonian conception of roles which Parsons and Shils took over into their dyadic model of interaction.

The Parsonian Dyad

The joint monograph 'Values, Motives and Systems of Action' (Parson and Shils 1951: Part II), written when Parsons was at his most behaviouristic, presents a discussion of roles in the context of dyadic interaction between 'ego' and 'alter'. The whole individual is seen as largely irrelevant to understanding the interaction process; the relevant unit is the role. The role is the segment of his total action which is relevant to the relationship in question. The main ingredient of the role is the 'role expectation'. Role expectations are what ego is expected to do in a given situation, both by himself and by others. Alter, of course, responds to ego's action, and alter's response constitutes a 'sanction' for ego. Sanctions may be for ego either positive, reinforcing and rewarding, or negative and punishing. If alter conforms to ego's expectations, he positively sanctions ego; if he deviates from his expectations, the sanction is negative. The relationship is reciprocal, for ego responds in turn to alter's actions. Ego's actions, in conformity to his role expectations, thus in return constitute sanctions for alter's actions. 'What are sanctions to ego,' write Parsons and Shils, 'are also role expectations to alter, and vice versa' (*ibid*:1951). The authors recognize that, initially, the expectations of ego and alter for each other's behaviour may not be identical. However, they suggest that within a continuing relationship, ego's and alter's interaction will gradually adjust into conformity with each other's role expectations. That is because each experiences the other's conformity as a positive sanction, which in turn is because, for each, the other's responses are the means of attaining whatever objectives they seek through the relationship. Underlying the scheme is an implicit assumption that it is always rewarding to conform to established social norms.

The Pattern Variables

That Parsons is concerned almost entirely with socially recognized and established roles, and is too eager to assume that even informal interaction tends towards such roles, is shown by the use he makes of the Pattern Variables in categorizing roles and role expectations. Parsons listed five dichotomous choices of modes of orientation (Parsons 1951:58ff.; Parsons and Shils 1951:76ff.). These are said to have had their origins in consideration of Ferdinand Toennies's conceptualization of pre-modern and modern societies as *Gemeinschaft* and *Gesellschaft*. In the course of studying the professions in the contemporary United States, Parsons realized that many supposedly *gemeinschaftlich* characteristics persist into a fully modern society. Relationships within the family remain intimate. The doctor combines the 'modern' characteristic of professional detachment with a 'pre-modern' rejection of the cash nexus as a basis for the quality of his service. This insight led Parsons to break down the Toennies dichotomy into five independently variable choices. The *Affectivity/Affective Neutrality* choice is concerned with whether the emotions are involved in a relationship or whether detachment is the pattern. (More accurately, since the emotions are always in some sense involved, it is concerned with whether immediate or deferred 'gratification' is sought.) *Diffuseness/Specificity* concerns whether the relationship involves the whole personality (as between husband and wife) or only a limited segment (as between shop assistant and customer). *Particularism/Universalism* poses the question: is a person's performance of a role judged by special criteria (again the wife—'beauty is in the eye of the beholder') or by generally accepted standards (a secretary's shorthand speed)? The *Ascription/Achievement* variable, borrowed from Linton, is also known as 'Quality/Performance': is a person considered suitable for a position by virtue of some quality, such as being the eldest son of the monarch, or because of some achievement like the acquisition of a degree or a diploma? And, finally, *Collectivity Orientation/Self Orientation* is self-explanatory, and closely related to the supposed modern trend to individualism and instrumental relationships.[1]

The primary constituents of role expectations, write Parsons and Shils, 'are analytically derivable from the pattern variables when these are combined with the specific types of situations' (whatever that might mean). It is difficult to see how it could be possible to substantiate the claim that there are five, and only five, relevant choices by which all actions may be classified.[2] Many sociologists have also found it more difficult to see the variables as dichotomous than as continua. Nonetheless, it cannot be denied that in a less than systematic way the pattern variables have been widely used by sociologists for characterizing the innumerable specialized and institutionalized roles found within the advanced division of labour of modern societies. But to describe a doctor's professional role as 'affectively neutral' is not in any way to explain why it is as it is and how the pattern became institutionalized.

Roles vary widely in the degree of their institutionalization. Parsons and Shils explain what this means as follows:

> By institutionalization we mean the integration of the complementary role expectation and sanction patterns with a generalized value system *common* to the members of the more inclusive collectivity, of which the system of complementary role-actions may be a part. In so far as ego's set of role expectations is institutionalized, the sanctions which express the role expectations of other actors will tend to reinforce his own need-dispositions to conform with these expectations by rewarding it and punishing deviance. [1951: 191, italics in original]

In plainer English, the role of shop assistant is highly institutionalized because everyone knows and accepts the usual patterns of action which consitute the minimum characteristics of the role. Therefore, the assistant and all her customers can judge whether she is adequately and consistently playing the role. Throughout his writings, Parsons is chiefly interested in this kind of role. That is why he adopts the Lintonian conception—'definitions of the situation' are ready made, and the standards of consistency are brought into the interaction situation from without. Ralph Turner speaks of this as *external validation* of a role. This happens when:

> the behaviour is judged to constitute a role by others whose judgements are felt to have some claim to correctness or legitimacy. The simplest form of such a criterion is discovery of a name in common use for the role. If the pattern of behaviour can be readily assigned a name, it acquires *ipso facto* the exteriority and constraint of Durkheim's 'collective representations'. [1962: 30]

But, with greater caution than Linton or Parsons and Shils, Turner immediately adds that

> Naming does not assure [sic] that there will be agreement on the content of the role; *it merely insures that people will do their disagreeing as if there were something real about which to disagree.* [my italics]

For the roles of shop steward and manager are well institutionalized, and specific examples of each may play their parts well. That does not guarantee that everything in the factory will run harmoniously—often quite the opposite. The fact that, in the short view at least, there is an objective conflict of interest between worker and employer (what is income to one is cost to the other) makes sure that role expectations have a certain obduracy not easily eroded. Parsons would point out that, even though the conflict between shop stewards and managers may be very real and sustained, it will usually take place within a matrix of agreement limiting the means by which the conflict is pursued.

This may well be true of most situations. But Elias (1970:79–83) warns us to remember that interaction can settle down to a stable pattern without any such moral component in expectations, a pattern based entirely on expectations in the probabilistic sense. Consider two tribes, both hunters and gatherers, who repeatedly encounter each other as they search for food in a tract of land. Food is scarce, and for reasons beyond their control and understanding—drought, for instance—it is getting scarcer. Conflict between the two tribes pursuing the same scarce resources breaks out and deepens; one tribe raids the other and kills a few of its members, and shortly afterwards a similar retaliatory raid takes place. Each tribe makes such arrangements as it can to defend its camps, but the war drags on. It may go on until both tribes are wiped out, until only one remains, or until both are so diminished in numbers as to make food supplies adequate once more. Or none of these things may happen, and the war just goes on and on. The tribes are clearly ecologically interdependent. Their interdependence stems from material circumstances, not from shared cognitions, norms or values. Nor do they acquire such shared orientations. They may not even speak each other's languages. Nonetheless, it is impossible to understand the actions, plans, goals or general ways of life of either tribe except by its interdependence with the other. This may be a limiting and rare case, but examples are not unknown. The possibility should be borne in mind as a safeguard against the over-ready assumption that relationships tend inevitably towards co-operation, harmony and equilibration.

Role-Taking: Process versus Conformity

Followers of Mead, though recognizing that where statuses are established, named and recognized (as they usually are in formal organizations) the Lintonian conception of role has a certain superficial plausibility, deny that the actor occupies a position for which 'the culture prescribes' a concise set of rules or norms. The formal organization such as a bureaucracy is a special case. Informal groups, whether in the laboratory or 'in the wild', show the role-taking process in its more general form. Roles correspond to a person's 'me's', which exist in relation to the roles of others, real or imaginary—father and son, leader and follower, 'me now' and posterity. The conceptions others have of their own roles in relation to oneself and of one's role in relation to themselves have to be discovered in the course of interaction. And the role-expectations may change and grow, the boundaries shift during or because of interaction. Even the most familiar roles, such as father and son, change. The roles of father in relation to son, and vice versa, are very different when the son is adult and the father retired from what they were between the young father and the boy. So the process is always tentative.

In task-orientated groups, newly formed in the laboratory of people hitherto unknown to one another, the process of role-formation and differentiation has repeatedly been observed.[3] Gradually there tend to emerge at least two recognizable roles: those of instrumental leader (who guides the group towards its prescribed task) and expressive leader (the guardian of group morale). These roles exist in relation to each other and to other members of the group. Yet they cannot be said to be in any sense culturally prescribed, and members of the group may indeed be largely unconscious of them. It is not easy to predict in advance *who* will assume these roles, though of course members do not enter such groups as *tabulae rasae*. Individuals' past experience, background and personality may increase the likelihood of their assuming the role. Even so, experience and personality count only *relatively* to those of others involved in the interaction—'in the land of the blind, the one-eyed man is king'. The process of tentative exploration is called, by Turner, 'internal validation' of role-taking (1962:29). It is, of course, supplemented in many situations by external validation—in formal, 'labelled' situations, roles are at least in part predefined. The Meadian, however, as well as the ethnomethodologist, would argue that they are never *entirely* externally defined.

Enough has been said to indicate that, in part, the Lintonian and Meadian conceptions of role draw attention to institutionalized and non-institutionalized roles respectively. This is not a dichotomy but a continuum along which roles vary. Yet this is not the whole story. Used with great care, the Linton view provides a sort of shorthand for what we observe in formal organizations and in the plethora of widely recognized specialities within the social division of labour. It represents a higher level of abstraction than the Meadian concept.[4] What in effect happens is that Linton takes the lowest common denominator of the behaviour which constitutes the role of shop assistant, bus conductor, medicine man or whatever—the minimum qualities by which people in general recognize the role as such. As noted in Chapter 1 (p. 34 above), the process of describing the common characteristics of a large number of people is likely to produce a picture close to the 'cultural norm'. But this procedure poses an acute danger of conceptual reification; it is a very short step from this process of abstraction to reifying the description and arguing that 'the culture prescribes that . . .'.

Plainly, external validation plays some part. But around the basic minimum of 'bus-conductorness' (the absence of which does draw down on itself sanctions, like the sack) every bus conductor elaborates. The jolly extravert conductor with a cheery insult for everyone produces quite different interaction patterns among passengers from the efficient but silent conductor. There is no real contradiction here, but the Meadian conception stays closer to interaction as it happens. And this is important, for no role actually observed is ever totally institutionalized. What George Homans calls the subinstitutional or elementary behaviour is never absent.

> [It] does not grow just in the gaps between institutions; it clings to institutions as to a trellis. It grows everywhere—if only because the norms established as institutions and the orders given in instituted organizations can never prescribe human behaviour to the last detail, even if they were obeyed to the letter, which they are not. Indeed the elementary behaviour helps to explain how and why they are disobeyed. [Homans 1961: 391]

Blau's famous study of the Federal law-enforcement agency (1955), in which agents were formally forbidden to consult colleagues other than superiors in deciding whether to take action against firms infringing the law, yet informally did so continually, is a classic illustration of the subinstitutional facilitating the operation of the institution. The equally famous 'bank-wiring group' of the Hawthorne studies (Roethlisberger and Dickson 1939), in which informally evolved norms against 'rate-busting' frustrated formal incentives to greater output, illustrates the possible conflict of the institutional and subinstitutional.

The Inadequacy of the Dyad

It has become something of a tradition to use the dyad to explain roles and interaction. Though intended for heuristic purposes, this is in fact seriously misleading, for the most interesting aspects of interaction cannot be explained in dyadic terms.

Role Conflict

This is one of the simpler phenomena which appear in situations involving three or more people. It is easy to see how conflict can arise between playing one role with one partner and another role with a second partner. William James commented that it is difficult to be both a philosopher and a philanderer (which shows how misleading it can be to generalize from personal experience!). James was thinking of our limited resources of time and energy, but also of the need for psychic unity. But conflicting role expectations are an everyday phenomenon. Suppose, in an examination, one student spotted a friend cheating. He might well disapprove strongly, but it is unlikely (not impossible) that he would take it upon himself to 'betray' the friend to the invigilator. But what would happen if the student were not a fellow examinee, but himself acting as invigilator (a situation apparently not so bizarre in American universities)? To report his friend would still, in some sense, be a breach of the friendship role, but not to do so would be to breach the role of invigilator. Implicit in the situation is the third party of the university authorities who have employed the invigilator. Taking the role of the other is not so simple—*which* other? Nor does the generalized other help much—the generalized other would be in the same dilemma. What the invigilator-student would do would depend on a number of considerations: his commitment to one role or the other, the risk of discovery by one party or the other, and so on. This situation has, in fact, been the subject of well-known studies (Stouffer 1949; Stouffer and Toby 1951).

Role-sets

Conflicting role expectations do not arise only through the temporary or accidental conjuncture of two roles such as friend and invigilator in the one person. They are permanent and inherent for the occupants of some positions. Gross, Mason and McEachern (1958) studied the School Superintendent (roughly the U.S. equivalent of Director of Education in Britain). As a public official, the superintendent has to deal with several distinct groups, including the elected members of the local School Board who are his employers, with parents as 'customers', and with teachers as subordinates. Each group tends to expect different things of him. For instance, School Board members necessarily have to worry about financial control, while teachers are concerned that he obtains for them good pay, conditions and teaching facilities, and the parents make all sorts of demands about the content and quality of their children's education. The superintendent typically cannot 'deliver the goods' entirely to one group's satisfaction without dissatisfying one or more of the others. But it is inherent in his position that he has to seek a *modus vivendi* with each.

It was with this kind of situation in mind that Merton (1957) developed the notion of the role-set. Starting from Linton's definitions, Merton postulated that each status (such as School Superintendent) involves not a single associated role but an array of roles, each relating the occupant of the status to a distinct category of associates. Merton asked what social mechanisms were available to reconcile the conflicting expectations and demands of members of the role-set, at least to the extent that the status in question became a workable proposition. He identified the following as among the most significant. First of all, the relationship may be of relatively less importance for some members of the role-set than others. For parents, membership of the Parent-Teacher Association may be peripheral relative to their occupational and home concerns, so that they may be less concerned to exert pressure on the School Superintendent than are the teachers, whose occupation is a more central part of their lives. Secondly, some of the members of the role-set may be less powerful than others. The School Superintendent may be able to achieve a degree of autonomy if no one group is sufficiently powerful to impose its will; to the extent that groups form coalitions, his chances are reduced. Thirdly, a useful degree of inconsistency may be possible because it is not observed; members of the role-set do not interact continuously with each other, and so, to an obviously limited extent, a person may present a somewhat different face to separate individuals and groups in the role-set—a technique familiar to politicians. Fourthly and conversely, if the conflicting demands are recognized by the different parties involved, they may in some circumstances not press their own demands in full but seek some form of compromise. Fifthly, if the status is one of many like it (there are many School Superintendents), associations of those similarly placed may develop codes of conduct, thus providing one form of what Galbraith (1952) called 'countervailing power'. Merton gives as an example the American Library Association's code on censorship, an aid to librarians withstanding public campaigns against the theory of evolution, sex, sociology or whatever. This is a manifestation of increasing institutionalization of the role. Sixthly, discontented parties may withdraw from the role-set, though this is not easily achieved in a highly institutionalized situation such as that of the School Superintendency which we have taken as our main example. Superintendent, board members and teachers cannot withdraw (if they resign, someone else has to take their place), and parents can only do so by the drastic expedient of buying private education for their children. Finally, though, it has to be said that none of these six mechanisms need inevitably come into action, and conflicting role expectations frequently have to be lived with as a continuing aspect of social interaction.

Games, Numbers and Social Complexity

It was Georg Simmel (1858–1918) who perceptively drew attention to the qualitative differences between the dyad and the triad, and more generally to the significance of numbers in social life (1950: Part II). People involved in a dyad, he pointed out, are aware that the relationship has no existence beyond themselves. If either one of them withdraws, there is nothing left. They are jointly responsible for collective action, and the actions of each are fully known to the other. Therefore they are fully involved in the relationship; in Parsons's terms, it is a diffuse rather than specific involvement. The introduction of a third party brings changes more decisive than a fourth or subsequent member. A triad survives as a dyad after a third member withdraws. One member can withhold knowledge from the other two, or two from one, and one can hold the other two responsible for collective action. Simmel suggested three kinds of triad in which the role of the third party differs from that of the other two people. The third man may be a conciliator or mediator between the two, if he seeks the welfare of the group as a whole. Or he may pursue his own interests in the role of *tertius gaudens*, exploiting their differences. Or he may pursue a strategy of *divide et impera*, not merely exploiting existing disputes, but actively creating them for his own advantage.[5] Compared with the qualitative changes introduced by the third party, Simmel contended, the appearance of fourth and subsequent parties has relatively diminishing impact. It merely complicates and enlarges the possibilities which may emerge, further dispersing knowledge and chances of control.

Even so, more than half a century later, a clear understanding of the impact of increasing numbers on social processes is perhaps the single greatest gap in sociological theory. Sociologists still tend to jump from discussing social interaction in the dyad, triad and small groups to 'social systems', 'institutions' and 'societies', gratuitously described as 'very complex'. In sociologists' *argot*, we lack a full understanding of 'micro/macro linkages', and find it difficult to conceptualize the appearance of 'emergent properties' of large groups. One of the clearest statements yet made, however, is contained in Norbert Elias's discussion of 'games models' (Elias 1970: ch. 3).[6]

Elias on Games Models

The purpose of Elias's models is to show how the interweaving of people's actions leads to the emergence of patternings seemingly independent of any individual's actions and beyond his control. The actions and responses of participants towards each other are to be viewed as moves in games. The games are used heuristically; they are highly simplified analogies to real social processes. Yet because real games *are* social processes, the analogy is a good deal less dangerous than the usual biological and mechanical analogies so often used in sociology. The games models are all based on trials of strength, and the first and simpler ones can be thought of as quite close to a real game like chess. Strength or 'power' in the game is not an absolute quantity, a substance of which each player has a store, but a quality of the relationship in question. In chess, skill is very obviously a relative thing even at the very highest levels.

1. Two-person games: (a) Imagine two people playing a game, in which A is a very strong player and B a very weak one. A therefore has a great deal of control and influence over B, and can actually force B to make certain moves. (Think of 'huffing' in draughts.) Yet, at the same time, B has a degree of power over A, for A has to take B's moves into account in making his own moves. Even famous chess players occasionally come unstuck by failing to anticipate the implications of a very inferior player's moves. Both players must have *some* strength or there would be no game. A's 'power' over B is the excess of his strength over B's strength, in this case a considerable excess.

A thus has a high degree of control over his opponent, being able to force him to adopt certain tactics. This also means that A has a good deal of control—though it is not absolute—over the course of the game *as such*, not only over whether he will obtain victory, but how, and how quickly.

(b) Suppose the discrepancy between A's and B's strength in the game diminishes, either because B quickly becomes more skilled, or because A tires, or whatever. Two things also diminish: A's ability to use his own moves to force B to make particular moves, and A's ability to determine the course and result of the game. B's chances of control over A increase correspondingly. But, as the disparity between the players' strengths is reduced, *the course of the game*

increasingly passes beyond the control of either. Elias explains it like this:

> Both players will have correspondingly less ability to control the figuration of the game, for it will become less dependent on each player's private plans and intentions for the game. But conversely, each player's general strategy in the game and his every move will be increasingly dependent on the changing figuration of the game process. The character of the game will change, gradually ceasing to be the accomplishment of an individual plan and becoming a social process. In other words, there will emerge from the interweaving of moves made by two individual people a game process *which neither of the two people has planned.* [Elias 1970: 85, his italics]

Predicting the state of even a two-person game like chess, say twelve moves ahead, is extremely difficult. There are numerous possible outcomes with differing degrees of likelihood. What is more, the probabilities change with each successive move.

2. Multi-person games on one level: (a) Imagine a game in which a very strong player A simultaneously plays separate games against a number of less skilled opponents, B, C, D . . . N. The weaker players do not co-operate with each other. This is a situation familiar to the chess world in exhibition matches given by master-class players. A's advantage in each separate game is very great, and each separately resembles model 1(a). The only difference might be that A's superiority might be undermined as the number of separate games increased; there is a limit to the number of separate relationships which can effectively be carried on simultaneously by one person.

(b) Suppose, however, that A plays a single game against a coalition of B, C, D, . . . N, each of whom alone is weaker than A. The balance of power is then much more indeterminate. If the weaker players can form a unified and harmonious coalition, their degree of control over A's moves and over the course of the game is likely to be enhanced. If the coalition is beset by inner tensions and disagreements, however, that is likely to reduce the advantages of the coalition and might, just conceivably, put A at a greater advantage than he was in the absence of the coalitions.

If the difference in strength between A and the united coalition of B, C, D, . . . N should diminish, the course of the game becomes less a direct outcome of either side's plans, just as it did in 1(b).

(c) Imagine a game in which two groups play against each other. The two sides are of roughly equal strength, and the rules favour neither side. With many players, there is a flurry of move and countermove. Neither side can quite determine either the other side's tactics or the course of the game. The moves of one player can be understood neither alone nor solely in relation to those of fellow team members, but only with respect to the whole game. Episodes acquire a certain fleeting structure of their own, and we use distinct terms to describe them. Achieving the overlap in Rugby, for instance, describes the structure and movements of the two lines of forwards, as teams and in relation to each other. The overlap is not a movement of either team alone, but is produced by the interweaving actions of team members as allies and opponents.

3. Multi-person games on several levels: Imagine a game in which there is a very large and growing number of players. We are now thinking of rather elaborate social processes. Perhaps it is inadvisable any longer to try to relate the model to any real-life game, unless it be the medieval village riots from which soccer claims ancestry. It becomes more and more difficult for any single player to put together a mental picture of the state and process of the game in which he is involved. That is very confusing, for every player needs such a picture in order to anticipate what will happen next and plan his next move accordingly. If the web of interdependence becomes too enormous, the individual can no longer make sense of the game nor formulate his strategy.

> If the number of interdependent players grows, the figuration, development and direction of the game will become more and more opaque to the individual player. However strong he may be, he will become less and less able to control them. Therefore, from the point of view of the individual player, an intertwining network of more and more players functions increasingly as though it had a life of its own. [Elias 1970: 88]

But, emphasizes Elias, just like those in the previous models, this is no more than a game played by many individuals. The difference is merely that, as the number of interdependent players grows and the game becomes more opaque and uncontrollable by any single player, the individual becomes gradually more *aware* of his inability to understand and control it. The sociology of knowledge concerns itself with this problem: how do people perceive and conceptualize the changing and growing webs of interdependence in which they find themselves bound up?

What of the structure of the game itself though? If players can no longer map out what is happening overall and plan their moves accordingly, the game is likely to become disorganized, and pressure builds up for the players to reorganize themselves. Several things may happen. The players may segment into several groups, who then continue to play the game independently. This sort of thing tends to happen in hunting and gathering societies, where the hunting bands tend always to remain quite small. Alternatively, the large group may remain but become organized more elaborately in a two-tier (or multi-tier) configuration. (In spite of better intentions, we seem to be making the Football League a model of society!)

In a two-tier game, not all the players any longer play directly with each other. Opposing sides still play against each other and test their relative strengths. But moves are made by specialized functionaries on an upper tier—leaders, delegates, representatives, negotiators, committees, élites, governments. Only these second-level players have direct access to the game. Yet they are not independent of the lower-level players, and are in fact involved in subsidiary games with the lower tier. Where the discrepancy between the strengths of first- and second-tier players is very great, we have an oligarchic situation.

The distinctive feature of an oligarchic game is that (as the word implies) there is a comparatively small circle of players on the upper tier. So each player at that level is once more able to picture the figuration of players and the course of the game, and to plan a coherent strategy by which to pick his way through the flurry of move and countermove. Yet though the game process may appear relatively transparent, it is, in fact, much more complex than anything observed in the earlier models; it is far more difficult for one player to steer the game in the direction he desires. For, even with only two tiers, several different balances of power have to be taken into account: between the top-tier players; between the top-tier players and the lower-tier players; between the lower-tier groupings; and within the lower-tier groupings. These are all interdependent. For instance, splits between upper-tier players may enhance the power of lower-tier groups. Or coalitions of upper and lower players against the strongest oligarch may stymie his chances of guiding the game his way. On the other hand, if there are two very evenly balanced coalitions, another upper-level player with relatively few allies on either level may be enabled to play the role of *tertius gaudens*.

If power differentials between the two levels diminish—for example, as lower-tier groups become better organized—the balances of power and the course of the game become even more indeterminate, fluid and beyond the control of any single individual or group. In an oligarchic game, the lower-level players may seem to exist for the benefit of the upper tier. But as the ties of interdependence between the two tiers increase, the opposite may seem closer to the truth. The upper-tier players become, more overtly, spokesmen for the lower groups. For each spokesman, his strategy with respect to lower-tier groups becomes as important as strategy towards others on the upper tier. The course of the game becomes still more opaque and still less susceptible to control and influence even by upper-level players. The significance of that is re-emphasized when it is realized that a two-tier game is a ludicrously oversimplified model of real societies involving millions of people and innumerable tiers.

Figure 3. Increase in number of possible relationships relative to number of individuals.

Number of individuals	2-person relationships	Increase	All possible relationships	Increase
2	1	–	1	–
3	3	2	4	3
4	6	3	11	7
5	10	4	26	15
6	15	5	57	31
7	21	6	120	63
8	28	7	247	127
9	36	8	502	255
10	45	9	1013	511

'All possible relationships' means all permutations of individuals, thus:

3 people = AB AC BC ABC = 4 relationships

4 people = AB AC AD BC BD CD ABC ABD ACD BCD ABCD
= 11 relationships

5 people = AB AC AD AE BC BD BE CD CE DE
ABC ABD ABE ACD ACE ADE BCD BCE BDE CDE
ABCD ABCE ABDE ACDE ABCDE = 26 relationships

(Simplified from Elias, 1970: 107.)

Elias demonstrates the potential complexity of human groups by the calculations set out in Figure 3. This shows how the number of possible alliances increases as the number of individuals increases. Three people can obviously be permutated into three dyads and one triad. Add a fourth person, and the number of possible dyads doubles to six, the number of possible triads quadruples to four, and there is one possible relationship between all four, yielding eleven relationships in all. And so on: by the time there are ten people, the calculations become unwieldy. Ten people, we need hardly add, is only a small human group, yet the structural possibilities within even such a small group are very large indeed. Relationships can be patterned into very diverse networks. Given the enormous complexity of networks involving more than a few people, it is hardly surprising that network analysis has not been very prominent in sociological analysis of large-scale societies. Elizabeth Bott did, however, carry out a well-known study of families and their social networks in London, and was led to distinguish between highly connected and dispersed networks. Figure 4 (p. 88) shows in simplified form what these terms mean; families replace individuals, and only six families are shown in each diagram. Bott's most interesting finding was that the more highly connected a family's social network, the more likely it was that the husband's and wife's roles would be highly 'segregated'—that they would have well-defined and separate tasks and activities, the wife cooking and cleaning, the husband holding the purse-strings and so on. Whether this finding is generally valid need not concern us; it serves merely to indicate the possible interest of network analysis, and points to the likelihood that the quality of interpersonal relationships is not independent of the figuration of environing social networks.

Unfortunately, it is plain that such painstaking mapping-out of social interconnections becomes impractical if the object of interest is the wider society of hundreds, thousands or millions of people. The image of a complex network can, however, usefully remain in the mind. The many kinds of social organizations of which sociologists speak—families, communities, associations, institutions—can be thought of as various kinds of knots and tangles, more or less highly connected networks strung together by more dispersed networks. Much of the most interesting work in mathematical sociology has been on ways of describing the various degrees and patterns of social interconnectedness. As yet, though, sociologists cannot for many purposes dispense with the mathematically less precise concepts like 'organization', 'institution' and 'community' when speaking of large-scale social networks. This is true not only of the patterns of thought used by sociologists, but of the means of discourse used by the general public, of the very terms they use to assimilate their experience.

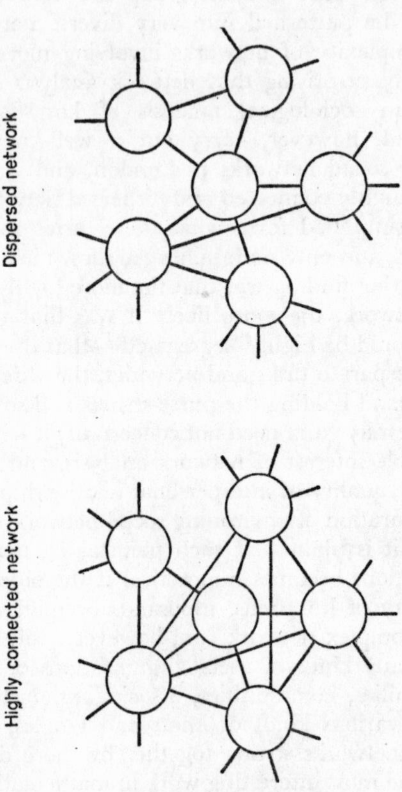

Highly connected network

Dispersed network

Figure 4 (adapted from Bott, 1955).

> Instead of players believing that the game takes its shape from the individual moves of individual people, there is a slowly growing tendency for impersonal concepts to be developed . . . These impersonal concepts take into account the relative autonomy of the game process from the intentions of individual players . . . as something not immediately controllable even by the players themselves. Metaphors are used which oscillate constantly between the idea that the course of the game can be reduced to the actions of individual players and the other idea that it is of a suprapersonal nature. [Elias 1970: 95]

Conclusions

It is important not to reify the concept of role, which is a second-degree construct created by sociologists for their own purposes; nevertheless, it is firmly grounded in the nature of social interaction. People and their roles are elaborately patterned through interaction into complex social networks. The analogy with games is a useful way of thinking about this process. The complexity of these networks of relationships is, however, so great that those enmeshed in them find it difficult to picture and explain their structure and dynamics, let alone to exercise control over them. This at once raises the question of how complex structures are co-ordinated and controlled, to the extent that they are co-ordinated and controlled at all. But before turning to the problem of social integration, we must first consider the nature of social power which, as the present chapter has already hinted, must play a considerable part in co-ordination and control within society.

Notes

1. This variable seems even more obviously continuous (as opposed to dichotomous) than the rest. The majority of actions are 'collectivity orientated'. But how broad is the collectivity in question in each case—one's family, one's country, or humanity in general?
2. See, also, Robert Dubin's article (1960) and Parsons's reply, 'Pattern Variables Revisited' (1960).
3. Amongst an extensive literature on this, see Benne and Sheats 1948; Bales 1950; Parsons, Bales and Shils 1953; Parsons and Bales 1955.

4. cf. Nadel 1957:106–20.
5. Simmel's influence can be clearly seen in later theoretical and empirical studies of the formation of coalitions in three-person groups. Theodore Caplow's work is especially prominent. See Caplow 1956, 1968; Vinacke and Arkoff 1957.
6. Elias does not use 'games models' in quite the same way as von Neumann and Morgenstern (1944) and their numerous followers. They tend to use *relatively* simple models very rigorously to demonstrate rational courses of action and winning strategies. Elias uses his models heuristically to show how, in progressively more complex situations, rational courses of action and winning strategies become steadily less easy to discern and more indeterminate.

4. Power

Though they use the term often enough, sociologists do not find it easy to define exactly what they mean by 'power'. Max Weber's definition must be the most frequently quoted. '"Power",' wrote Weber (1968:I, 53), 'is the probability that one actor within a social relationship will be in a position to carry out his will despite resistance, regardless of the basis on which this probability rests.' This definition has two great merits. Weber saw that power must be stated in terms of probabilities, not certainties. In a whole series of matches, it is likely that a First Division football team would establish itself as more 'powerful' than a Fourth Division opponent; but, in a single decisive encounter in a knockout competition, it occasionally happens that the 'weaker' side wins. More important, Weber firmly located power within social relationships, not as a quality of an individual. Power cannot be assessed as an absolute quantity—it is always relative. Furthermore, as social relationships are never static, neither are the balances of power which they involve. Power should be seen as a process, ever shifting, developing, changing. Perhaps 'power' should be a verb, not a noun, for it leads us to look for something static and fixed. This has often been noted:

> Power in social life is somewhat analogous to energy in the physical world. . . . We talk freely about the uses of energy and power, but when we attempt to specify more precisely what either of these phenomena is, we encounter difficulties. The main reason is that neither energy nor power can be directly observed or measured. Their existence, nature and strength can only be inferred from their effects. [Olsen 1968: 172]

What is power and when is it not power? Sociologists have not been able to agree. Suppose one person suggests to another that it would be a good thing if the latter did so-and-so. Suppose, further, that the suggestion is well received, that it is willingly, even eagerly, carried out, not to please the person who suggested it, but because it was a good idea in itself. We should be reluctant to describe this case of willing compliance as an exercise of power. But what if it required some persuasion to convince the second person that the course of action were desirable? He might at first resist, but change his own evaluation of desirability. Should we describe this as an instance of the exercise of power, as the phrase 'the power of persuasion' might suggest, or should we call it something else, such as 'influence'? At the other extreme, to meet Weber's requirement of resistance, some sociologists have been inclined to define the exercise of power as involving the use or threat of negative sanctions—'You may not want to do this, but I can make things unpleasant for you if you don't.' It is generally agreed that the polar case of power is 'physical coercion'. A man holding a gun and demanding 'your money or your life' seems an entirely unambiguous illustration of the meaning of power. Yet the outcome of this situation—surrender of the wallet—is highly predictable only because the vast majority of people would consider death too high a price to pay for the contents of their wallets (which would no doubt be taken after their death anyhow). Historically, of course, we know that even the threat of death is not always sufficient to bend another to one's will. The heretics burned by Bloody Mary at Smithfield valued their souls more highly than their lives.

It is apparent that to exercise power in a social relationship, it is necessary to have some control over whatever it is that others desire, or over the means by which these desires may be fulfilled. Yet control is always a matter of degree; it consists merely of the ability to alter the balance of costs and benefits of two or more courses of action, *as they are perceived by the other person.* The threat of a horrible death by fire might well have shaken most people's theological convictions; but for those whose convictions held, Queen Mary did not hold the keys to heaven, and the benefit of salvation still exceeded the costs of execution. In the last resort, some freedom of action remains even to the person subjected to physical coercion. Even coercion merely alters the probabilities of various outcomes (from the observer's point of view) or their relative costs and benefits (from the point of view of the person subjected to coercion).[1] It emerges that there is little point in defining 'power' entirely in terms of the deployment of negative sanctions. That would mean that while successful blackmail was an exercise of power, successful bribery was not—for bribery involves positive sanctions. Positive

sanctions suffice as well as negative ones in altering the balance of advantage between courses of action. Power, then, is best viewed broadly as the process by which some actors in social relationships are able to carry out their will by changing the balance of advantage of alternative courses of action for others in the relationship. This perspective on the nature of power has been most closely approached by the exchange theorists.[2]

Social Exchange Theory

Although its key ideas were anticipated by earlier writers, and though they represent the adaptation of well-established theories from economics to sociology, social exchange theory in its present form appeared on the scene only quite recently. Its major statements were made by Homans (1958, 1961), Thibaut and Kelley (1959) and Blau (1964). Homans deserves the chief credit, but I shall mainly discuss Blau's formulation, because it is the most ambitious and offers most hostages to fortune. Discussion of social exchange must precede consideration of the theory of power which rests on it.

The basic assumption of exchange theory is that men seek many rewards which can be obtained only in interaction with other people. They enter new social relations because they *expect* to find them rewarding and continue to participate because they *do* find them rewarding. For the moment, it does not much matter what exactly it is that they seek, although Blau's reading of Erving Goffman's analyses of everyday interaction leads him to give prominence to the rewards of social approval, deference, 'status', and the like, as well as to more tangible rewards like practical assistance.

Homans and Blau share a favourite illustration of the social exchange principle. Consider two men (and only two at this stage) working in an office, one of whom is well experienced and fast at his work, the other less able or less experienced. The latter would welcome some assistance and advice from the expert.[3] The expert is quite able to help the non-expert, yet any assistance he gives costs him something. He has his own work to do, and time and effort spent helping the non-expert means that he has to work longer at his own tasks than otherwise. This work foregone represents the 'opportunity cost' to the expert of the assistance he gives. Now, unless giving advice to the non-expert is defined as part of the expert's job by his superiors, and unless the expert feels some moral responsibility to give free advice or finds it inherently self-satisfying to do so, Blau assumes that the advice will only be given if the expert receives something from the non-expert in return for the cost incurred. What can the non-expert give in return? Blau suggests that he can accord his benefactor social approval, esteem or 'status'. Let us assume that the expert likes the enhancement of his own status which accrues from the non-expert's expression of esteem. He will thus be prepared to give up some time from his own work to obtain 'status'. ('Status' is not the ideal word, since it tends to connote a static rank. Here it should be thought of as meaning a *flow* of esteem or approval.) The situation from the expert's point of view can then be shown as an indifference map, representing his preference between combinations of 'status' and accomplishment in his own work, which he can achieve by allocating his time between his own tasks and giving assistance (Fig. 5).

Each 'indifference curve' AA', BB', CC' DD', in Figure 5, is a line drawn through all combinations of work and 'status' between which the expert would be indifferent, and with which we may therefore infer he would be *equally* satisfied.[4] (Think of them as akin to isobars on a weather map, linking points of equal pressure.) Thus,

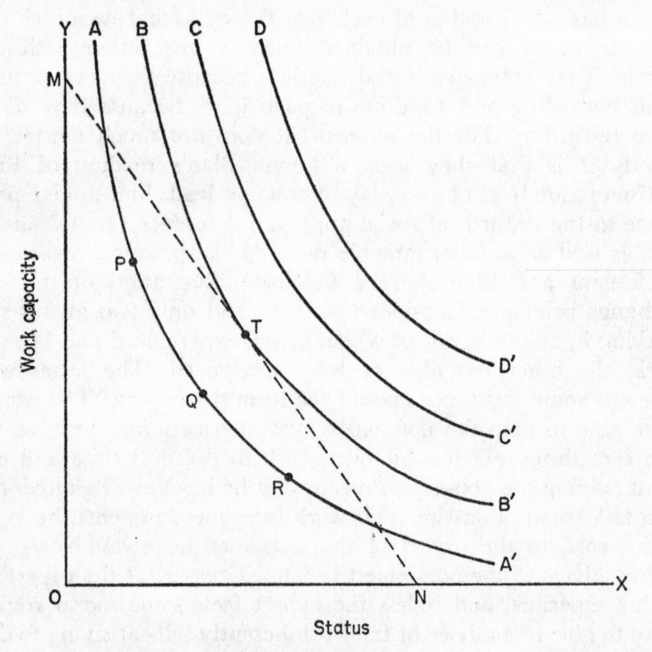

Figure 5. The expert's indifference map.

at point P, he gets more of his own work done (or has to work less hard at it) than at point Q, but receives less 'status'; at point R he receives more 'status', but has remarkably little time left in which to do his own work. However, he is *equally* satisfied whether he is at P, Q, or R, because all lie on the same indifference curve AA^-.

Indifference curves are convex to the origin because of the principle of the *diminishing marginal rate of substitution.* The marginal rate of substitution is measured by the slope of the indifference curve. The slope at point P is steep; this is because when he is giving most of his time to his own work but receiving little 'status' from the non-expert, the expert is willing to give up a relatively large amount of his time to obtain some 'status'—he substitutes 'status' for work. However, when he is receiving quite a lot of approval at point Q, he will be conscious of the need to spend time on his own work, and the next marginal unit of 'status' will seem of less value to him, so he will divert only a little time from his own work in order to obtain it. This is represented by the decreasing slope of the indifference curve. At point R, the non-expert would have to be quite obsequious to elicit more advice!

Curve AA^-, however, is only one of an infinite number of possible indifference curves on the map. Only four are shown in Figure 5, just as a weather map shows only a few of the infinite number of possible isobars—satisfaction, like air pressure, is a continuous not a discrete variable. Though the expert is indifferent between the combinations of work and 'status' represented by P, Q and R on the Curve AA^-, he would prefer to be at *any point* on curve BB^-, and still more on curve CC^-, and better yet on DD^-. That is because any point on a higher indifference curve represents a combination of more work *plus* the same amount of 'status', or more 'status' *plus* the same amount of work, or more of both, compared with any point on any lower curve. We assume that people prefer more of one or the other or both to having to give up some of one in order to obtain more of the other reward.

What determines which is the highest achievable indifference curve? This is where the 'time-constraint line' MN enters the picture. If the expert spends all his time on his own work, he will do a maximum of OM work. If on the other hand he did none of his own work at all but spent all his time advising the non-expert, he would receive a maximum of ON units of 'status'. The line joining M and N is tangential to indifference curve BB^- a point T, and so BB^- is the highest attainable curve. The expert would thus not settle for any of points P, Q or R when he could reach T.

Now let us bring the non-expert more fully into the situation. We could draw an indifference map for him, too, with 'status' and advice on the axes; each time he seeks advice and expresses his gratitude to the expert by according him 'status', the non-expert implicitly reduces his own status. Just as the expert has to trade off between his own work and the 'status' he obtains by giving advice, so the non-expert has to balance the value of advice against the loss of status in obtaining it. When the expert complies with a request for advice, he increases the non-expert's work capacity and reduces his own. When the non-expert reciprocates for the advice by expressing his esteem for the expert, he raises the expert's 'status' while reducing his own. Their resources of 'status' and work capacity can now (at least in Blau's view) be added together, and the non-expert's indifference map 'tilted over' on top of the expert's to form what is known in economics as a 'box diagram'. This is shown in Figure 6, where the expert's indifference curves are represented by solid lines and the non-expert's by dotted. The box diagram now purports to show that where the non-expert can obtain advice only from the expert, and the expert 'status' only from the non-expert (a situation of 'bilateral monopoly'), both parties can attain higher indifference curves and higher satisfaction by exchanging advice and 'status'.

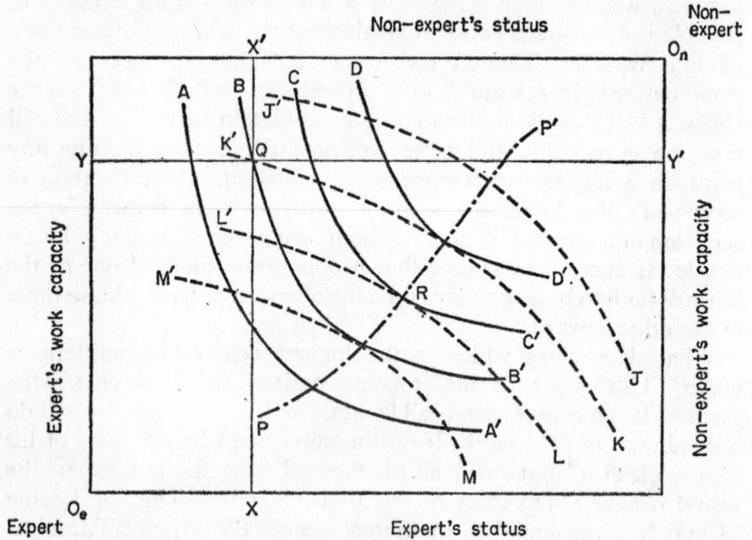

Figure 6. The case of bilateral monopoly.

Before any exchange takes place, the non-expert is entirely dependent on his own limited work capacity ($O_n Y^-$), while the expert is receiving only such esteem ($O_e X$) as might be supposed to accrue to someone recognized to be highly competent. This situation is represented by point Q, where the expert is on indifference curve BB⁻, and the non-expert on *his* indifference curve KK⁻. By increasing their exchange of advice and esteem, it would be possible for them to reach a point such as R, where both are on higher indifference curves, respectively CC⁻ and LL⁻. Both thereby profit from the exchange. The point R is one of tangency between one of the expert's curves and one of the non-expert's. All such points are joined by the curve PP⁻, called the 'contract curve' (or 'Pareto optimum'). At all such points, the slope of the two indifference curves is the same, indicating that the marginal unit of esteem is of the same value to the expert as the marginal increment of advice to the non-expert. Where exactly on the contract curve trade will take place depends on the bargaining strength of the two men, and perhaps also on the fair rate of exchange, if such a rate is recognized and if the two men feel they ought to abide by it. But,

> Whereas moves that profit both parties are possible from any point that is not on the contract curve, once they are on the contract curve no move is possible that does not disadvantage one of the two (or both). [Blau 1964: 175]

Three people cannot be shown on a box diagram, but it is easy to see what would happen if a third person, also a non-expert in need of advice, were installed in the office. If the one expert remained the sole source of advice, advice would become more scarce, and its 'price' bid up by competition between the non-experts. Either of the non-experts would have to accord the expert more 'status' to elicit the same amount of advice as before. Conversely, the introduction of a third person who happened to be expert would reduce the price of advice to the non-expert.

Exchange and Power

So far we have been talking about freely reciprocated exchange, in which bargains were struck and services of equal value exchanged. In these circumstances, each has some measure of control, of power in fact, over the actions of the other, even though one may be temporarily or permanently in the stronger bargaining position. Blau, however, is particularly interested in situations where transactions are not fully reciprocal. If one person is unable to reciprocate in full measure, he becomes indebted to his benefactor. Unreciprocated benefactions, says Blau, produce differentiation of status. A man who has resources at his disposal with which he can meet other people's needs, can use them to attain power over others, subject to four conditions. First, the other people must not have resources which the benefactor wants, or there will simply be mutual exchange. Secondly, the recipients must not be able to obtain the benefit from any other source—the benefactor must have some degree of monopoly power. Thirdly, the recipients must be unable or unwilling to take the benefit by force. Fourthly, they must not undergo a change of values which enables them to do without the benefit they originally wanted. So control over total food supplies, for example, would be a considerable source of power, though control over the supply of butter would be of little avail if margarine were plentiful. It should also be remembered that some services are akin to capital goods; it is quite likely that the more advice the non-expert receives, the more he will learn and thus be able eventually to do without advice in the future. Nevertheless, if these four conditions are met, Blau contends, indebtedness is met by acceding to the creditor's wishes, and this creates power differentials. The benefactor has more control over the actions of the recipients than the recipients have over the actions of the benefactor. It has to be emphasized once more that power is always relative. It cannot even be measured by discrepancies in resources, for the power which resources bestow depends among other things on their relative dispensability to the people who lack them.

How does this situation differ from ordinary mutual exchange? According to Blau, the distinction lies in who has discretion over repayment. In the office, the non-expert could choose when to lay on the social approval in return for advice; if he did not repay, the supply of advice would merely be discontinued. In a power relationship, Blau suggests, the return of compliance is made when the supplier of the original benefit, the creditor, demands it. In the office situation, the expert merely received 'status', not obedience. Yet by this account, submission to another's power rests on the subordinate having a sense of obligation, recognizing indebtedness and lack of balance in the exchange of services. Locating who has discretion over repayment in no way explains *why* some relationships are balanced, some unbalanced, exchange. In the end, it seems, the subordinate's sense of obligation rests entirely on participants' judgements of 'fair rates of exchange', whether these judgements are peculiar to the participants themselves or commonly accepted in the social group or society. There is no 'outside', independent rule which can distinguish power from exchange situations. This suggests the need for a closer look at the assumptions of Blau's book.

Critique

The first thing that has to be said is that Blau's direct borrowing of the trappings of economic analysis gives social exchange theory a wholly false air of precision. This is particularly true of his discussion of bilateral monopoly (see Heath 1968). Quite how the expert's supply of assistance and the non-expert's supply of 'status' are to be measured is not very clear. A rough-and-ready measure of the flow of advice would be the amount of time spent on giving it, but that might be very misleading as a measure of the flow of 'status'. And for each unit of 'status' that the expert receives, does the non-expert lose an exactly equivalent unit? It is not even obvious that the two men's work capacity can simply be added together. If the expert can solve $O_e\ Y$ problems and the non-expert $O_n\ Y^1$, it is not certain that by co-operating they will in practice solve precisely $O_e\ Y + O_n\ Y^1$ problems together. What Blau presents in this case is little more than an analogy with economic transactions, and analogies are often misleading. Homans, at least, recognizing the limitations imposed on social exchange theory by difficulties of measurement, refrains from the use of over-elaborate diagrams. His propositions merely take the form,

> ... '*x* varies as *y*', which says that the value of *x* increases with any increase in the value of *y* but does not say just how much it increases. Our present degree of precision in measuring the variables warrants this much precision in our propositions but no more. [Homans 1961: 57]

With his more modest propositions, Homans is none the less able to build a model of surprising rigour and predictive power, as Maris (1970) has shown.

Blau himself contends that there are differences other than measurability between social and economic exchange (1964:92–7). Obligations in social transactions, he says, are usually not specified in advance; on giving a dinner party for friends, one cannot bargain with them about the date and menu for when they will return hospitality. But then risk is present in many economic transactions too. Next Blau argues that social exchange, in contrast with economic exchange, tends to engender feelings of gratitude; yet, as he notes, the distinction is blurred if, for example, one is granted a loan on privileged terms. Thirdly, 'in contrast to economic commodities, the benefits involved in social exchange do not have an exact price in terms of a single quantitative medium of exchange ...' (1964:94). But this is misleading. Economists would define an economic commodity merely as one which is scarce and desired. Blau's distinction is not between social and economic transactions, but between monetary and non-monetary transactions. (Almost any durable physical commodity could, of course, serve as money.) Blau is really raising the problem of measurement again: money serves as a precise, cardinal-scale measure of value, and it is this which is missing in what he calls social transactions.

Blau does, however, raise a more important point when he says that, in social exchange, the rewards are frequently intrinsic to the relationship rather than extrinsic.

> Deep intrinsic attachments fundamentally alter the social transactions in interpersonal relations. The basic difference is between associations that are considered ends-in-themselves by participants and those they consider means to some further ends. [Blau 1964: 35–6]

If social relationships are ranged between extrinsic and intrinsic poles, purely monetary relationships exemplify the former, and love relationships the latter. Intermediate are many kinds of social relationships which are, at least in part, intrinsically valued for themselves. But the polar case of love is crucial. Blau argues that though his theory can be applied to the exchange of small favours between couples, it cannot be applied to the main goal, the relationship itself.

> Extrinsic benefits constitute objective criteria for comparing associates, choosing between them, and abandoning one in favour of another. They are independent standards for determining whether a person's choice of associates is rational or not ... [However] an individual's subjective judgement that an association is intrinsically rewarding for him cannot be considered wrong in any meaningful sense ... only value judgements apply to associations that are intrinsically attractive. [1964: 36–7]

Since so many associations and activities are intrinsically attractive, the question must now inevitably be asked whether the whole of social exchange theory is not tautological. Blau recognizes this to be the central question.

> ... the assumption of exchange theory that social interaction is governed by the concern of both (or all) partners with rewards dispensed by the other (or others) becomes tautological if any and all behaviour in interpersonal relations is conceptualized as an exchange, even conduct towards others that is not at all oriented in terms of expected returns from them. [1964: 6]

Blau therefore defines the scope of his theory as encompassing 'all striving for rewarding social experiences, including the desire to further humanitarian ideals or spiritual values, as well as the pursuit of personal advantage and emotional satisfaction' (1968:452), and 'particularly *wertrational* as well as *zweckrational* conduct' (1964:5). But he excludes behaviour induced by physical coercion, motivated by irrational drives (such as to squander money) or even in conformity with internalized moral values (1968:453–4).

Actually, Blau need not have made these exceptions—which is just as well, as they are not very well defined. The main point is that exchange theory is inevitably tautological so long as we do not have independent evidence of the actor's motives or intentions. This is a characteristic that it shares with its intellectual ancestors in the utilitarian tradition of social thought. For instance, commenting upon James Mill's utilitarian 'Essay on Government' in 1829, Macaulay wrote:

> What proposition is there respecting human nature which is absolutely and universally true? We know of only one: and that is not only true but identical; that men always act from self-interest. . . . But in fact, when explained, it means only that men, if they can, will do as they choose. . . . If the doctrine, that men always act from self-interest, be laid down in any other sense than this—if the meaning of the word self-interest be narrowed so as to exclude any one of the motives which may by possibility act on a human being, the proposition ceases to be identical: but at the same time it ceases to be true. . . . Nothing can possibly be inferred from a maxim of this kind. When we see a man take something, we shall know it was the object of his desire. But till then we have no means of judging with certainty what he desires or what he will take. [1889: 180]

Macaulay was wrong in suggesting there is no way of knowing a person's motives except by observing a particular act, but quite right in suggesting that we must have knowledge of motives independent of observing that act. *Post hoc* explanation leads to tautology.

When discussing Alfred Marshall, Parsons (1937:132) pointed out that traditional economics takes wants as 'random'—it does not seek to explain why people want what they do, merely the actions which follow from their desires. Social exchange theory is similar, as both Homans (1961:4) and Blau (1968:457) recognize. It does not explain why people in different societies and social groups—even people *within* one social group—pursue the diversity of rewards which they do. It is still necessary to study social customs and culture to gain insight into what people value and to what kinds of power they will respond. But social norms and internalized values *determine* action no more and no less than, in the end, physical coercion does. They merely make some outcomes more likely than others. Given this kind of information, the place of exchange theory is a more limited one of explaining the dynamics of certain kinds of social interaction, as Homans is well aware:

> Naturally the rewards created and distributed in a street gang are not just like those in a hunting band; but given the difference in rewards, the propositions describing the behaviour of individuals realizing rewards of some kind through face-to-face transactions are probably much the same for all groups. [1961: 6]

The scope of exchange theory's contributions to sociology has, in the past, been rather overstated. Yet it has great virtues. It very firmly indicates that the influence or control which people exercise over one another's actions in a relationship is rarely one-sided. Control is usually reciprocal to some degree, though one party may have much greater control over the actions of a second than vice versa. And exchange theory also encourages a marginalist view of the operation of power resources as inducements and deterrents. Finally, it shows that the intentions, perceptions and evaluations of *both* sides involved in a balance of power must be taken into consideration to predict its outcome, even though one side may be much weaker than the other. When people exercise power, they deploy resources to influence others, but it is the motives and evaluations of *the latter* which determine whether they will constitute negative or positive sanctions as well as how much purchase these sanctions will have over their actions. As Blalock (1967:214) states, 'Resources depend primarily on the motivation and goals of the person over whom power is being exercised, whereas mobilization is a function of the goals and expectations of the persons exercising the power.' The germ of that idea is caught in the proverb, 'You can take a horse to water but you can't make it drink.'

Resources for Power

What resources can be used in the exercise of power? Weber's definition is explicitly and deliberately unspecific. *Any* resources can be used which alter the balance of advantage of another person's action in the direction desired by he who deploys the resources. Resources can be used either to make the desired course of action more attractive (positive sanctions) or to make other courses of action less attractive (negative sanctions). That we deploy our resources in this way does not necessarily mean that we shall succeed in carrying out our will—our resources may not be sufficient to tip the balance far enough, especially if the other's resistance to our will is based on *wertrational* commitment to an absolute principle. We should all like to think, for example, that no one is rich enough to 'buy' the Lord Chief Justice or Chief Justice of the U.S. Supreme Court. Some sociologists would not count such an unsuccessful attempt to exercise power as an example of power itself. Thus Bierstedt writes that 'power is always successful; when it is not successful it is not, or ceases to be, power' (1950:733). We can make our definitions as we please, but some are more useful than others. Bierstedt's is really a verbal trick which unnecessarily restricts our attention only to certain outcomes of a wider social process—the deployment of inducements and deterrents to bend others to our will, successfully or unsuccessfully.

The resources which may be deployed in this way are of infinite kinds—whatever constitute inducements and deterrents *to those subject to them*. Among resources discussed by sociologists are income, property, sacramental and magical capacities, bureaucratic office, access to information, knowledge, scarce skills and charisma. Listing possible power resources would be a purely taxonomic exercise, were it not that sociologists have asked two related types of probing question about them. First, they have asked what kinds of society engender what kinds of interests, goals and wants among members, realizing that this is of crucial importance in determining what kind of resources will enable their controller to exercise most power in each kind of society. The relationship between wants and power is seen particularly clearly in Riesman's *The Lonely Crowd*. Tracing the evolution of American 'social character' from 'inner-directed' to 'other-directed' in an age of high mass consumption, Riesman seeks to show that changes in what Americans value had consequences for the types of power resource to which they respond, and therefore for the distribution of power in American society (1950:Part II). With greater historical sweep, Weber shows the intimate connection between the prevailing values and interests of a society and the forms of domination found in it. One of the themes of his sociology of religion, for instance, is the link between the structure of society, its beliefs, its members' conception of their interests, and its type of leadership.

Secondly, some writers have not contented themselves with a taxonomy of power resources but have sought to show that some resources are 'more basic' than others, which are in some way reducible to the basic forms. If anything is most basic, Mao Tse-tung surely got it right when he said that 'power grows out of the barrel of a gun'—but only because death is a higher price than most people are prepared to pay for most things. Marx's thesis that economic resources are the basic source of power is even more famous. The ownership of capital, the means of large-scale industrial production, concentrated in the hands of a comparatively few entrepreneurs, gave them overwhelming power over workers, any of whom alone had control only over his labour power, an insignificant fraction of total labour resources. It is still a matter of controversy whether the growth of organized labour and the proliferation of scarce skills among workers has significantly shifted the balance of economic power. Many Marxists would be inclined to argue that these factors are somehow superficial and that ownership of capital still remains the decisive power resource in capitalist economies. One thing, though, is indisputable—in modern societies money has a special place among resources for power. Everyone wants money because it has value in exchange for so much else, and so it has a particularly wide scope as an inducement.

Authority and social organization are best seen as two more kinds of power resource, though this is perhaps not a conventional view. They occupy a special position because they cross-cut other power resources—they can reinforce the exercise of power, no matter what its other bases. So far, the exercise of power has been depicted as the deployment of resources as inducements and deterrents, and compliance with power as a calculation of costs and benefits. Not that calculation need be rational in any sense of the term. Nor need it even be conscious; as economists point out, it is not necessary that people think in terms of marginal utility for the theory to predict the outcome of their actions. This view of power can take us quite a long way. Legitimacy, however, is a new element in the situation. Resources can yield domination to which people comply for their own advantage, without considering it legitimate (Weber 1968: I, 212–13). Domination which the dominated regard as legitimate, as morally justified in terms of their values, is usually called *authority*. Legitimacy can be thought of as an element in the minds of those who comply, which alters their evaluation of the costs and benefits of compliance or non-compliance. People are very likely to comply with the orders of a man with a gun; they are perhaps still more likely to do so if they think he has a legitimate reason for having the gun and for giving orders. But legitimacy and means of coercion are functional alternatives which can be traded off against each other;

the more the police have *authority*, the more their powers are regarded as legitimate in a given community, the less frequently are they likely (*ceteris paribus*) to have to brandish guns there. The dominator may also, of course, consider his power legitimate, though this does not enhance his power one jot. What does enhance his power is his success in promoting his legitimacy in the eyes of those over whom he would exercise power.

Weber distinguished three pure types of authority by the grounds upon which they claimed legitimacy (1968: I, 215). They were (a) rational-legal authority, (b) traditional authority and (c) charismatic authority. Rational-legal authority rested upon 'a belief in the legality of enacted rules and the right of those elevated to authority under such rules to issue commands'. Traditional authority rested on 'an established belief in the sanctity of immemorial traditions and the legitimacy of those exercising authority under them'. Finally, charismatic authority rested on 'devotion to the exceptional sanctity, heroism or exemplary character of an individual person, and of the normative patterns or order revealed or ordained by him'. It will be seen that these three types of authority are related to Weber's four ideal-types of action (see pp. 24–26 above); in fact, the distinction between traditional and rational authority runs into the same difficulties at the margin as did that between traditional and rational action. The boundaries of charismatic authority, which is related to affectual action, are also susceptible to blurring, so that it becomes a dustbin for whatever refuses to fit into the other categories. Nevertheless, it cannot be denied that when Weber explores how these three kinds of claims to legitimacy are embodied in typical institutions, the result is highly illuminating. Out of the notion of authority flow some of Weber's most celebrated discussions. Bureacracy is the exemplar of rational authority. Patriarchalism, patrimonialism and feudalism are among its traditional precursors. Charismatic authority has repeatedly created social movements through history; it is a revolutionary force in State and Church, but inevitably becomes transformed and 'routinized' into one of the other forms of administration with the departure of the charismatic leader. Discussion of all this occupies the whole of the third volume of *Economy and Society*.

Yet it is less important to categorize the forms of legitimacy than to appreciate the effect of any form—which is to amplify, even to multiply, the potential of other power resources, whether guns, money, property or magical gifts. Certain resources for power exist only in a legitimate form. For example, high social status may in some circumstances be a power resource. Status situation, however, 'is determined by a specific, positive or negative, social estimation of honour' (Weber, 1968:II, 932), and clearly 'positive estimation of honour' implies legitimacy by definition. Similarly, a religious leader can only bring supernatural sanctions (like the threat of damnation) to bear on a believer, for they do not constitute sanctions to the atheist. On the other hand, these necessarily legitimate forms of domination need not be considered legitimate by the *entire* community in order to be felt by the entire community. The priest may not be able to cow the atheist by threat of damnation, but if many do accept his authority, he may be able to incite them to ostracize or even to lynch the atheist.

Which brings us to social organization. For a leader or ruler to dominate a large number of people permanently, he normally needs a special inner group, a trusted and disciplined staff, to carry out his orders (Weber, 1968:I, 212). Such henchmen may adhere to the leader purely out of self-interest; but, if so, domination is likely to be unstable and periodically prone to Byzantine intrigues and squabbles. Greater stability will result if the staff at least accept the leader's dominance as legitimate, whether on rational, traditional or charismatic grounds. Whether or not they themselves are based on legitimate authority, such administrative groups constitute a power resource conceptually distinct from the legitimacy of domination in the eyes of *all* those subject to it. But they act upon other power resources in the same way as legitimacy, enlarging the span over which power may be exercised.

Organization formalizes chains of command and improves co-ordination, stabilizing power resources as plant roots fix sand-dunes, and increasing the predictability and probability of success in the exercise of power. In discussing the 'distribution of power' in the political community, Weber (1968:II, 927–39) concentrated on the organization of three kinds of power resource—economic, honorific and politico-legal. Weber did *not* write about 'class, status and power', as if power were a separate dimension of stratification. And in spite of W.G. Runciman's efforts (1970:102–40) to prove Weber's medieval preoccupation with the number three, I can see no evidence that Weber intended these three prominent kinds of resource (economic, honorific and legal) to be exhaustive of all possibilities. Indeed, elsewhere, he spoke of military and religious power resources and corresponding social organizations, without any implication that these could be 'reduced' to other more basic power resources. Nevertheless, Weber did give special treatment to three kinds of social organization which emerged on the basis of these three kinds of power resource. He spoke of classes (in the economic order), status-groups (*Stände*—in the social honorific order) and parties (in the politico-legal order). The circumstances which facilitate the formation of these patterns of organization, and the collective action they in turn make possible, will be discussed in the next chapter.

For present purposes, two general effects of the social organization of power should be noted. First, organizations formed to express the interests or ideals of one group frequently stimulate organization to express antithetical interests and ideals. Secondly, organization based on one kind of power resource may make possible the acquisition of other kinds of resources. For instance, class organization to express economic interests may give rise to class-based political parties, acquiring political domination to reinforce the control of economic resources. Economic groups may also acquire social honour; in England, for instance, the aristocracy has never been so closed to the *nouveaux riches* as the nobility of many other countries. Religious and status-groups may acquire economic and political power, as in India and Northern Ireland. Military and political power may be the stepping-stones to economic resources, as in Latin America (and even in the U.S.A., where politicians rarely seem to retire poor). C. Wright Mills's celebrated book *The Power Elite* (1956) was an attempt to demonstrate the coalescence of a single (albeit loosely organized) military–industrial–political complex at the pinnacle of American society. These correlations and transformations of power resource should not, however, be taken for granted. Social and historical circumstances determine which of them are more and which less likely to occur. Weber, for one, was more cautious than Marx in generalizing about the sources of power in any and all societies.

The Creation and Distribution of Power

One consequence of the lack of agreement among social scientists concerning the notion of power has been a rather curious debate between advocates of the 'zero-sum' conception of power and the 'non-zero-sum' conception. This can be traced back at least to Talcott Parsons's essay of 1957, 'The Distribution of Power in American Society' (in Parsons 1969:185–203), in which he accused C. Wright Mills of inappropriately adopting the zero-sum conception in *The Power Elite*, though Mills himself did not use that term.

The terms 'zero-sum' and 'non-zero-sum' perhaps contribute more confusion than clarity to understanding the issue at stake. 'Zero-sum' is a term used in games theory to describe a situation in which the winner gains what the loser loses, so that the sum of gains and losses is zero. It applies exclusively to closed systems in which the players gain nothing from, nor lose anything to, people outside the game, and in which the game itself creates no additional payoffs (such as the enjoyment of playing). By analogy, the zero-sum conception of power is that if one person or group 'has power' of x units, then those over whom power is exercised must have $-x$ units.

There are a number of objections to this analogy (which is Parsons's, not Mills's). First, it is confusing that power, in this context, seems to refer both to participants' relative strength in the game *and* to the rewards for which they are playing. And then the exercise of power is hard enough to observe, let alone to measure on a ratio-scale. Both of the terms zero-sum and non-zero-sum imply a zero in the scale. If these points seem too pedantic, it should be remembered that a zero-sum game is artificially closed; most real relationships are open. Each party to one trial of strength may, in an open system, enlist the support of allies, so that the amount of power resources in play is indeterminate and fluctuating. The value of the winner's gains may exceed the value of his opponents' losses—or be less, in a pyrrhic victory. Furthermore, in a complex social network of relationships, a person or group may be weaker in one bilateral relationship, but stronger in other bilateral relationships within its network. Power relationships may indeed be intransitive: A may win against B, and B against C, yet C win against A. How all these pluses and minuses are to be summed up is not clear.

The terms zero-sum and non-zero-sum are little more than emotive metaphors. What separates advocates of one from the other is their interest in two different aspects of power relationships. Those who favour the zero-sum image are interested in how potential power resources are distributed in society at a given time, and the probabilities of one person or section being able to achieve their will in face of opposition. They are interested in 'power *over*' others. On the other hand, those like Parsons who favour the non-zero-sum image are interested in 'power *with*' others—how it is possible to attract the support and consent of sufficient others to achieve collective objectives. Parsons suggests a parallel with the study of the distribution of wealth and the production of wealth respectively. Let us now look at his own non-zero-sum conception of power in more detail.

Parsons, Power and Money

By restricting the meaning of 'power' entirely to legitimate forms, Parsons has advanced a fascinating analogy between the creation of political power and the creation of credit by the banking system.[5] Parsons's definitions in this field are idiosyncratic, at variance with other writers and with the terminology used so far in this chapter. 'Power' he defines as the

> generalized capacity to secure the performance of binding obligations by units in a system of collective action. . . . [The] power of A over B is in its legitimized form the 'right' of A, as a decision-making unit involved in the collective process, to make decisions which take precedence over those of B, in the interest of the effectiveness of the collective operation as a whole. [1969: 361, 370]

As Parsons recognizes, this preoccupation with legitimacy makes his conception of power much narrower than other writers', and certainly than Weber's. Why then put such stress on legitimacy? Parsons argues that complex societies simply could not function if, on every single issue, leaders had to convince every single follower that a decision was in the follower's interest. That situation, says Parsons, would be rather like a barter economy where, if A has cattle and wants sheep, he has to find someone else, B, who *both* has sheep *and* wants cattle. Money makes possible more flexible, indirect exchange: A sells cattle to B, who has no sheep, in exchange for money, which he then uses to pay C, who *does* have sheep for sale. The money is a token of no value in itself, but facilitiates trade if A, B and C all have *confidence* that others will accept money in exchange for other goods—sheep and cattle—which do have value. In the same way, Parsons argues, legitimacy facilitates collective action; it gives leaders 'the right to claim loyal co-operation, within institutionalized limits, *without prior specification of the expected performances* ... the rights to make binding decisions ...' (1961 :67–8, his italics). This is not inconsistent with our earlier remarks about legitimacy as a power resource, but we must remember that Parsons has defined away those situations in which people comply out of self-interest, because they get something—if only a quiet life—out of compliance.

Is it true then that a gain in 'power' by unit A necessarily implies corresponding losses by other units, B, C, D . . . ? Parsons's analogy with money yields the answer 'sometimes yes, but more usually no'. Banks are central institutions in the circulation of money; but they also *create* money. To put the matter in a nutshell, because there is very little risk that depositors will demand repayment of more than a small fraction of total deposits at any one time, the banker can lend to borrowers at interest far *more* than he retains in cash deposits. If the public increase their deposits by a given amount, it is possible for the banking system to multiply the initial deposit by several times that amount.[6] The credit thus created is an addition to the total money supply; the currency notes and coin issued by the government represent only a small fraction of the total money in circulation. The system rests on confidence—the banker's confidence that depositors will not simultaneously demand repayment of all deposits, and the depositors' confidence that the banker is prudent and will not take undue risks in investing their money. Both, in turn, rest on confidence in the productivity of the economy; the banker's loans to business are secure because businessmen use them to increase output, which brings them more profit, and enables them to repay the loans with interest. Conversely, a fall in deposits leads to a contraction of credit and falling output.

In democratic political systems, says Parsons, this process finds its analogy in the generalized grant of power which puts the elected leadership in positions akin to that of the banker. The public's 'deposits' of trust in the leadership permit the leaders to take and implement decisions over and above the specific policies enumerated in an election manifesto. This increases the amount of trust in circulation (if the decisions meet with public approval), and this stimulates increased output of 'effectiveness'. ('Effectiveness' means the implementation of decisions and fulfilment of promises, Parsons's analogue to the 'real' output of economic goods and services.) A decline in public trust will lead to a contraction of the leaders' 'power' and a decline in the output of 'effectiveness'.

A most interesting by-product of this analogy is Parsons's view of political 'inflation' and 'deflation'. In economics, the term inflation means a general rise in prices and a fall in the value of money. Vastly over-simplifying a still live issue in economic theory, this occurs when the total output of the economy fails to keep pace with the money supply—'too much money chasing too few goods'. The analogy, says Parsons, is a political leadership which builds up public expectations by promising a great deal, 'without the necessary organizational basis for fulfulment of expectations having been laid' (1969:392). 'Power', like money, then apparently loses its value. Parsons does not explicitly give an illustration of this, but the experience of many developing nations might fit. There, the people's expectations, stimulated by independence, by first contact with the products of industrial technology, and by the politicans themselves, are frustrated because the infrastructure for their fulfilment has not been laid. The politicians—literally and figuratively—cannot deliver the goods. The result is often political instability and revolution.

What of deflation, which in economics signifies a general fall in the price level and therefore a rise in the value of money? Parsons draws a parallel between 'financial panics' and the episode of McCarthyism in the U.S.A. in the early 1950s. (Twenty years later, the Watergate scandal would presumably be another example.) As Senator McCarthy and his associates spread distrust and suspicion in ever-widening circles with their allegations of Communism in high places, the public lost confidence in their leaders, withdrawing their 'deposits' of trust. It became more and more difficult for government to proceed. Again, Parsons is not very lucid on this, but I suppose he had it in mind that while the 'quantity of power' in circulation was low, the value of power to those who had any was high. The leaders who were distrusted were joining the bread line, so to speak, while McCarthy and other Republicans who were still trusted as 'patriots' were placed in a very powerful position.

There is, however, something very suspect about these extended verbal analogies. Parsons's insight that trust, confidence or legitimacy facilitates collective action may well be valid. Yet, even accepting this, the economic analogy is very confusing. 'Inflation' and 'deflation', which describe the movement of prices, tend to be conflated with 'boom' and 'slump', which describe the movement of output. Financial panics tend to occur at times of inflation, but the loss of confidence in money can cause slumps. So I think it would be possible to draw an equally diverting analogy between McCarthyism and, for instance, the great German monetary collapse of 1922–3. Then, public confidence in money spiralled away (just as McCarthy's allegations led to a spiralling loss of confidence) and the Mark was finally worth one hundred-millionth of its pre-war value, while production slumped and unemployment soared. This, however, was a case of hyper-inflation, not deflation, so it is the opposite to Parsons's analogy. I put it forward certainly not as a serious contribution to sociological theory, but to illustrate the dangers of enslavement to amusing and bemusing analogies.

Fascinating as it is, Parsons's view of power is little more than a homily on legitimacy as a power resource. The real world is even more untidy than Parsons's models. There are as many ways of acquiring and creating power as there are power resources. One does not acquire property by the same means as one acquires legitimacy. Entrancing as they are, analogies like Parsons's are no substitute for going out to see how 'power' works in the real world. But even that is not so simple as it sounds.

The Elusiveness of Power: A Case-Study

To illustrate the practical difficulties of research on the exercise of power, it is as well to choose studies ambitious for rigour rather than scope. In preference to theses on the 'distribution of power' in whole nations, I choose Robert Dahl's *Who Governs?* (1961), a study of politics in New Haven, Connecticut. Dahl's theoretical objective was to refute earlier 'community power' studies whose authors had expected to find a single ruling élite group and, in consequence, had tended to find them. Dahl believed that the correct hypothesis to start from was that no single group 'had power' in a community. For present purposes, though, this need concern us less than the difficulty of conclusively proving anything either way.

Dahl began his search for power in New Haven by looking at two obvious power resources, trying to identify the Social and Economic Notables. These he defined by criteria quite independent of political activity—those who attended annual 'high society' coming-out celebrations, and the directors of the largest businesses. It immediately emerged that these two categories hardly overlapped at all; the big businessmen did not include many of the New Haven patricians. Nor did many members of either group hold political offices; indeed the patricians seemed to have little contact with decision-making at all, and disappear from the study. Status was evidently not much of a power resource in New Haven politics.

Was it possible, however, that economic magnates had great influence on decisions behind the scenes? Dahl next looked at who was involved, officially and unofficially, in decision-making in three separate areas of public concern: (a) political nominations, (b) public education (siting and quality of schools, teachers' salaries and so on), and (c) urban renewal (city centre redevelopment). Interestingly, different groups of people were involved in each of these three areas, so there appeared to be no single power élite. The crucial issue, however, was urban renewal. This was the question which most dramatically affected the distribution of economic resources, which hit most people in the pocket.

Urban renewal had been an issue in New Haven since the 1940s, but it had made little progress. Too many people were likely to be adversely affected, and piecemeal redevelopment seemed the only possibility. Then a new mayor, Mr Lee, came to power with urban renewal as the lynchpin of his programme. At first businessmen refused to co-operate. But Lee drew their attention to the large-scale Federal aid available for urban renewal, and succeeded in pressurizing one businessman to head an Urban Renewal Commission. Others joined him, and eventually the commission came to include representatives of all the big interests likely to be affected—business, trade unions, Yale University. Lee invented the commission to approve his development plans and to 'sell' them to the groups involved—its members were to act as opinion leaders. Dahl asserts that Lee and his top aides took all the decisions, and that the commission never challenged his plans in any major detail. Dahl therefore infers that there was no single power élite in New Haven, nor any veto-group (to use Riesman's term) which could block initiatives inimical to its interests. The mayor and his assistants were the most powerful people, and they owed their power to having been elected and to their skill in persuasion and putting together coalitions of interested groups to get things done.

The weakness of the study is that Dahl did not fully succeed in coming to terms with the problem of 'covert power'. Unfortunately, the evidence that the commission of leading citizens never overruled Mayor Lee is ambiguous. It *could*, indeed, mean that Lee always persuaded them that his policies were right. It could also mean that Lee never submitted to them decisions which he thought they would reject. In other words, did he trim his policies in advance to suit their anticipated wishes? And what else might have edged them towards acquiescence? Dahl himself records that the prospect of massive Federal aid flowing into the town helped to sweeten local economic interests. Finally, why was it so vital to recruit the representatives of economic interests in the first place? The mayor, of course, was working within an established power structure, to which concessions probably had to be made. Given only the price at which a deal was made, it is not easy to infer which party, buyer or seller, struck the better bargain.

This is not to argue that Dahl's study is worthless or his conclusions wrong. On the contrary, *Who Governs?* is certainly one of the best studies of power in communities, and Dahl's interpretation (on which brevity has inflicted injustice) is probably more plausible than those of earlier writers. Yet the absence of firm evidence on the extent to which Lee and the members of the Commission each made concessions to the other, vitiates any strong inference as to who played the stronger hand in the game.

The conclusion we must draw concerning theories about the exercise of power is the same as in the case of exchange theory. It is necessary to have *prior* knowledge of what people are seeking, what they value, what are their goals, motives and purposes, *independent* of what we may infer from observing their actions in the bargaining or power situations. It is notoriously risky to draw conclusions from the facial expression of a poker player. We must also specify what power resources they have and how they bring them to bear. Unless we have this informtion, theories about power, as about exchange, court tautology.

Notes

1. There is, perhaps, a distinct category of instances in which resistance is overcome by removing the opponent from the scene of action altogether—by killing or imprisoning him for example—so that he no longer makes either a positive or negative contribution to the attainment of the objective in question. But where objectives are achieved in spite of opponents' continued resistance, or because power is exercised to secure their acquiescence or even co-operation, there is no clear-cut point at which to divide 'power' from 'coercion'.

2. See also Simmel's remarks on power (1950:182) and the propositions advanced by Blalock (1967:139–42; 214).

3. The study which originally inspired this illustration is reported in Blau, 1955, esp. ch. 7. Homans discusses it at some length (1961:359–77).

4. Economists try to avoid speaking of 'utility' or 'satisfaction', since these cannot be measured on a cardinal scale, while combinations of commodities can. However, since advice and esteem are not very easy to measure cardinally either, it is perhaps pretentious for sociologists to have such fine scruples, and Blau does, in fact, talk about utility. For a thoroughgoing critique of Blau's use of economic analysis, see Heath (1968). For a fuller explanation of indifference curve analysis, see Samuelson (1961:450–56), or any other introductory economics textbook.

5. This analogy received its fullest statement in Parsons's 1963 essay 'On the Concept of Political Power', reprinted in Parsons, 1969: 352–404. See also ibid., pp. 405–522 for his related views on 'influence' and 'value-commitments' as related 'media of exchange'. For a fuller critique of Parsons on 'power', see Giddens (1968) and esp. Coleman (1963).

6. The credit multiplier works like this: suppose a bank receives £100 in new deposits, retains £10 and lends £90. The next bank receives the £90 as a new deposit, retains £9 and lends £81, and so on through many stages. The total credit created on these assumptions would be given by the formula

$$\Delta M = \frac{1}{r} \times \text{new deposits}$$

where M is the quantity of money and r the proportion of deposits retained at each stage. So if each bank retained 10 per cent of new deposits, the multiplier would be 10, and the initial deposit of £100 would create £1,000 of new credit. Economists no longer believe in fixed and mechanistic multipliers, but the basic logic remains sound. Needless to say, the mechanism can also work in reverse—the withdrawal of deposits causing a contraction of credit by a negative multiplier.

5. Social Integration

We are frequently told that the central question of sociological theory is why there is order in society. In one sense, this is undeniable. It is necessary to sociology, as to any other discipline pretending to yield reliable and cumulative knowledge, that there be order in its subject-matter. This means only that orderly, regular patterns can be discerned in social phenomena. It is only regularities which make possible description and explanation, in social science as much as in the natural sciences. Sociologists have therefore been able to find order and regularity not only in stable societies and smoothly functioning organizations, but in bitter social conflict, in bloody revolutions, and in periods of rapid, unplanned and superficially chaotic change. Law and order may break down in orderly, regular ways. Needless to say, order in this sense of regularity may be quite imperceptible to participants, and only become apparent to a sociologist faced with data on many similar situations: for example, on communities shattered by natural catastrophes (Barton 1969).

But this is a red herring. This is not the sense of 'order' in which 'the problem of order' is said to be central to sociological theory, and it is important to keep the two meanings distinct. By 'the problem of order' is meant the question posed by Thomas Hobbes (1651): why do men co-operate with each other in society? Why is there not a continual 'war of everyone against everyone', as each individual pursues his own self-interest by whatever means, including force, that are at hand? Why is life not, in consequence, 'solitary, poor, nasty, brutish and short'? How, in other words, is a degree of *harmony* in society achieved? In the past, sociologists have tended to espouse one or other of the contradictory answers proposed by political philosophers. Social order is the result of some people being able to coerce others into obedience; or it rests on general agreement among the members of society; or it stems from their striking bargains with each other which are to everyone's individual advantage as well as the collective advantage. But it is unhelpful to see these viewpoints as mutually exclusive. For the sociologist, social order must be a matter for empirical investigation. It is obvious that each of the old philosophical views has a grain of truth in it, for each comes near to describing what is observed in some societies, or parts of societies, of different types, at different periods of history, in particular circumstances. But each, as a 'theory' of social order of universal validity, is laughable. To avoid the air of unreality which used to pervade some sociological discussions of social order, it is as well to remember that social harmony is very often *not* achieved, and that social order and disorder are very much relative terms. The actual state of relative order to disorder in a particular society or part of society is the outcome of complex forces of dependence and interdependence, of co-operation and conflict, of strength and weakness, of alliances and cleavages between people and groups. Central to any understanding of these forces is that aspect of the structure of societies called the division of labour.

Specialization, Interdependence and the Division of Labour

In *The Wealth of Nations*, the most celebrated of all discussions of the division of labour, Adam Smith described the advantages of specialization in human activities. Consider the pin-makers' shop, said Smith (1970:109–10; orig. 1776). About eighteen separate operations were involved in making each pin. A single worker carrying out each and every operation—drawing and cutting the wire, sharpening the point, forming and attaching the head, and so forth—could make no more than twenty pins in a day. Yet ten men working together in one of the primitive 'manufactories' of Smith's day, each specializing in one or two operations, could between them produce perhaps 48,000 pins a day. Together, they could produce at least 240 times as many pins as if they each worked separately. Little wonder that Smith considered the division of labour a chief cause of 'the wealth of nations', and that it has been carried forward without apparent limit in industrial societies. Nor is the division of labour of only economic significance. The less elegant terms 'role differentiation' and 'structural differentiation' signify sociology's recognition that increasing specialization of activities is not confined only to the sphere of production.

For the economist, the chief interest of the division of labour is the vast multiplication of output of goods and services it makes possible. The sociologist, too, should not lose sight of the great incentives there are to specialization. Even if the increased output is distributed very unequally, it is quite likely that, in factual *economic* terms, everyone concerned will be better off. For the problem of social order, however, increasing specialization as such is of less significance than its inevitable corollary: the growing web of interdependence which it spins through society. People's position in the division of labour both makes others dependent on them, and simultaneously makes them dependent on others; it is a source both of power and of constraint. The degree of power and dependence varies widely. On the one hand, everyone who performs some specialized task on which others depend has some resources for power. The resources are obvious in the case of the owner of a factory producing some general necessity, especially if he has a degree of monopoly power in the product market and monopsony power in the labour market. They are least obvious in the case of the unskilled labourer, whose labour power is a drop in the ocean, whose place may readily be taken by someone else, and who is not even organized into a union with some degree of monopoly power.

On the other hand, in an industrial society, the overwhelming majority of the population directly produce for themselves no more than an infinitely small fraction of individual needs. Even the most powerful are dependent on countless others. Concomitant with an advancing division of labour, then, is a great lengthening of what may be called 'chains of interdependence' (Elias 1970) or 'interaction chain length' (Blain 1971, Kemper 1972). Chains or networks of interdependence may include a few dozen people in a hunting and gathering band, or they may stretch across the world to hundreds of millions of people in contemporary society. The longer are the chains of interdependence, the smaller will be the proportion anyone will know personally of those with whom he is interdependent. Contacts are more frequently indirect than direct and face-to-face. All this is implicit in such classical discussions of social solidarity as those of Toennies and Durkheim (Blain 1971). But their famous dichomoties between *Gemeinschaft* and *Gesellschaft* and mechanical and organic solidarity, fruitful as they certainly have been, tend to distort our perception of what is essentially a continuous not a dichotomous variable. Except in the very smallest of social units, a proportion of relationships are indirect. This proportion rises as the chains of interdependence lengthen, but even in the largest-scale societies, knots of *gemeinschaftlich* relationships inevitably remain within the wider *gesellschaftlich* network.[1]

What therefore constitutes 'social order' in complex networks of interdependence? Essentially it is *calculability*. People have to rely for many of their needs on people who are anonymous to them; their trust cannot be based on personal knowledge of everyone involved. If the network does not prove reliable, people may cease to contribute to it and become more self-reliant, and certainly fall into contention with each other. Chains of interdependence may break and the division of labour regress, as they did in Europe during the decline of the Roman Empire. A rapidly advancing division of labour may be equally disruptive. Rapid structural differentiation often outstrips the process of social integration, and brisk social change is often accompanied by marked social conflict. This brings into focus the two-fold significance of the division of labour for social order. Advanced specialization raises the question of how the activities of countless individuals are to be co-ordinated sufficiently to maintain the web of interdependence. The corollary is that the interdependence which specialization entails is a powerful source of constraint on individuals' activities. We shall examine first the problem of collective action, then that of constraint.

Collective Action

Collective action is an achievement in the face of great obstacles. Why it is theoretically problematic can be seen if we consider a group in which each member is a free agent and has his own scale of preferences for collective objectives. Suppose every member's participation is essential to the attainment of any objective. Now it is easy to see that if a particular objective is desired by no one, no action will be taken to achieve it; and if it is equally desired by everyone, collective action will not be very problematic. But consider the much more probable situation in which some want one thing, others another. Suppose members face three possible alternative objectives of collective action, A, B and C, and are asked to rank them in order of preference. Person *x* ranks them A, B, C; person *y* ranks them B, C, A. It can then be seen that, with only two people involved, it is already impossible to construct a *collective* ordinal scale of preference (A, C, B, or C, B, A, etc.) which satisfactorily aggregates and reflects the two individual scales. Next let us introduce a third person *z* with preferences C, A, B (Figure 7)[2]. It may then appear that the deadlock can be broken by a simple voting rule. But still more paradoxical effects then appear. Suppose the alternatives are offered in pairs. The first choice is between A and B; A wins with two votes. Then the choice lies between A and C; C wins with two votes. The paradox is that, had the initial choice lain between B and C, B would have been chosen; then B would have been chosen in preference to A. It seems unreasonable that collective decisions should hinge on the order in which alternatives are offered —though timing very often is important in real life.

Figure 7.[2]

Rank	Actor x	Actor y	Actor z
1	A	B	C
2	B	C	A
3	C	A	B

This is only to touch on an old problem in welfare economics and a growing body of work in mathematical sociology.[3] Even this simple heuristic model, however, makes it possible to characterize (or perhaps to caricature) the ways in which the traditional 'theories' of social order tried to solve the problem of collective action. The so-called 'conflict' view is that conflicts over collective objectives are endemic and continuous, and that collective action takes place chiefly because some people have the power resources to impose their preferences on others. The 'consensus' view denies, in effect, that people's preferences are independent of each other; socialization tends to produce similar scales of preference. Or it inculcates an acceptance either that some people's views *should* take precedence over others', or of a voting or decision rule which, in spite of imperfections, is accepted as binding. The 'exchange' perspective takes a broader view; there are numerous collective decisions and actions, and no one can expect to be satisfied every time. But people are prepared to participate in one action to which they are relatively indifferent or even antipathetic so that, when it comes to matters about which they care more, others will assist them. The activities of Congressmen in 'log-rolling'—exchanging support for each other's measures in order that each can build up an alliance to push through his own pet legislation—are a good example. The exchange view is in effect a sub-species of the consensus view, for it implies some degree of agreement underlying the exchange process.

Interdependence and Constraint

The 'consensus' and 'conflict' traditions of thought are also associated with very different views of constraint which the division of labour imposes on individuals. The two views are epitomized in the ideas of alienation and anomie, derived respectively from Marx and Durkheim. The two traditions are agreed that society, social relations and institutions constrain and shape the individual's activities, and that the division of labour is especially significant in this context. But they evaluate the fact very differently and draw opposite conclusions. Sociologists have used the concepts both of alienation and anomie extensively in research. In trying to use them in a reasonably value-free way, however, they have noticeably transformed both in a similar direction, so that in some usages the two words are almost synonyms.

Both 'alienation' and 'anomie' have come to be used rather loosely.[4] This is especially true of alienation, which some writers have used quite indiscriminately. Schacht (1971:139) remarks that Erich Fromm 'seems to refer to almost everything of which he disapproves as an instance of "alienation". He disapproves of a great deal; so it is not surprising that he finds alienation to be "all-pervasive" '. In Marx and Durkheim, alienation and anomie both refer primarily to characteristics of social structure, not to subjective feelings of the people enmeshed in it. Anomie essentially means the absence of norms or *common* standards of behaviour and aspiration, and in this sense is a quality observable only in the group, not in the individual. Durkheim first used the term to describe a situation in which the division of labour is ill-co-ordinated, and where people's roles and responsibilities are poorly defined. A situation of general disorganization and conflict results (1933:353–73). Later he used it to describe one of the situations to which suicide was a potential response. For Marx similarly, alienation was an objective property of certain patterns of social organization. Labour in a broad sense ought to be a basic form of self-expression and self-fulfilment. But the progressive division of labour in capitalist society prevented this. It fragmented skills, and more and more of a worker's time and energy was absorbed in narrower and narrower activities. What obscure phrases like 'the worker is alienated from the product of his labour' really boil down to is that labour is not performed for its own sake as an end in itself, but only as a means of subsistence. This is so because the division of labour structures and restricts opportunities for alternative action. The mere fact of employment is not essential for alienation; a self-employed farmer forced by economic circumstances to toil long hours, and unable to do the things he would really like to do, would be as alienated as a factory worker.

> A man's labour is truly 'his own labour' for Marx only when it is 'spontaneous', 'free and self-directed activity'. It is his own only when it reflects his own personality and is prompted by his own need to build or create or do something of his own choosing. It must, in short, be precisely what he wants to do. [Schacht 1971: 90–91]

Hence Marx's famous remark that in communist society it would be 'possible for me to do one thing today and another tomorrow, to hunt in the morning, fish in the afternoon, rear cattle in the evening, criticize after dinner, *just as I have a mind,* without ever becoming hunter, fisherman, shepherd or critic' (1947 :22, my italics).[5]

Though alienation and anomie are to be seen as objective properties of social structure, both clearly also have social psychological implications (Lukes 1967). And these implications reveal antithetical views of social constraint. Although no one was more conscious than Marx of the power of social institutions to shape men, his discussion of alienation implies that he had some conception of human needs and potential existing independently of social influences. Capitalist society interferes with the free development of this potential.[6] But why should men raised in capitalist society not *choose* to do the kind of jobs which exist in it, and find them satisfying? Do not all societies shape their members' behaviour and personalities, and all, even if there is an infinite variety of social patternings, impose constraint? Durkheim's discussion of anomie represents a continuation of precisely this line of thought. The implication here is that the individual becomes psychologically disorientated and disrupted in the absence of firm social guidance. The anomic suicide illustrates this most clearly; one of Durkheim's most inspired suggestions was that sudden good fortune (for example windfall wealth) is as effective as bad fortune in shattering accustomed standards of behaviour and aspiration, and it could, equally, drive some people to suicide. So although, as Horton (1964) argues, alienation and anomie express Marx's and Durkheim's common condemnation of rampant economic individualism, they also express opposing views of human needs. To put it a little simplistically, Marx concluded that less, and Durkheim that more, social control and constraint were desirable for human well-being.[7]

In trying to make practical use of the concepts of alienation and anomie in their research, sociologists have tended to make them more exclusively psychological, and to play down the structural implications. To distinguish the psychological from the structural or 'sociological' sense of anomie, McClosky and Schaar (1965) speak of 'anomy', and Srole (1956) chose the term 'anomia'. These are subjective feelings to be measured by responses to attitude-scale items. Similarly, Nettler (1957) and Blauner (1964) assess the extent of 'alienation' by individuals' attitudes. In consequence, the two ideas have increasingly converged. Inspecting the attitude-scale items used by Srole to measure 'anomia' and by Nettler to measure 'alienation', the difference between what they purport to measure is not immediately striking. Thus the psychological interpretation makes it possible to amalgamate anomie and alienation and merely distinguish several varieties of some generalized psychological *Angst*. The best-known attempt to do so is that of Seeman (1959). Seeman identifies five distinct dimensions of 'alienation': powerlessness, meaninglessness, normlessness, isolation and self-estrangement. Normlessness is superficially closest to Durkheimian anomie, but in fact all five dimensions refer to the subjective feelings of the individual, not to any external conditions of his social existence.

The structural conception of anomie is, however, by no means dead. In his essays on deviant behaviour (mentioned above, p. 30), Robert Merton (1968:185–248) conceives of anomic situations as arising through the inadequacy of socially structured opportunities for the attainment of the goals to which cultural values encourage individuals to aspire. Interestingly enough, however, Merton does not doubt the existence of clear cultural values, even if some people are pressured into rejecting them. We must take this as our cue to examine the view of social structure associated with 'consensus theory', which emphasizes the vital part which common values and norms play in social integration.

On Consensus

Few sociologists would wish to deny that groups of people who interact with each other over a period are likely to evolve normative regularities in their behaviour together. The study almost inevitably used to illustrate this is the Hawthorne 'Bank-Wiring Group' (Roethlisberger and Dickson, 1939), in which norms limiting the maximum output were observed to develop within the work-group apparently from fear of reductions in piece-rates. A norm, in this sense, is plainly something more than an average; it is a standard of behaviour to which people adhere to a greater or lesser extent. But why do they adhere to them? Talcott Parsons (1951:37) clearly recognized the two main possibilities: conformity for the sake of expediency, and conformity in response to moral commitment. Expediency better explains the behaviour of the bank-wiring group and many other cases, but having recognized the possibility of merely expedient conformity, Parsons virtually drops it from his work. For Parsons, the great proponent of the consensual view of social order, moral commitment to shared norms and values becomes an almost mystical element in social life. Almost mystical, because it is often difficult to see how his all-embracing conception of the social order can be shown to be either true or false.

Social structure, for Parsons, is made up of roles, norms, values and collectivities (1961 :41). We have already discussed (p. 73ff) his model of dyadic interaction, which purports to show that, in any continuing interaction, the actors must conform to each other's role expectations and establish stable co-operation. On these shaky foundations, Parsons erects a huge edifice. Norms and values are the building-blocks. The distinction between the two is relative. A *norm* Parsons sees as an element in the expectations of particular roles, defining them as the rules of chess define the moves of the various pieces. Wherever there is 'role differentiation', norms 'define the rights and obligations applicable to one role but not to another' (1961 :42). Everyone may recognize and even accept the norms, but not everyone is bound by them because people occupy different roles. To recognize the norms defining the role of bus conductor does not mean that everyone is expected to behave as a bus conductor. In contrast, *values* 'are shared by the members over and above their particular roles'. For instance, in a factory, the production engineer may be expected to concentrate on maintaining the quality and output of the product, the accountant to be concerned to keep down unit costs, and the personnel manager to see harmonious labour relations as the great virtue. These three role-specific norms may to a degree conflict with each other in specific circumstances. Yet each may be seen as a reflection of the engineer's, the accountant's and the personnel manager's *shared* commitment to the value of efficient production, and of their *common* goal of maintaining the prosperity of their firm. The difference between a value and a goal, incidentally, is that between a signpost and a destination; the former is a general conception of the desirable, the latter a specific and desired situation. Of *collectivities*, less need be said; if everyone in the factory shared the aforesaid values, it would be described as a collectivity. With his customary eloquence, Parsons defines a collectivity as a 'system of . . . interaction of a plurality of role-performers ... normatively regulated in terms of common values and of norms sanctioned by these common values' (1961:42).

Since the difference between norms and values is relative and a question of scope, what is a value at one level may be a norm at another. As Parsons sees it, norms within one group of roles are legitimated by more general values which transcend these particular roles; but these values may themselves be relatively specific norms which are legitimated by still more general values at a higher level. Thus is constructed a hierarchy of values of ever-increasing generality, up to the core values of the well-integrated society. Looked at the opposite way, it is a giant moral syllogism. In a society of millions of members and countless roles, the topmost values which hold the whole edifice together (if they do) must be of impressive abstraction; so, as often as not, Parsons consigns them safely to the realm of religion. Parsons's collaborator, Edward Shils, has written more explicitly on the 'central value system' of society, which

> ... partakes of the nature of the sacred. In this sense, every society has an 'official' religion, even when that society or its exponents and interpreters conceive of it, more or less correctly, as a secular, pluralistic and tolerant society. [Shils 1961: 117]

The central value system consists of the values and standards espoused and more or less observed by those in authority, and it always 'legitimates the existing distribution of roles and rewards'. It rests 'on the need which human beings have for incorporation into something which transcends and transfigures their concrete individual existence' (1961:121). However, Shils does not suggest that every member of any society subscribes to the central values. Rather there is a minimum level of acceptance of authority in society, which presumably disintegrates if the minimum is not met. But with spreading webs of interdependence, the central institutions of modern societies increasingly impinge on the whole population, and Shils sees them as more integrated by common values than pre-modern societies.

It is a mistake to dismiss consensus out of hand as a factor which, in many circumstances, promotes social integration. Yet it is a difficult task to investigate the beliefs which people actually hold and which actually guide their actions. In consequence, the claims made by Parsons and his followers for the unifying power of shared values often seem too sweeping and empirically ill-founded. Alvin Gouldner (1971 :140) pointed out that

> Parsons never allows moral values to become just one other variable in the social equation. Paradoxically, however, neither does he ever mount a full-scale and systematic exploration of the nature and functioning of moral values.

For as soon as attention is turned to the practicalities of social life, numerous difficulties to any solution of the 'problem of order' exclusively in terms of value integration become obvious.

First, it is implicit in Parsons's view of a hierarchy of norms and values of ever-increasing generality that the topmost and most widely spread are also the most abstract, vague and unspecific. They can therefore be used to legitimate any social structure and none in particular. Parsons himself notes (1951:293) that revolutionaries appeal to the same abstractions of 'democracy' and 'justice' as do the upholders of the status quo. He chooses to interpret this as evidence that the overt conflict is the top tenth, so to speak, of an iceberg of underlying unity; but it might as easily be taken as evidence of the inability of common commitment to abstract ideas to maintain social cohesion. If values are signposts, general consensus on the value of 'democracy' or 'justice' is about as useful as a signpost in Piccadilly Circus pointing towards Sydney.

Secondly—a related point—in many particular situations two or more general values may conflict with each other. Lipset (1964) identifies 'achievement' and 'equality' as two key values in the American credo; but as often as not, opportunities for 'achievement' mean competition for unequal rewards. Mann (1970:424) points out that, in such circumstances, it is likely that 'cohesion results precisely because there is no common commitment to core values'. Thus, less privileged groups may be more tolerant of inequality just because they are *less* committed to achievement.

Thirdly, 'negative consensus' may contribute more to social cohesion than 'positive consensus'. Jack Douglas (1970) emphasizes the significance of 'accommodative morality' in complex, pluralistic societies. The diversity of tastes and commitments which abounds in pluralistic societies is facilitated by a general value of privacy—embodied in the privacy of the home, countless private clubs and associations, and in the anonymity of the city. In so far as there are notional goals at all in a country like the United States, Douglas argues, they are 'least common denominator goals', of which he mentions economic growth, national security and health as the three most obvious. Their significance is that they are each necessary as a condition of Americans individually pursuing their great diversity of more specific goals.

Fourthly, it should not be too readily assumed that consensus on values promotes social harmony irrespective of the content of these values. As van den Berghe (1963) pointed out, 'consensus on norms such as extreme competition and individualistic laissez-faire, or suspiciousness and treachery . . . , or malevolence and resort to witchcraft is hardly conducive to social solidarity and integration'.

Fifthly, need consensus be about the central institutions of society? There is abundant evidence that only small minorities can give expression to a reasonably articulate set of beliefs about social institutions (Converse 1964), yet it tends to be assumed that even the inarticulate have absorbed the general values. Yet social cohesion may owe much to more mundane mechanisms. Speaking of the average member of industrial societies, Mann (1970 :435) writes : 'his normative connections with the vast majority of fellow citizens may be extremely tenuous, and his commitment to general dominant and deviant values may be irrelevant to his compliance with the expectations of others'. On this view, social integration is due less to a great hierarchy of ever more general shared values than to a principle of social inertia; as William James observed, habit is 'the great flywheel of society'. At any rate, quite complex patterns of social interaction may continue, not because participants share any very specific values concerning the broad organization of society, but because their relations are pervaded by less ethereal feelings like trust, and because everyone gets something out of their mundane relationships.

The significance of trust between parties to exchange relationships has long been recognized. Systems of ceremonial exchange in primitive societies, discussed by Malinowski (1922) and Mauss (1954) among others, serve to generate trust and alliances, which promote social cohesion as well as trade in 'real' commodities. How then does social exchange start? Alvin Gouldner (1960) suggested that the 'norm of reciprocity' ('treat others as you would like them to treat you'; Matthew 7:12) is a cultural universal and acts as a 'starting mechanism' for social transactions. Such a norm may, indeed, be found in every society, but as Blau (1964 :92) comments, moral commitment to it probably only reinforces tendencies which stem from the very logic of interdependence. For, where people are interdependent with one another, it is merely prudential and expedient behaviour to follow the principle of reciprocity, no matter what one's moral feelings. That is not to deny that every culture contains countless standards as to what constitutes fair exchange in particular situations. It is noteworthy that, in extending his theory of social exchange from face-to-face bargaining to the level of macro-structures, Blau finds it necessary, like Parsons, to posit commitment to more general values.

On Conflict

If agreement of one sort and another is found in every society, so is conflict. Lewis Coser (1956), building very directly on the work of Simmel (1955, orig. 1908), has done a great deal to overcome the assumption common in post-war American sociology that conflict is necessarily something destructive or pathological. Perhaps he went too far and painted too rosy a picture of the consequences of conflict. For it must never be forgotten that conflict often creates chaos out of order. History shows too plainly how conflict within and between societies can destroy complex organization, reverse the division of labour and reduce standards of living. Yet conflict takes many forms and has many consequences; it is certainly nonsense to see consensus and conflict simply as opposites. C. H. Cooley (1918:39) put the matter in a nutshell when he observed that 'conflict and co-operation are not separable things, but phases of one process which always involves something of both'. The same scarce resources which require co-operation to produce become as often as not the focus of conflict over how they shall be distributed as rewards among those who helped to produce them. Then again, the very experience of close co-operation can set up tensions between the co-operating individuals and groups.

Conflict is rarely unlimited. Some measure of agreement is usually evident even between antagonists. There is generally at least a minimal consensus on 'the rules of the game', on the means which shall and shall not be used in the conflict. In pressing a wage claim, for instance, a strike is accepted as a legitimate means of affecting the outcome, while shooting the manager is not. Even wars, though they may no longer be fought with eighteenth-century textbook exactitude, usually proceed on some ground rules. The revue *Beyond the Fringe* caught the flavour of modern war with a prediction of 'Forty million dead bodies strewn all about the place . . . which is almost the maximum score permitted by the Geneva Convention'. As Simmel emphasized, conflict is a *relationship* between opponents.

Conflict may or may not be accompanied by hostility and animosity between the parties to it. Where conflict is the expression of emotional hostility, it becomes an end in itself. Hostility may, perhaps, be directed impersonally against all members of a minority race, but intimate personal relationships are particularly likely to give rise to violent hostility. (Murder is most often a family affair.) On the other hand, where conflict is pursued as a means to an end—as a trial of strength over the allocation of resources, for example—it is possible that the parties may feel little bitterness towards each other. Much depends on how the parties define the situation. Ideology may intensify conflict by representing it in terms not of personal or sectional interests, but of broad ethical principles. Then again, it may render the conflict less bitter and hateful. When opponents are seen only as prisoners of social situations, they ought scarcely to be hated so much. Not that people are always consistent. Arthur Koestler (1945:227) observed that Marx 'taught that man's mental make-up is a product of his environment, yet showered invectives on everybody who, in obedience to his environmental conditioning, couldn't help disagreeing with him'.

It is not a simple matter to generalize about the consequences of conflict, either within groups and organizations or between them. Conflict *within* groups may destroy them as units capable of collective action, or it may actually assist them. A family row may clear the air and a strike may, on occasion, be settled to the satisfaction of both parties. On the other hand, families do break up, and strikes often end in greater discontent and lower productivity than when they started. Conflict is more likely to serve as a safety-valve or to resolve clashes of interest when there is already an underlying unity present. The more secure the matrix of agreement within which conflict takes place, the more internal conflict the group may be able to absorb. Paradoxically, then, the correlation between consensus and conflict may be positive, not negative (Coser 1956:81). Thus a well-integrated organization may be able to encourage internal conflict as a source of ideas which can be put to fruitful use. But, again, much depends on the type of organization. What may be true of, say, an advertising agency, is not necessarily true of a religious or political sect. The latter often show monolithic agreement, but they typically cannot tolerate much internal conflict. They require unanimity and total involvement of their members, so that when disputes break out on outwardly trivial points of dogma, they can be extremely bitter and the outcome may be cataclysmic fissuring of the group.

Conflict *within* groups and conflict *between* groups are related in complex ways. First of all, conflict, and even just passive hostility between groups, serves to define group boundaries and makes it clear who is one of 'Us' and who is one of 'Them'. Though overt conflict between castes was rare, Simmel noted that 'the Hindu social system rests not only on the hierarchy, but also on the mutual repulsion, of the castes' (1955:18). Conflict with an external enemy may strongly promote internal cohesion. If no external enemy is immediately at hand, leaders have long known the advantages of finding one. Shakespeare's Henry IV, having waded through bloodshed to a throne, proposed a crusade from motives not entirely religious.

> . . . those opposed eyes
> Which, like the meteors of a troubled heaven,
> All of one nature, of one substance bred,
> Did lately meet in the intestine shock
> And furious close of civil butchery,
> Shall now, in mutual well-beseeming ranks,
> March all one way, and be no more oppos'd.
>
> [*Henry IV*, Part One, I, i]

Jews and other scapegoats have often fulfilled the same function as the Saracens. However, a qualification is again needed concerning the power of external conflict to promote in-group unity. Coser (1956 :93–4) contrasts the proverbial unity of Great Britain during the Second World War with the deep schism in France; the French nation was so deeply divided before the war that the war's effect was to shatter society, not unify it.

Membership of 'in-groups' and 'out-groups' is not always at all clear cut. In open, pluralistic structures, an individual is a member of many groups. This not only means that he is less likely to be totally involved as a personality in any one of them, but that he will participate in a variety of inter-group conflicts, the lines of which cross-cut each other. As a result, people who are antagonists in one conflict are allies in another. The 'web of group affiliations', as Simmel's translator so appropriately phrased it, thus serves to moderate the intensity of conflicts. An offshoot of this idea is the notion of *cross-pressures*. It has often been suggested that individuals who belong to two or more groups which pull their loyalties in contrary directions react by feeling less intensely about the issue in question. This was one of the major conclusions drawn from studies of voting in American elections (especially Berelson, *et al.* 1954). A voter whose family was strongly Republican, but whose occupational colleagues were strongly Democrat, might resolve the contradictory pressures of his immediate associates by becoming indifferent or wavering. In a rather different sense, a person was also said to be cross-pressured if his social background placed him in conflicting categories. For example, if Catholics tend to vote Democratic and businessmen Republican, a Catholic businessman is cross-pressured. This is a much weaker sense of cross-pressure, for it by no mean implies that Catholic businessmen are necessarily surrounded by two conflicting but politically homogeneous groups of face-to-face associates. The cross-pressure effect would only be detectable from large-scale survey data. Some doubt has been cast on the potency of cross-pressures, at least in this second sense (Horan 1971; Sperlich 1971), but in so far as they do not exist they tend to moderate the intensity of social conflict.

All these propositions about conflict, though empirically contingent, are, in Franklin Roosevelt's phrase, 'very iffy'. According to circumstances, conflict between groups may promote social cohesion or disruption; internal conflict may case schism or be a sign of basic unity; ideology may intensify conflict or reduce it. Simmel's and Coser's propositions suggest things to look for in particular research situations. They are essentially formal, as were our earlier remarks on consensus, and say little about the likely subjects of social agreement and disagreement.

Group Interests, Group Consciousness and the Structure of Conflict

Some of sociology's most exciting propositions have, however, been very much concerned with not only the form but also the content of consensus and conflict in historical societies. In this, Marx and Weber, and more recent writers in their tradition, offer a marked contrast to Simmel.

Marx

To say anything about Marx is to step into a minefield of ideological controversy, and any brief statement is bound to be disputed by someone. With that warning, let us nonetheless proceed. Marx is usually thought of as one of the greatest writers on social conflict. So he was, yet he was equally concerned with the conditions which promote consensus as those which lead to conflict. It is true that he saw little prospect of society-wide harmony, except in the communist society of the future, about which he said precious little. But he was much concerned with the circumstances in which men in similar social situatons would recognize their common interests and unite in groups capable of collective action in pursuit of their interests.

Marvin Harris (1968:4) has perhaps come closest to summing up in one sentence Marx's basic perspective of materialism:

> This principle holds that similar technologies applied to similar environments tend to produce similar arrangements of labour in production and distribution, and that these in turn call forth similar kinds of social groupings, which justify and co-ordinate their activities by means of similar systems of values and beliefs.

The essential insight is that the material basis of a society—its modes of production and economic organization—generate a finite number of social groupings, the members of each of which share a similar social situation and therefore have interests in common. These groupings, however, are mere categories—Dahrendorf (1959) was later to call them 'quasi-groups'—and their members are by no means necessarily *conscious* of their common situation and interests. There may, therefore, be considerable conflict between segments of the same grouping. Marx asked how social categories could become conscious of a common identity and unite against other groups.

Marx was, however, not so much interested in the formal and abstract process as in the particular case of the genesis and dynamics of capitalist society. The structure of interests changed during its growth. Marx did not have a romantic utopian image of the past; he saw that the proletarian and bourgeois classes had a common interest in the overthrow of the remnants of feudalism, and wrote glowingly of the vigour with which the bourgeois entrepreneurs transformed the economy (Marx and Engels 1968 :36ff.). As industrialization proceeded, however, the interests of the two classes came to be at odds. The workers might fail to perceive this, and retain a false conception of their true interests, but economic forces gradually drew them into conflict with the bourgeoisie. In the early capitalist economy, many groups persisted whose class affiliation was ambiguous—the artisan whose special skills were in short supply, the self-employed craftsman, the small factory-owner who worked alongside his men. Marx, however, predicted the increasing polarization of society into two camps. The petty bourgeois would disappear, prosperity making him a true bourgeois, or lack of it a wage-slave; with him would disappear the ambiguities of interest and the cross-cutting ties between the classes. Why was this to happen? Marx's argument is essentially economic. The logic of machine production and economies of scale would dictate larger and larger productive units, driving out the self-employed craftsman and the small factory owner (if he did not himself expand). Machines would also make many hitherto scarce skills redundant, and make men into unskilled machine minders. With labour increasingly homogeneous, its strength in the market would decrease. The reserve army of the unemployed, any member of which could do a job as well as the unskilled labourer then in employment, would bid down wage rates, leading to mass pauperization.[8] Furthermore, Marx accepted the view of the competitive process advanced by Ricardo and the English classical economists. Competition between entrepreneurs would be so fierce that profit margins would leave little room for the indulgence of humanitarian delusions; an employer who paid more than the market wage would soon be driven into bankruptcy. (Twentieth-century economists have suggested that the growth of economic units and the emergence of oligopolistic markets make such strict market discipline unlikely.)

Suffering itself would assist the emergence of class consciousness, and make evident the advantages of solidarity, of collective action to multiply the industrial bargaining power of the workers, and eventually to overthrow the capitalist system. Militancy would be especially likely to emerge, for example, in mining villages, where the workers share a common lot in a homogeneous community. In contrast, difficulties of communication would prevent the emergence of the peasantry, who are scattered across the countryside, as a self-conscious class (Marx and Engels 1968:171–2). The extent to which external leadership is necessary to catalyse class-consciousness has long been in dispute between Marxists such as Lenin and Rosa Luxemburg. Marx, however, firmly predicted increasing organization along class lines for collective action, at first in trade unions for industrial objectives, later broadening to concerted political action for the overthrow of capitalism.

That Marx's prognostications have not all proved accurate is accepted even by many Marxists.[9] Why have the lines of conflict in capitalist society not become deeper and more clear-cut? The answer seems to lie partly in social developments which Marx did not entirely foresee, but also partly in theoretical difficulties in the notion of objective class interests.

Weber

Many of Weber's differences with Marx centre on the notion of interests. Certainly the sociologist may observe that a category of people share a common situation in some respect. But can such people be said to have objective interests as a group, interests which they may or may not perceive 'correctly'? Weber was extremely sceptical about the validity of any definition of individual or group interests except as they appeared to the individuals themselves. He protested at

> that kind of pseudo-scientific operation with the concepts of class and class interests . . . which found its most classic expression in the statement of a talented author that the individual may be in error concerning his interests, but that the class is infallible about its interests. [1938: II, 930]

Though he did not by any means reject all of Marx's analysis of class, Weber saw nothing inevitable in the emergence of class consciousness and collective class action. A category of people could be said to have a common class position in so far as the life chances of its members were determined by their similar position in the market. Nevertheless:

> The class situation and other circumstances remaining the same, the direction in which the individual worker, for instance, is likely to pursue his interests may vary widely . . . In the same way, the direction of interests may vary according to whether or not social action of a larger or smaller portion of those commonly affected by a class situation, or even an association among them, e.g. a trade union, has grown out of the class situation, from which the individual may expect promising results for himself. The emergence of an association or even of mere social action from a common class situation is by no means a universal phenomenon. [1968: II, 929]

The common situation may not be recognized at all. Or it may produce nothing more than similar *individual* reactions, taking the form of low morale, unorganized and perhaps semi-conscious go-slows, or, at most, sporadic individual acts of sabotage. Whether anything more substantial results—'class actions' such as wildcat strikes, or the more permanent organization of associations with class objectives—hinges on historical and cultural circumstances. Most important, the connection between the causes and consequences of the class situation must be 'transparent'. In Chapter 4 (pp. 84–85 above), it was noted that, as social networks increase in complexity, they become 'opaque'—the individual finds it more difficult to put together a mental picture of all the interconnections involved. No matter how great the disparities between the life chances of different groups, no great discontent or conflict need result as long as their causes and consequences remain unrecognizable and unexplained to the people involved.[10] Since Weber did not suppose there were only two class situations in society—the market would continue to differentiate the life chances of those with different kinds of property and various kinds of skills—he saw little reason why causes and consequences of life chances should necessarily become more transparent.

Moreover, Weber recognized that common economic situations were not the only bases for collective social action. Categories of people who shared a common status, religion, ethnic background or political outlook could also enter as units in social conflict. Of particular interest were people who shared a common 'status situation'.

> In contrast to the purely economically determined 'class situation', we wish to designate as *status situation* every typical component of the life of men that is determined by a specific, positive or negative, social estimation of *honour*. [1968: II, 932, his italics]

Sharing a common 'style of life', status-groups are normally conscious of their common status situation. Such groups as the Boston Brahmins would be examples of status-groups, but the caste system in which the original Brahmins figure illustrates the most extreme form of status-group stratification. Status distinctions are, of course, most often correlated with economic inequality, but 'the notion of honour peculiar to status absolutely abhors that which is essential to the market: hard bargaining' (1968:II, 937). Which principle gets the upper hand? Weber suggests that, where there is little economic change and a stable pattern of allocation, status-groups will tend to form and tend to impede the development of free markets. Where the economy is rapidly changing (and this can stem from the impact of change from outside the society), status will tend to be undermined by the market and class be more prominent as a basis for social action. In relatively stable situations, various power resources (economic, honorific, political-organizational, and so on) are probably distributed in much the same way; in periods of rapid transition their distribution may be discrepant, with the economically powerful perhaps not being accorded high status.

Changes since Marx

If Weber's discussion suggests reasons why patterns of social conflict have remained more complex than Marx expected, there have also been a number of specific social trends which have, so far, frustrated Marx's predictions. They fall into three groups.

(1) First, there have been several developments in industrial

economies which have tended to fragment and diversify the distribution of interests and, it is argued, to create more quasi-groups rather than fewer.

For one thing, though it is true that, in some industries, technology has reduced the worker to an unskilled machine minder, the broader trend of the division of labour has been to make labour more heterogeneous rather than homogeneous. This is the trend which Dahrendorf (1959:48) refers to as 'the decomposition of labour'. More workers have skills which cannot quickly be learned, so they cannot easily be replaced and are able to command high wages. Even relatively unskilled groups may occupy such strategic points in the division of labour that, if well organized, they have immense bargaining power. In short, there are many groups of employees who have an advantageous position in the labour market, and this differentiation does not facilitate class solidarity.

A related development has been the emergence of the so-called 'new middle class'—the salaried occupations ranging from high bureaucrats to lowly clerks. They now form a much larger proportion of the labour force than in Marx's day, and in some technologically most advanced industries actually outnumber the manual workers. Some of them earn less than some manual workers, others much more. To which class do they belong? If they earn their living entirely by selling their labour, they might be considered objectively 'working class'. But we know that this fails to coincide with the subjective identification of most of them. David Lockwood (1958) made what now seems an obvious point that the 'work situation' of particular groups—the 'significant others' they encounter in their work—influences their group identification. We should not, for example, expect domestic servants to form a hotbed of militancy.

On the opposite side of the market there has been a corresponding 'decomposition of capital' (Dahrendorf 1959:41). This is the frequently discussed 'separation of ownership and control' which has occurred since Marx's day, made possible by the spread of the joint-stock, limited liability company. Economic units have become larger, yet their ownership has become more dispersed through shareholdings, while practical control has passed to salaried bureaucrats. There is a large literature in sociology and economics on the extent of this development and its implications for economic motivation and social relations (see Nichols, 1969). For his part, Dahrendorf argued that Marx's view of ownership and non-ownership of capital as the great divide in society was excessively legalistic. What is now important, said Dahrendorf, is not whether people legally own capital, but their relationship to authority and control. In any 'imperatively co-ordinated association' (1959:167), there was a 'command class' and an 'obey class'. It is not very clear how, in a multi-tier chain of command, one decides the zero-point dividing those in authority from those in subordination. Within a complex division of labour, few people escape a considerable degree of constraint. In any case, Dahrendorf's view would give much weaker predictions about the lines of conflict in society as a whole than did Marx's. Since, in a pluralistic society, a man may belong to many groups, being in authority in one and taking orders in another, the 'theory' gives no guidance as to whether certain lines of conflict will become more salient than others, or how groups will coalesce in alliances for common objectives. If there are *n* 'imperatively co-ordinated associations' in a society, Dahrendorf in effect said, it may contain an indeterminate number of classes up to 2*n*. Perhaps this is the only general assertion which a cautious man might make.[11]

(2) A second group of factors have impeded the crystallization of quasi-groups as self-conscious entities capable of collective action in conflict with others.

A sense of society-wide consensus, even if it be only a limited sense of common membership in one society, is said to impede the emergence of full class consciousness. T. H. Marshall (1950) traced the growth of what he called rights of citizenship in Britain from the seventeenth century. 'Civil' rights of citizenship—equality before the law—were followed by the gradual extension of political rights to all adults, and more recently by 'social' rights of citizenship as embodied in the provisions of the Welfare State. As a whole, it is argued, this process has achieved the 'civic reincorporation' of the working classes, who no longer feel themselves 'outside' a system which exists for the benefit of others. Associated with this tendency (whether as cause, effect, or both) has been the increasing institutionalization of class conflict. Lipset (1960:220) speaks of 'the democratic class struggle', and Dahrendorf remarks that,

> Instead of a battlefield, the scene of group conflict has become a kind of market in which relatively autonomous forces contend according to certain rules of the game, by virtue of which nobody is a permanent winner or loser. [1959: 67]

Free collective bargaining illustrates this *par excellence*, and serves, on the whole, to prevent industrial conflict spilling over into the serious political conflict Marx predicted. (As governments in Britain, the United States and elsewhere have, for macroeconomic reasons, increasingly intervened in collective bargaining, it remains to be seen whether the insulation of spheres of conflict is a long-term phenomenon. Affluence, too, has often been said to dampen down discontent and discourage class conflict, though, as Goldthorpe, Lockwood, *et al.* (1969) have argued at length, the relationship between economic prosperity and political outlook is far from simple.

(3) Finally, individual social mobility is a factor which may, in some ways, be seen as an alternative to inter-group conflict. Seeking to explain why there was no strong Socialist party in the United States, Sombart suggested as early as 1906 that abundant opportunities for individuals to make good—to use the system—would reduce demands for changing the system. Dahrendorf goes further and suggests that 'individual competition and collective action are in principle mutually convertible, that they are basically equivalent expressions of the same great social force, contest' (1967:19). In other words, the individual discontented with his lot can, in an open and pluralistic society, strive with some hope of success to change his situation *by individual effort.* However, inequalities of many kinds restrict most individuals' chances of realizing their interests alone, and therefore there are, even in the most open societies, probably limits to the extent to which individual mobility can supplant collective action in groups.

Conclusions

The big, bold, traditional and ideologically charged 'theories' of social integration and conflict increasingly appear like dinosaurs ill-adapted to the complexity of contemporary societies. As *Weltanschauungen* they retain their emotional appeal, and there is a note both of satisfaction and regret in Dahrendorf's conclusion that 'the social structure of interests no longer guides us directly to the parties and platforms of political conflict; interests seem to get "lost", or perhaps satisfied, before they ever appear in the arena of group antagonism' (1967:14–15). The Parsonian concern with the social structure of values is no more adequate. If sociologists remain interested in 'social order' as a general problem, it is because they are salvaging particular insights from old systems and subjecting them to relatively modest empirical tests. It is likely to prove more fruitful to formulate well-defined propositions of limited scope, identifying what factors, present in what strengths and combinations, tend (*ceteris paribus*) to change the level of consensus or conflict, harmony and disharmony.

Notes

1. cf. the discussion of Parsons's Pattern Variables, pp. 73–74 above.
2. Reproduced from Coleman (1966).
3. See, for example, Mishan (1960), Coleman (1966, 1972, 1973), Olson (1965), Arrow (1951, 1967).
4. Marx himself spoke of alienation in several senses. For a careful analysis of these and pre-Marxian usages, see Schacht (1971), ch. 1–3.
5. How this freedom of choice is to be made compatible with the degree of co-ordinated specialization and interdependence necessary to support the present population of the globe, Marx never spells out in much detail.
6. Herbert Marcuse (1964:6) gave very crude expression to what amounts to a myth of the noble and pre-social savage: 'In the last analysis, the question of what are true and false needs must be answered by the individuals themselves, but only in the last analysis; that is, if and when they are free to give their own answer. As long as they are kept incapable of being autonomous, as long as they are indoctrinated (down to their very instincts), their answer to this question cannot be taken as their own.' It is not obvious why Marcuse is in a better position to know what is good for us; the sinister overtones are too audible to require amplification.
7. This is simplistic because Durkheim's treatment of altruistic suicide makes it plain that he felt that social constraint could also be excessive. 'Durkheim argues in effect that the relations of suicide rates to social regulation is curvilinear—high rates being associated with both excessive individuation and excessive regulation' (Coser 1971:134).
8. Marx argued that unemployment would be created by the deficiency of demand due to the extraction of 'surplus value'; the details of this need not concern us. However, Marx's assumptions about the power of the 'reserve army' need to be qualified. In a

competitive labour market (in the absence both of trade unions and collusion between employers), wage rates would not necessarily fall as far as the 'minimum subsistence level' (see Samuelson 1961 :617–19). The presence of trade unions or collusion between employers could alter the equilibrium wage level by shifting respectively the supply and the demand schedules for labour.

9. See Kissin (1972) for a brief review of recent Communist thinking on 'State Monopoly Capitalism'.

10. Opacity is very often associated with social stability. There is considerable evidence that most people most of the time do not pay much heed to the distribution of rewards in society as a whole. They compare their lot not with groups remote from them and vastly better off than themselves, but with people known more directly who are a little better off or a little worse off. They experience deprivation not in absolute terms but in relation to particular reference groups or to accustomed standards. Runciman (1966) used this idea of 'relative deprivation' to explain why the British were not more discontented with social inequalities. On the other hand, it is implicit in Durkheim's discussion of anomie that the deregulation of people's customary aspirations by violent social or economic changes can increase their sense of relative deprivation. J. C. Davis (1962) used this insight to explain the incidence of revolutions. Abrupt social change tends to make social processes more transparent, and so opacity may, in part, be a consequence as well as a cause of stability.

11. Dahrendorf later (1967) rejected this approach. Though it is not easy to test the hypothesis that relationships to authority are the prime determinant of group consciousness, Lopreato (1968) did attempt to do so. His findings were not favourable to Dahrendorf's original hypothesis.

6. System Integration

'. . . if all functions that actually tend to maintain the system are manifest functions (i.e. recognized by the participants) there ceases to be any real difference between functional and causal analysis'.
William R. Catton, Jr (1964: 919)

Without any great effort of ingenuity, we have come so far with scarcely a mention of the notion of 'social system', still less of 'structural-functionalism'. It seemed best to avoid that rich vein of confusion as long as possible.

The basic idea of functionalism is that of a *system*. A system, according to the dictionary, is no more than 'a complex whole, set of connected things or parts, organized body of material or immaterial things'. In short, the kernel of functional analysis is the idea of a social system consisting of interdependent constituent parts. At its simplest, this involves the idea that the presence or the value of one variable in a system imposes a degree of constraint on the range of possible variation in other components of the system. Or it involves the equally simple proposition that a change in one component of a system will be followed by changes in other components. For instance, it has been suggested that if a society has an industrial economy, it is unlikely that it will also have, or long retain, an elaborate pattern of prescriptive kinship relations; among the reasons for this belief is that an industrial economy demands social and geographical mobility of labour, and an extended family would be incompatible with this. It is a short step from this hypothesis of interdependence between the institutions of society to suggesting that a particular institution (such as the nuclear family unit consisting of husband, wife and offspring) fulfils certain 'functions' (such as the socialization of infants) for the wider social system. This could be equally well expressed by saying that one institution has certain *consequences* for other institutions with which it is interdependent. The word 'function' as used in sociology can usually be translated as 'consequence' and the gain in clarity of thought achieved thereby is considerable.

Why should such innocuous ideas be as controversial as they undoubtedly have been?[1] Broadly speaking, there are two reasons. First, functionalism came to be identified with the consensual view of social order; many writers have used 'functionalism' as virtually synonymous with a predilection for consensus. Secondly, the slipshod logic of many functionalist theories has earned them well-deserved criticism.

The consensual view of society is not logically inherent in a functional or systemic approach. Analytically they are separate issues, though in the history of sociology there are good reasons for confounding them. For one thing, Talcott Parsons and such influential followers as Kingsley Davis, Wilbert Moore, Marion Levy and Neil Smelser, whom Lockwood (1964) proposes we call 'normative functionalists', combined the functional approach with an emphasis on consensus, normative integration, shared values and so on. Then it must be admitted that sociologists who derive social order from interpersonal consensus will also find appeal in the image of smoothly intermeshing and harmoniously compatible institutions at the higher level. Lastly, as I shall argue below, to assume value consensus is one possible route of escape from the invalidly teleological mode of reasoning which plagues functional explanations.

In spite of this, Lockwood suggests that it is fruitful to draw a distinction between normative functionalism and general functionalism, between the problems of social integration and system integration. That of social integration, as we have seen in Chapter 5, concerns the level of harmony and disharmony, or of co-operation and conflict in a society or social group. The fact that we have discussed this without reference to the mysteries of functionalism and social systems gives some support to Lockwood's distinction. System integration, on the other hand, is more generally concerned with the causal links of interdependence between groups and institutions. Causal interdependence certainly need not imply social harmony. In Chapter 3 (p. 76) we mentioned a hypothetical (but not unrealistic) case of two tribes whose actions each helped to determine the way of life of the other, yet whose relations were not in the least harmonious. They were at war, and might well stay at war for a long time, being none the less systemically interdependent. Coser (1956) discussed social conflict within an essentially functional framework, as did Gluckman (1955). Indeed, for all his attention to social conflict, Marx himself took an essentially systemic view of society. What could be more systemic than Marx's discussion of the complex links between economic arrangements and other social institutions, or his view that, given certain characteristics of the substructure, the range of likely variation in the superstructure of beliefs and political institutions is limited? The Marxist theses may or may not be entirely valid, but there is no denying that they contain the basic functional insight—that of institutional interdependence.[2] It could be argued that one reason why Marx and Engels poured such scorn on the 'utopian' socialists was precisely that the latter had failed to make a functional analysis of society, and therefore failed to locate the point of maximum leverage for social change, and consequently to show how their new society could be made to grow out of the old.

If even Marx can be enlisted as a systems theorist, it is not surprising that Parsons has claimed that 'general agreement exists regarding ... the concept of system' (1961:33). Kingsley Davis (1959) went even further and announced that functional analysis is merely 'another name for sociological analysis'. In the very minimal way in which we have so far defined systems and functionalism, this may be true. But such arguments involve a certain sleight of hand. For functionalists have historically used the idea of 'social system' in a rather more specific sense. Let us first examine systems analysis in general before looking at the particular form of it identified with functionalism.

Systems Analysis

'The concept of system is nothing but an application of the criterion of logical integration of generalized propositions.' So says Parsons (1961:32), and rightly, though it would be unfortunate if we were led to believe that Parsons himself uses the concept of social system only in this general, logical sense.

The systemic view is useful—indeed necessary—whenever we are confronted with a situation of other than simple mechanical causality. Sociology is not often blessed with situations where item A has an effect on item B, which in turn affects item C, with the simplicity of one billiard ball hitting another. More often than not, a number of variables are causally interrelated with each other in complex ways. A may have an effect on B and C, and C may affect D, but A is itself affected by the reaction of B and D, and so on. In his work on race relations, Blalock (1967, 1970) identifies a large number of variables involved in the patterning of minority group relations. His preliminary identification of the causal links is shown in Figure 8.

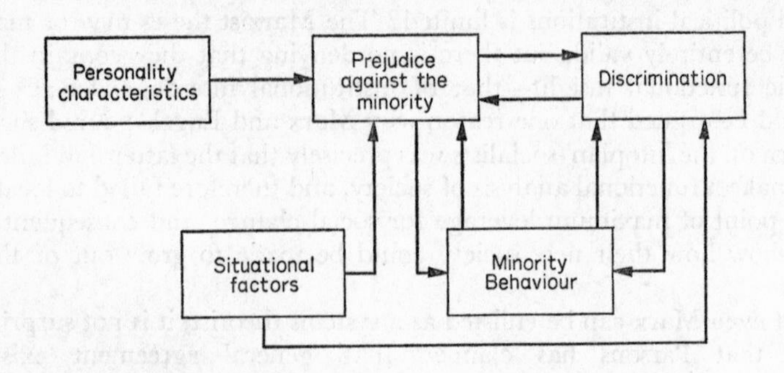

Figure 8 (from Blalock, 1970:276).

These major variables can be further broken down; for example, discrimination can be analysed into educational discrimination, occupational discrimination, political discrimination, residential exclusion, social exclusion and so on, again all interrelated in far from simple ways (Figure 9). Merely to abstract these variables from the empirical evidence, and to find ways of measuring them, is a considerable intellectual achievement in itself.

Yet it is not good enough, faced with such a situation, to put it all down to a vague 'reciprocal causality' or to say that 'everything determines everything else'. We must attempt to trace the exact nature of the links between each variable or 'part' of the system. It is no simple matter, under non-experimental conditions where variables cannot be manipulated at will, to disentangle these complex causal systems involving large numbers of variables. The usual approach, however, is to use sets of simultaneous equations called 'structural systems' (Blalock 1964:52ff.). Having selected a set of variables as of theoretical interest, each variable must be treated as a possible independent variable, and a separate equation written for each of them. Thus the relationships between the various kinds of discrimination in Blalock's example could be written as follows:

(1) Residential exclusion	$R = f_1(E, O, P)$
(2) Educational discrimination	$E = f_2(R, P)$
(3) Occupational discrimination	$O = f_3(E, P)$
(4) Political discrimination	$P = f_4(E)$
(5) Social exclusion	$S = f_5(R, E, O)$

These relationships are represented in Figure 9.

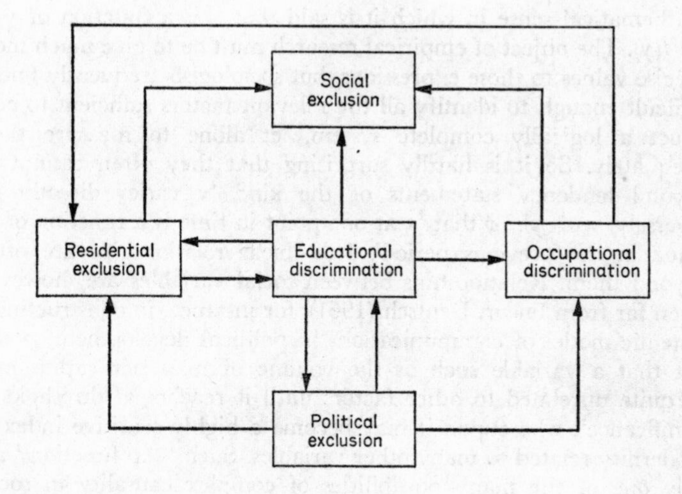

Figure 9.

This is not the place to explore the niceties of how it is possible to test such a structural system against data and to make causal inferences from multiple regression techniques; Blalock has lavished attention on this.[3] It is not, however, merely a matter of esoteric methodology, but a central logical problem of the social sciences. Economists have long struggled with the reciprocal links between macroeconomic aggregates of consumption, saving, investment, income and the demand for money. In a celebrated review of Keynes's *General Theory,* Reddaway set out its basic argument in four simple equations which are now found in every elementary economics textbook, and in form they are not unlike those in the sociological example above. Superficially, however, they presented a puzzle, as Reddaway observed. 'Are we then reasoning in a circle?' he asked. 'The answer is no, we are merely faced with the inevitable difficulty of trying to describe a system where the four variables *mutually* determine each other.' (1964: 106, his italics; orig. 1936.)

The equations used above by way of illustration are of the mathematically simplest kind. They are functional statements only in the mathematical sense in which it is said that x is a function of y or $x=f(y)$. The object of empirical research must be to give much more precise values to those expressions, but sociologists frequently find it difficult enough to identify all the relevant factors sufficient to construct a logically complete system, let alone to measure them adequately. So it is hardly surprising that they often cannot go beyond tendency statements of the kind 'x varies directly (or inversely) with y', or that 'x at one point in time is a function of its value in the previous period'. Non-linear relationships are often beyond them. Relationships between social variables are, however, often far from linear. Deutsch (1961), for instance, in constructing a systemic model of communications in political development, points out that a variable such as the volume of mail per capita may be quite unrelated to other factors until it reaches a 'threshold of significance', whereupon it may become a highly sensitive index of modernity related to many other variables. Such 'step functions' are only one of the many possibilities of complex causality in social systems.

There is no point in underestimating the difficulties of making causal inferences from the empirical study of complex social systems. But there is equally little point in baulking the issue, as happened in the past. The sound strategy seems to be to begin from simple models and attempt to make them progressively more consistent with the evidence, using the model, of course, as a guide to what further evidence is required. Economics has built up an impressive body of theory starting from initially very simple mathematical foundations. The simpler models, incidentally, generally do not assume any tendency to equilibrium, except in the very limited sense that, if none of the variables is further disturbed, stasis will set in (see Machlup 1958), and they may even predict explosions or the disintegration of the system.[4] In contrast, sociologists have tended to *assume* from the outset that many social phenomena could only be represented by something altogether more complicated, a *goal-directed* or *teleological system*, the parts of which behave in such a way that certain features of the system are maintained constant. Unfortunately, this kind of model is so complex that it has rarely been rigorously demonstrated to be appropriate to any particular empirical phenomena. So it has remained very much at the level of assumption. Why the assumption should have been made requires an examination of the history of functionalism and the peculiar place therein of the biological analogy.

The Biological Analogy

The analogy between the groups and institutions within society and the parts of an organism goes back at least to Aristotle, who wrote in the *Politics* that:

> ... every state consists, not of one, but of many parts. If we were going to speak to the different species of animals, we should first of all determine the organs which are indispensable to every animal. ... In like manner the forms of government are composed not of one, but of many elements. [1905: 152–3]

Just as an animal needed certain organs if it was to survive, so the various groups in society each contributed in their own way to its survival. This analogy recurs time and again in social thought. It was very prominent in the work of Herbert Spencer. It was evident in Durkheim's writings, especially perhaps in his discussion of 'normal' and 'pathological' states of society, in *The Rules of Sociological Method* (1938:ch. 3), even though, in the same book, he expressed some incisive criticisms of this mode of reasoning. And the biological analogy left its mark on the writings of A. R. Radcliffe-Brown (1881–1955) and Bronislaw Malinowski (1884–1942), the generally acknowledged founders of modern anthropological functionalism.

Radcliffe-Brown and Malinowski were fond of emphasizing their differences from each other. Radcliffe-Brown was more explicitly a follower of Durkheim, and called himself a structural-functionalist; Malinowski tended increasingly to appeal to psychological arguments and called himself a functionalist *tout court* to distinguish himself from the hyphenated school of thought. None the less, the similarities between them are now more striking than their differences. Both were in revolt against evolutionary and diffusionist interests which dominated anthropology in the nineteenth century and persisted into the twentieth. Their revolt was not a total one; both Radcliffe-Brown and Malinowski accepted that, on the whole, societies had tended to evolve from simpler to more elaborate structures, and that customs diffused geographically from one society to another. Historical evidence in literate societies gave ample evidence for these processes. What they did deny was that we were ever likely to have reliable historical evidence about how preliterate societies had developed. In the absence of reliable historical data, it was possible only to speculate about the past, and such exercises in 'conjectural history' diverted attention from important questions about what actually could currently be observed of preliterate societies in the field. Why, for instance, did a society appear to have adopted one custom from a neighbouring tribe, but not another custom equally available for diffusion? Malinowski and Radcliffe-Brown particularly objected to the interpretation of any quaint custom of which the meaning was not immediately apparent as a 'survival' (like the redundant appendix in the human body) from an earlier stage of development. One such case was that of the 'joking relationship' between mother's brother and sister's son among the patrilineal BaThonga (Radcliffe-Brown 1952:15–31; orig. 1924), which had previously been interpreted as a survival from an earlier stage of matrilineality and matriarchy. But how were customs like this to be explained without reliable information about their origins in the society's past?

In slightly different ways, Radcliffe-Brown and Malinowski gave the same answer. To use a pair of jargonistic terms, *diachronic* analysis was to give way to *synchronic*. Speculation about the past was to be abandoned in favour of analysing the society in its present state, as a unit made up of interrelated parts.[5] Particular customs were to be interpreted in terms of their contribution to the maintenance of the system.

> The function of a particular social usage is the contribution it makes to the *total* social life as the functioning of the *total* social system. Such a view implies that a social system (the total social structure of a society together with the totality of social usages in which that structure appears and on which it depends for its continued existence) has a certain kind of unity which we may speak of as a *functional unity*.[6] We may define it as a condition in which all parts of the social system work together with a sufficient degree of harmony or internal consistency, i.e. without producing persistent conflicts which can neither be resolved nor regulated. [Radcliffe-Brown 1952: 181; orig. 1935, my italics]

Thus the celebrated joking relationship was interpreted not as a survival from a hypothetical matriarchal stage, but as part of an existing pattern of relationships with mother, father, father's sister and so on. And it was shown to contribute to the maintenance of the Thonga lineage system. This illustrates the main virtue of the 'postulate of functional unity' as a working hypothesis in field research. It acts as an antidote to excessive ethnocentrism when confronted with some 'quaint' custom, and directs attention to its possible positive role within an existing pattern. Yet what exactly is explained? It is not so much the joking relationship which is explained as the maintenance of lineages. More exactly, Radcliffe-Brown did not explain how the joking relationship originated, and did not claim to, but rather the pattern of continuity once it had been established.

Radcliffe-Brown was quite clear that this 'concept of function applied to human societies is based on an analogy between social life and organic life' (1952:178). Observing that Durkheim had defined the 'function' of a social institution as the correspondence between it and the *needs* of the social organism, he noted that, like all analogies, this one had to be handled with care. Can societies have needs? There are a number of striking differences between societies and organisms, notably that if a constituent element no longer functions as it did previously, societies generally change their structure but do not die out. Animals in parallel circumstances tend to keel over. Disparities of this kind caused Radcliffe-Brown some hesitation, but not much, in speaking of social needs.

> . . . to avoid possible ambiguity and in particular the possibility of a teleological interpretation, I would like to substitute for the term 'needs' the term 'necessary conditions of existence', or, if the term 'need' is used, it is to be understood only in this sense. It may be here noted . . . that any attempt to apply this concept of function in social science involves the assumption that there *are* necessary conditions of existence for human societies just as there are for animal organisms, and that they can be discovered by the proper kind of scientific enquiry. [1952: 178, his italics]

So began the great paper chase for the 'functional prerequisites of a society'. Radcliffe-Brown's own conception of what these were, though shadowy, remained at the structural level—family systems and the like. Certainly he rejected explanations in terms of universal biological or psychological needs. Malinowski (1944), however, late in his life constructed an elaborate set of 'basic needs' of a bio-psychological kind, though allowing that they found expression in very diverse social and cultural arrangements. The details need not concern us, but an interesting aspect of his argument is that every established social pattern must make some contribution to satisfying one or other of these needs. This came to be known as 'the postulate of universal functionalism'.

The great objection to such reasoning is that constants cannot explain variables. We know that the diversity of human cultures is very great. If then we concede that all men have basically similar bio-psychological make-up, we still have to look for the variable factors which interact with standard human beings to produce the diversity we observe. Candidates may include environmental factors, history, pure chance, and permutations thereof. Such glum thoughts did not, however, prevent sociologists joining in the hunt for functional prerequisites, exigencies and whatever.

Among the first to do so was the distinguished group usually abbreviated to Aberle, *et al.* (1950). Succinctly, Aberle and his colleagues first defined what they meant by society, then suggested four circumstances in which a society so defined would cease to exist and finally produced a long list of the things which were, in their view, necessary to prevent this eventuality. Their definition of a society was 'a group of human beings sharing a self-sufficient system of action which is capable of existing longer than the life-span of an individual, the group being recruited at least in part by the sexual reproduction of the members'. A great deal hinged on this definition, especially on the obscure phrase 'sharing a self-sufficient system of action'.

Given this definition, it does not take any great deductive skill to see that a society will cease to exist in four circumstances: (a) the biological extinction or dispersion of the members; (b) the total apathy of members (disintegration of the 'system of action'); (c) the war of all against all; and (d) the absorption of the society into another society. Ignoring such nagging doubts as whether it is useful to regard Scotland as ceasing to be a society at the Act of Union in 1707, it was then possible to produce a list of nine functional prerequisites which had to be fulfilled if a society was to continue. These were:

(1) Provision of an adequate relationship to the environment and for sexual recruitment.
(2) Role differentiation and role assignment.
(3) Communication, especially through language.
(4) Shared cognitive orientations.
(5) A shared, articulated set of goals.
(6) The normative regulation of means.
(7) The regulation of affective expression.
(8) Socialization.
(9) The effective control of disruptive behaviour.

Most of these points are, of course, banalities. But here is normative functionalism with a vengeance. The scheme shows much more clearly than did Radcliffe-Brown or Malinowski how the biological analogy can be used to prop up the consensus view of society. Of course, if society is defined essentially as consensually integrated, it is scarcely surprising that most of the 'functional prerequisites' are variations on a consensual theme.

Aberle's article antedated Talcott Parsons's own formulation of a similar set of ideas, which eventually took the form of the four functional exigencies of Adaptation, Goal-Attainment, Integration and Latency-alias-Pattern-Maintenance-and-Tension-Management, first put on public exhibition in *Working Papers in the Theory of Action* (Parsons, Bales and Shils, 1953).[7] These are, in effect, a reworking of Aberle's prerequisites in a more general and abstract form. The main difference is that Parsons says that his apply not just to whole societies but to any social system within a society. The *form* of Parsons's argument is, however, identical to that of Aberle. What Aberle and his colleagues really said was that *if* a set of phenomena meets their definition of a society, and *if* it is surviving, *then* it will contain features that meet their nine prerequisites. And Parsons is saying that *if* a set of social phenomena meets his definition of a social system and is surviving, *then* it will contain features that can be classified into his four functional problems. Unfortunately, over the years he has seemed increasingly to assume that virtually anything can be fitted into the schema, and the benefits to be obtained from doing so have become increasingly obscure.

The 'AGIL' scheme is usually displayed in that best of all possible diagrams, the four-cell box (Figure 10). The Internal/External division separates those activities which are concerned with mediating relationships with the environment from those maintaining its internal structure. The Instrumental/Consummatory distinction points to the difference between ends and means. Some activities are concerned with the achievement of goals either external or internal to the system. Others are concerned with the provision of the means by which these ends can be attained.

The function of *Pattern-Maintenance* refers to the 'imperative' of maintaining the stability of patterns of institutionalized culture which define the structure of the system. The process of socializing children, as the main process by which the shared values of the social system are inculcated, clearly belongs in this box. Also involved are all those activities from coronations to reunion dinners by which the sense of common identity is ritually and symbolically reinforced.

	Instrumental	Consummatory
External	A Adaptation	G Goal-Attainment
Internal	Pattern-Maintenance and Tension-Management L	Integration I

Figure 10.

Integration is concerned with the mutual adjustments of interrelated units in the system. Socialization merely prepares individuals for participation in groups; integrative mechanisms are still necessary to ensure their co-ordination. Integration involves the 'normative regulation of means', as in patterns of legitimate authority and in mechanisms of social control.

Goal-Attainment is concerned with the allocation of personal and other resources to achieve different goals. Usually there are many goals, so they have to be ranged in a scale of priorities.

Adaptation covers those activities by which the social system adapts to the social and non-social environment. In particular, it is concerned with the provision of disposable facilities independent of their relevance to a particular goal. The difference between adaptation and goal-attainment is relative. The *goal* of a steel firm is the production of steel; but steel is a generalized resource from the point of view of the economy, so the steel firm is adaptive with respect to society's broader goals. This illustrates Parsons's Chinese-box conception of social systems. The economy, for instance, can be seen as the adaptive sub-system of society; but it can itself be analysed in AGIL terms, and the capital market then, in turn, becomes the adaptive sub-system of the economy. And so on *ad infinitum* (see Parsons and Smelser 1956).

Having dutifully, if rather briefly, outlined the AGIL scheme, I must add that I do not believe it is very useful in sociological explanation. Smelser, one of the few people other than Parsons to employ it, did make some play with AGIL in his *Social Change in the Industrial Revolution* (1959), but as Homans convincingly argued (1964), his Parsonian boxes did not enter at all into his final explanation of the social changes he observed. AGIL might alternatively be regarded as an analytical device potentially useful in facilitating comparisons. Aberle, *et al.*, remarked that they were 'concerned with *what* must get done in society, not *how* it is done'. The highest aspiration of proponents of functional prerequisites and suchlike would therefore seem to be not to explain why one social system is as it is and different from another, but merely to suggest that different systems may fruitfully be compared because they fulfil equivalent functions. The AGIL scheme, however, is far too vague and elastic-sided to serve even for this limited purpose of taxonomy.

Before beginning a critique of functionalism, let us take one conspicious example of functionalist explanation to illustrate the worst pitfalls of the method. Davis and Moore (1945) propounded what came to be known as the 'functionalist theory of stratification', arguing that 'stratification' was a 'functional necessity' in society. A controversy ensued over the next two decades.[8] Actually, Davis and Moore said nothing about stratification in the sense of strata with discernible boundaries or self-identity. They were in fact concerned with the unequal distribution of rewards which, it is true, is observed in practically every known society. Their argument can be stated very briefly. It was that some positions—doctors and so forth—have greater 'functional importance' for society, and require more talent or training than do others. Society therefore 'has to' reward these positions more than others.

> Social inequality is thus an unconsciously evolved device by which societies insure [*sic*] that the most important positions are conscientiously filled by the most qualified persons.

Davis and Moore did not explain how the 'functional importance' of jobs was to be assessed empirically, other than by observing how much they were paid, which would be tautological. Indeed, it is not clear what *is* explained. The focus is mainly on the consequences of inequality for the allocation of labour, and precisely how inequality arises is left implicit. In so far as the theory has a valid kernel, it is no more than a sociological gloss on the marginal-product theory of wages of half a century earlier. However, as we shall shortly see, there is pregnant significance in the remark that stratification (like Topsy?) 'unconsciously evolved'.

Merton's Critique of Functionalism

Though certainly not the last word on this subject, Robert Merton's essay on functionalism (1968:73–138, orig. 1949) promoted greater clarity and is already a classic. Merton focused attention on three assumptions to which we have already alluded, and which are very often implicit and sometimes explicit in functionalist reasoning: the postulates of functional unity, universal functionalism and indispensability. Exposing these as unwarranted, he advanced a number of conceptual innovations by which functionalism could be made more defensible.

The influence of the biological analogy is nowhere clearer than in the postulate of functional unity. The image of the whole social structure of society forming a single well-integrated and consistent whole in which 'particular social usages' contribute to the maintenance of the 'total social system' is a very organismic one. Merton wryly notes that the sea anemone, though an organism, is so poorly integrated that when it moves off from a rock, it may easily leave a part of its 'foot' behind; how much looser is the integration of most socio-cultural systems. 'Functional unity' may have had certain merits as a rough working hypothesis guiding field-work in small-scale and fairly static societies,[9] but as a practical matter it simply cannot be assumed that 'everything influences everything else' in society. In complex societies, particular social institutions often have a high degree of 'functional autonomy', and can change without necessarily causing widespread repercussions. The degree of functional integration is itself a variable to be investigated, and that means mapping out the links by which one social pattern has consequences for another.[10] It follows that it is not sufficient simply to say that something is 'functional'; *which* items of social structure it helps to maintain must be specified.

Nor are there any better grounds for upholding the postulate of universal functionalism—the assumption that any and every continuing social pattern or custom must have positive functions, contributing to the maintenance of the established way of life and therefore to the welfare of members of the society. Nineteenth-century anthropologists may have been too ready to dub as 'survivals' any patterns not immediately comprehensible. Yet not to recognize that such *non-functional* patterns may sometimes exist is to fall into the trap which ensnared Clyde Kluckhohn when he tried to explain the retention of the useless buttons on men's jacket sleeves. He said that their function was to maintain tradition, which made people feel comfortable. But what tradition were they maintaining? Only that of having buttons on their sleeves. And if people like the tradition of having buttons on their sleeves, why did they give up the tradition of wearing top hats? This kind of reasoning is plainly specious.

More important, Merton pointed out that established social institutions, far from helping to maintain other institutions, may often undermine them. To take one example at random, in developing countries if the schools and universities turn out educated people faster than the economy can absorb them into suitably satisfying employment, the consequence may be frustration leading to greater political instability. These 'negative' consequences Merton calls *dysfunctions*. Of course, one and the same social process or institution may be functional for one aspect of social structure (serving to maintain it in its established form) and dysfunctional for another (serving to undermine it). Using the concept of dysfunction is, however, very hazardous. The very prefix *dys-*, from the Greek for 'bad', is most unfortunate, carrying with it the implication that any activity which promotes change is to be regretted. Sociology may be able to explain certain kinds of social change, and it may be able to say whether members of the society will consider them bad or good, but it can conjure up no general proof that change is 'a bad thing', like some king in *1066 and All That*. Common sense none the less suggests that hardly anyone considers all change bad. Freer sexual attitudes, for instance, may undermine traditional patterns of marriage—or at least there are vocal groups who believe they do and consider it a bad thing. The same changes in sexual morality may, however, equally be dysfunctional for the prostitution industry, any reduction in the scale of which is likely to be considered a good thing by the same vocal groups. If the concept of dysfunction is to be used at all, it must be used strictly to refer to consequences which serve to promote change, not, as it too frequently is, as a pompous sociological epithet for anything of which the sociologist disapproves.

Merton's third point of attack was on the 'postulate of indispensability'. The notion of functional prerequisites and system needs has often led to a Panglossian chain of thought. If a social pattern is well established, it must be meeting the needs of the system, and therefore it must be indispensable, and everything is to the best in this best of all possible worlds. This is obviously fallacious. Even if we acknowledge that a social institution fulfils a function and meets a need very satisfactorily, might not the need have been met equally well by a range of different institutions? Given, for instance, a basic 'need' for government, why are some societies totalitarian, some liberal democratic? Merton introduces the complementary concepts of *structural constraints* on the one hand and *functional equivalents* or *alternatives* on the other. Though a fully industrial economy may preclude an elaborate clan system (structural constraint), it may be quite compatible with a whole range of less rigid family patterns (functional alternatives). Kerr, *et al.* (1962), argued that in the long term a totalitarian political sysem is incompatible with a complex industrial economy, essentially because the rational allocation of resources requires individual freedom of initiative in the economic field, and that this must spread to the political. Others, on the contrary, have argued that there are functionally equivalent ways of achieving rational allocation in a command economy, or that economic freedom can exist alongside political regimentation.

Merton claims that the idea of functional equivalents 'unfreezes the identity of the existent and the inevitable'. This is true. Yet it does not entirely dispense with the troublesome notion of functional 'needs', and this remains the central problem of functionalism.

The Problem of Teleology

Durkheim's work is by no means free from all functionalist fallacies, but he did express very clearly the dangers of reasoning from 'needs'.

> To show how a fact is useful is not to explain how it originated or why it is what it is. The uses which it serves presuppose the specific properties characterizing it, but do not create them. The need we have of things cannot give them existence, nor can it confer their specific nature upon them. It is to causes of another sort that they owe their existence.[11] . . . We must seek separately the efficient cause which produces it and the function it fulfils. [1938: 90, 95]

If social customs and institutions are to be explained as arising in response to some need, the implication is that they are goal-directed or purposive. In other words, the explanation is teleological. Now, as was argued in Chapter 2, individuals are capable of purposive action, and teleological accounts of individuals' behaviour may be quite legitimate. So there is no difficulty if we can point to individuals who have recognized a social need and taken action to meet it. For instance, it is arguable that in late nineteenth-century England there was a social and economic 'need' for mass elementary education. How did it come to result in the 1870 Education Act? The question could perhaps be answered by establishing in what ways the 'need' became obvious, who recognized it, what power resources were at their disposal, and how they overcame opposition.

But it cannot be seriously argued that all, or even most, social customs and institutions have been consciously and deliberately created in full knowledge of all their consequences. There is often a discrepancy between the subjective motive and objective consequence. The reason participants give for a custom may not coincide with what the sociologist can observe to be its consequences. Merton gives the example of the Hopi rain dance. In times of drought, the Hopi gather to perform a ritual dance, with the professed intention of magically causing rain. Meteorologists, we may anticipate, would have no great faith in this as a causal mechanism. However, the ritual does appear to promote a general feeling of social solidarity, so the effort is not entirely wasted. Merton therefore draws a distinction between the *manifest* functions or dysfunctions (those intended and recognized by the participants) and *latent* functions or dysfunctions (those neither intended nor recognized). The Hopi ritual apparently had only latent functions, for the intended consequences did not come about.

The distinction between the manifest and the latent consequences of a social custom or institutional pattern is of great significance in sociological analysis, and has passed into general use. But it in no way resolves the problem of teleological explanation—it merely defines it more narrowly. Explaining patterns whose consequences are manifest—even if manifest only to a powerful minority—is no problem. The manifest consequence is also their cause. Unfortunately this does not in the least help to explain why a *latent* need, recognized by no one, should give rise to any social pattern. At this point it would be useful to be able to hypothesize something like a Jungian collective unconscious, but such metaphysical entities are, by general assent, out of court. Yet to explain a social institution as an unconscious response to a social need, as Davis and Moore did with social inequality, is to adopt an almost equally illegitimate form of teleology. Collectivities have no group mind, and therefore cannot merely be assumed to be goal-directed and purposive.

Three Escapes from Teleology

There are, however, three possible ways in which teleological explanation of collective behaviour, organizations or institutions may be justified if there is sufficient empirical evidence. Not surprisingly, Talcott Parsons has made use of all three arguments, which become very entangled in his work. They are: (a) consensus on common goals; (b) cybernetic mechanisms in society analogous to the common thermostat; and (c) evolutionary processes akin to natural selection.

Consensus Again

Of consensus, little more need be said. The association between functionalism and consensus theory has been extremely close. The more nearly people think alike and share common values, the more nearly is it possible to treat them as equivalent to a single individual acting purposively in pursuit of goals. Alfred Schutz put it rather better:

> The concept of functionalism—at least in the modern social sciences—is not derived from the biological concept of the functioning of the organism. . . . It refers to the socially distributed constructs of patterns of typical motives, goals, attitudes, personalities, which are supposed to be invariant and then are interpreted as the function or structure of the social system itself. The more these interlocked behaviour patterns are standardized and institutionalized, that is, the more their typicality is socially approved by laws, folkways, mores, and habits, the greater is their usefulness in commonsense and scientific thinking as a scheme for the interpretation of human behaviour. [1962: 61–2]

Schutz was, I think, a little too generous to 'modern' functionalism. Two reservations must be entered. First, as was emphasized in Chapter 5, the extent of social consensus has to be established empirically; it cannot be merely assumed for the convenience of being able to treat social systems as goal-directed. Secondly, if a set of people is shown to be pursuing some common goal, to have some common purpose, this is some sort of explanation of their activities. But if these activities have latent functions, to demonstrate that there is consensus in no way establishes why a pattern of behaviour with such happy consequences should so fortuitously have been hit upon.

To demonstrate that there was an omnipotent dictator or a highly unified élite with clear objectives of its own and the power to achieve them would equally justify treating a social entity as goal-directed. However, as was argued in Chapter 3, social networks of any complexity are more difficult to control than the would-be Machiavellis involved in them often imagine. That is because complexity makes them opaque and the consequences of actions are difficult to anticipate. Yet many sociologists who are hostile to consensus theories are ready and eager to detect guiding élites in equally dubious circumstances. Merely to assume that a collectivity is goal-directed by a powerful élite is to make exactly the same mistake as merely to assume that it is goal-directed by virtue of value-consensus. In both cases, the assumption has to be justified by empirical evidence, and as we have seen in Chapters 4 and 5 respectively, neither the distribution and exercise of power nor value-consensus is particularly easy to investigate.

Cybernetics

Cybernetics is the study of communication and control mechanisms in machines and living creatures. The most familiar example of a cybernetic mechanism is a simple thermostat, a heat-sensitive device which, through an electrical circuit, controls a central heating boiler. The thermostat is set to a desired temperature, and the boiler then heats the house to the point where the thermostat responds by breaking the circuit and cutting out the boiler. The temperature then falls until the thermostat switches the boiler back on again. The house temperature therefore fluctuates about the desired level, its amplitude and frequency of oscillation depending on the sensitivity of the thermostat, the thermal properties of the heating system, and so on. This system constitutes a simple kind of feedback loop, by which the results of each stage of the cycle become the causes of the next. The system therefore simulates a simple kind of purposeful behaviour, seeming steadily to pursue the goal of the desired temperature, as if it were turned on and off by an individual reading a thermometer. Indeed, according to Mead's account (see pp. 13–18 above), the purposeful behaviour of individuals *is* a kind of cybernetic phenomenon, made possible by the symbolic anticipation of the outcome of actions feeding back into the decision-making process.

In the body, there are similar self-regulating, 'homeostatic' mechanisms by which, for example, the body temperature is maintained despite quite wide variation in atmospheric temperature, and the constituents of the blood are also maintained within narrow limits. Analogies drawn between these biological mechanisms and social processes by the physiologists L. J. Henderson and W. B. Cannon had a strong influence in the 1930s on sociologists including Talcott Parsons. So it is not suprising that Parsons has sought to make functionalist teleology respectable by looking for cybernetic processes in society. However, he tends to overlook some of the demanding logical requirements of this kind of explanation.

Sifting through Merton's essay, and discarding extraneous matter like functional needs, the philosopher Ernest Nagel finds that functional statements are 'appropriate in connection with systems possessing self-maintaining mechanisms for certain traits, but seem pointless and even misleading when used with reference to systems lacking such self-regulating devices' (1956:251–2). Functionalists, according to Nagel, have implicitly used a 'directively organized' or 'goal-seeking' system model. Again however, it is far from sufficient merely to assume that a set of social phenomena is directively organized. Empirical evidence for the existence of feedback and self-regulating mechanisms has to be produced and explained in the usual way, and the logical requirements for doing so are extremely stringent. Rudner (1966 : 109) doubts whether they have been met 'in many (if any) of the works in which, to date, social scientists purport to be giving functional explanations'.

Simple heuristic examples can, however, be suggested. Economic processes, for instance, are often to some extent self-regulating. Avoiding the more controversial market mechanisms, consider a situation in which a wage agreement ties pay to a cost-of-living index. If the prices of some important goods rise, the workers' purchasing power falls slightly until the cost-of-living index responds, whereupon the wage rises again to restore the former value. That would be very much a consciously created feedback mechanism. Cancian (1960) suggests that a small group of people trying to solve problems through discussion can be seen in similar light. Problem-solving can be treated as the goal to be maintained, and it may be a function of two kinds of activity: 'task-orientated' and 'emotional-supportive'. As the group works hard, tempers fray and problem-solving is jeopardized. So a period of relaxation and joking follows in which the conditions conducive to problem-solving are re-established. Small group studies do, in fact, show that this kind of oscillating group process is common. But why should this self-regulating pattern emerge? People may not be fully conscious of alternating the types of activity, but the goal of problem-solving is obviously a manifest purpose, and the changes of mood are seemingly unconscious or semi-conscious responses.

Yet Rudner is probably right that valid teleological explanations of the cybernetic kind are still few and far between in sociology. Parsons has made extensive use of cybernetic jargon, speaking of 'input-output' and 'cybernetic hierarchies of control'. He sees Pattern-Maintenance as the highest level of control in AGIL, and cultural systems as the highest level of control over social, personality and organismic systems, each level being linked to the others by feedback loops. What this means, except that Parsons is a philosophical idealist who wants to hedge his bets, is difficult to say. Walter Buckley (1967) ruminated on cybernetics and General Systems Theory, but seemed to achieve little more than a translation of old ideas into new jargon, and much the same can be said about Etzioni (1968). These three authors share a commendable desire to avoid over-simple single-factor conceptions of social causality, but seem to have borrowed little more than the imagery of cybernetics.

Evolution

A third way in which social organization may appear to respond and adapt unconsciously to latent 'social needs' is through some process of evolution. There may be social processes equivalent to natural selection, and this can give the appearance of purposeful, even planned, change.

Consider the case of the moths which changed their colour. Certain species of hitherto light-coloured British moths have been observed to be becoming darker in industrial areas of the country. Formerly their habitat may have been silver-birch trees, on which they would be inconspicuous. On sooty buildings (or sooty birch trees) they would, however, be very conspicuous, and be eaten by the birds. So they become darker. But it is not plausible that they held a council of war and decided to change colour. Rather, natural selection must have been at work. By some random process, a proportion of darker moths must always have been bred; but on silver birches, they would tend to be spotted and eaten more quickly than the lighter members of their species, so bred less, ensuring the preponderance of lighter moths over darker. On black buildings, of course, the opposite happens: the darker moths survive longer and breed more, so the strain gradually becomes darker.

Social analogies to this process have all the time been implicit in functionalist sociology. Evolution was very much explicit in Spencer, and though it is true that Radcliffe-Brown and Malinowski rebelled against their evolutionist precursors, it is highly misleading. Though they rejected speculative reconstruction of the past of nonliterate societies, their assumptions of functional unity and universal functionalism depended absolutely on their belief that natural selection of social customs and institutions was at work. Synchronic analysis of social institutions as a unified, well-integrated, well-adapted system made sense only if natural selection could be assumed to have eliminated the poorly integrated and ill-adapted. This, too, is the significance at which we previously hinted of Davis's and Moore's remark that social inequality is 'an unconsciously evolved device by which societies ensure . . .'. Though badly expressed, what this implies is that unequal societies, like dark moths on sooty buildings, thrive better than egalitarian ones.

Evolution has also come to the fore in Parsons's later work (1964, 1966, 1971). Restoring Spencer to the list of sociology's founding fathers, he has written a great deal about the structural segmentation and differentiation by which societies become more complex in organization. The implication is usually that the more differentiated and complex the patterns which emerge, the better the society's chances of survival. The main thrust of Parsons's evolutionism is on crucial social and cultural innovations which have constituted 'adaptive upgrading' for the societies which spawned them or subsequently adopted them and have given these societies an advantage in the evolutionary process. Among these critical breakthroughs in social organization, he particularly lists social stratification, bureaucratic administration, money and the market complex, and the democratic association. Even more emphatically, and even less surprisingly, he sees cultural, especially religious, innovations as the keys to world history. Now the assumption that natural selection operates on social institutions can be overworked. Unless the selective mechanism (parallel to the birds picking out moths) and the way in which an innovation placed its possessors at an advantage (akin to that of the darker moths) is specified in detail, the thesis becomes tautological. Unless we have an independent standard by which to judge how well integrated a system is, the mere fact that it has survived does not indicate perfect integration; it may mean simply that, so far, it has met with no particular threat from its environment.

None the less, used with care, evolutionary ideas can be useful, and in contexts less grand than global history. Take for example Joan Woodward's research (1958) on the relationship between management structure and commercial success in a sample of English manufacturing firms. Commercial success was broadly defined, and several different measures were used, including profitability, share of market, rate of growth, labour relations record and rate of labour turnover. Preliminary analysis of the results showed that there was no straightforward correlation between organization and any of these measures of success. There was an enormous range of differences in organizational structure. The number of tiers in the organizational tree ranged from two to twelve, and spans of control from two to nineteen. These differences were not related in any simple way even to the size of the firm—the variations seemed random.

The crucial insight which produced order out of this chaos was that technology and the nature of production objectives had to be taken into account. It appeared that the type of production—whether single units to a customer's individual specification, or mass production of cars on an assembly line, or flow production in an oil refinery or paper works—placed rather different constraints on management structure. Grouping the firms in terms of the technology they employed—broadly into unit and small-batch production, mass production, and continuous-flow production—produced some order in the data on management structure, irrespective of size. The median number of tiers and the median span of control differed markedly for each technological class. But, more interestingly, the commercially more successful firms tended to have management structures which approximated to the median values *for their technological class,* and the least successful firms diverged most from these medians. How is this finding to be interpreted?

In this specific context, it does seem possible to speak meaningfully of the 'demands of the technical situation' or organizational needs. It seems likely that, in unit production, where the product is being made to the customer's requirements, there has to be close consultation between the customer, the designer, and those who design and cost the product. So a relatively fluid organization without remote and inflexible chains of command is an advantage. In mass production on assembly lines, and still more in process production, routine production decisions can in contrast be delegated far down the line. Once production is started, the main objective is to keep it going; after the design stage, there is probably little need for consultation between designers, sales and production staff. These differing 'situational demands' are consistent with Woodward's finding that the median number of tiers in the administrative chart was least in the case of unit production, more in mass production, and greatest in process production.

Now, asks Woodward:

> Are those responsible for building the organization in successful firms consciously aware of the demands of the technical situation, and does this affect their decisions? The findings suggest it is unlikely. In only three firms was there any definite evidence that organization was determined by a systematic analysis of 'situational demands'. [1958: 38]

Fortunately, in this particular situation, it is easy to point to an analogy to natural selection in market forces. One reason why the most successful firms approximated to the median organizational patterns for their technological type was, presumably, that these by chance produced the best commercial results; the market 'encouraged' those forms whose structure most closely met the latent 'needs' of the situation. Yet it would be unwise to assume that market discipline was perfect, or to rely entirely on unconscious adaptation to the economic environment in explaining these findings. Managers may not have been fully aware of the relationship between technology, organization and commercial success. But they were striving for success, and it is probable that successful organization was, in part, intentional creation, part a latent consequence of trial and error. In studying complex figurations of human actions, the simple dichotomy between latent and manifest consequences becomes a little blurred. It should be remembered that people, unlike moths, can think about their situation, and even if they perceive only part of it, their actions may not be entirely inappropriate.[12]

Functionalism: The Indispensable Second-Best

It will have been noted that, even where it is plausible that some process akin to natural selection is at work, we are told nothing about how evolutionary changes are first initiated. In the fable of the moths, nothing was said about why some darker-coloured moths should have been bred in the first place. Similarly, in sociology, it may be possible to point to an institutional innovation which gave a society, a group or even a firm some definite advantage over its rivals in certain specific circumstances. Yet, unless we can pinpoint how *people* came to make the innovation in the first place, the explanation often seems incomplete. Darwin himself knew little of genetics and mutation; that missing element in the theory of evolution was supplied rather later. In sociology, the corresponding missing element in most functional explanations is an action interpretation of the pattern. Without it, the explanation is unsatisfactory and incomplete. As Weber pointed out, 'action in the sense of subjectively understandable orientation of behaviour exists only as the behaviour of one or more *individual* human beings' (1968:I, 13, his italics). Interpretation in terms of objective functions or consequences of patterns of collective behaviour should be complemented wherever possible by interpretation in terms of participants' ends-in-view. They may have extremely diverse motives, have no clear conception of the figuration formed by the interweaving of their actions, and still less of its dynamic consequences, but these facts are worth knowing. Weber saw the functional perspective as second-best, but still appreciated its importance.

> First this functional frame of reference is convenient for purposes of practical illustration and for provisional orientation. In these respects it is not only useful but indispensable. But at the same time if its cognitive value is overestimated and its concepts illegitimately 'reified', it can be highly dangerous. Secondly, in certain circumstances this is the only available way of determining just what processes of social action it is important to understand in order to explain a given phenomenon. [1968: I, 15]

Functionalism must obviously be stripped of excrescences such as over-generalized functional requisites, equilibrium, homeostasis, and tendencies to unjustified teleology. These arose mainly in response to the absence of historical evidence in non-literate societies. The prevalence of such evidence in literate societies makes it all the easier to discard these logical foibles. What is left when they have been discarded may not be functionalism, but it is indispensable. It is little more than the interdependence hypothesis, common to the Marxist as much as to the functionalist tradition. Historical and action analysis is not an alternative to systemic analysis, but is most fruitful precisely when combined with it.[13] It is exactly because the consequences of people's activities often do not coincide with what they intended that it is essential to make a systemic analysis of the causal links within social organization.

Notes

1. See Demerath and Peterson (1967) for a collection of articles which amply demonstrates the wide ramifications of the controversy over functionalism.

2. Several authors have noted a convergence between functionalism and Marxist sociology, especially the more orthodox Iron Curtain sociology. See van den Berghe (1963), Gouldner (1971) and Friedrichs (1970).

3. Structuralists have also used algebraic notation to represent social systems. Leach (1961) has recommended the use of topological mathematics to represent kinship systems. However, Leach's object is to represent the underlying structure in order to facilitate comparative analysis; having done so, his explanation is still of an essentially functional, synchronic kind.

4. As does the Harrod-Domar growth model in its simplest form.

5. Harris (1968:526) argues that this programme led to the neglect of such historical data (from earlier travellers, for example) as did exist concerning some pre-literate societies.

6. This 'postulate of functional unity' is frequently contrasted with the American anthropologist Lowie's description of culture as a thing of 'shreds and patches', but this remark is misleading as a guide to Lowie's views; he did not despair of finding *any* regularity in cultural phenomena.

7. For the story of the rise and fall of Parsons's functional requisites, see Sklair (1970).

8. The successive contributions to the debate are surveyed by Huaco (1966).

9. Just how static actually were the societies studied by anthropologists in the early twentieth century is in dispute. An unchanging 'traditional way of life' before the impact of civilization was perhaps too readily assumed. And where stasis was observed, it may often have been the fairly recent product of the policies of the colonial power, especially in British Africa.

10. On functional autonomy, see Gouldner (1959). The degree of integration was always an empirical variable for Sorokin too, who distinguished between four modes of integration of socio-cultural phenomena: (a) mere Spatial-Mechanical Adjacency; (b) Integration in Relation to a Common External Factor; (c) Causal-Functional Integration; and (d) Logico-Meaningful Integration (Sorokin, 1937:ch. 1).

11. The causes 'of another sort' do not always materialize. As Percy Cohen (1968:41) neatly remarks, 'it could be argued that men need a way of settling all disputes without violence; but they do not have one'.

12. This draws attention to a significant difference between biological and social evolution. Organisms do not *genetically* pass on to their offspring behaviour useful within their environment which they have learned during their lifetime. Biologically, the 'inheritance of acquired characteristics' is not possible. But, as Konrad Lorenz (1966:205) notes, 'Conceptual thought and speech changed all man's evolution by achieving something which is equivalent to the inheritance of acquired characters.' Conceptual thought and speech do not grant men perfect knowledge and foresight; they do not eliminate latent consequences. What they do is to speed up the process of innovation and the transmission of acquired knowledge.

13. For some suggestive remarks along these lines, see Goldthorpe (1964).

Conclusion

Irony and Sociology

One of the principal ingredients of great literature is irony. Characters in both tragedy and comedy fail to perceive the full significance of the situations in which they are caught up, and find themselves perversely mocked by—as it seems—fate. Their good deeds precipitate disaster, or evil intent is frustrated by circumstance. We savour irony because we, as observers, are granted greater knowledge of the situation than have the actors in it.

If the plots of real life lack the elegance of literature, they frequently abound in irony. More often than not, people's knowledge of the structure of the social situations in which they are entangled is imperfect. This is something more than the ubiquitous margin of uncertainty in another person's response. It is a facet of the social distribution of knowledge that the facts of the situation may be incompletely known to any of the actors; even if they each pool their particular knowledge, they may still not possess every piece of the jigsaw puzzle. There may be links in the system, interdependencies unrecognized by anyone, and the system may play tricks on those enmeshed in it. The frequent inadequacy of the stock of knowledge and systems of relevance at the actor's disposal means that social actions very often have consequences unforeseen by the actor. It may be that, had the actor foreseen these consequences, he would have considered them desirable, and would have intentionally committed the action none the less. It may be that he would have considered them undesirable and therefore, if they outweighed the benefits of any desirable consequences, have refrained from the deed. There is also a large class of unforeseen consequences to which the actor would have been quite indifferent even had he anticipated them. As long as he does not foresee them, however, all three kinds of consequence remain, in Merton's famous phrase (1936), 'unanticipated consequences of purposive social action'. As an entirely separate matter, if any of these three types of unintended consequence help to maintain some aspect of the social *status quo*, the functionalist could call them latent functions; and if they undermine it, latent dysfunctions. But that is not now our concern.

The most dramatically ironic of the unanticipated consequences of social actions are the special cases of the self-fulfilling and self-contradicting prophecies. In both, actions initially based on false premises have paradoxical outcomes. Merton (1968 : 457–90) gives several examples of the self-fulfilling prophecy. American trade unionists earlier in the century often excluded blacks from union membership, in the belief that they accepted lower wages than whites, acted as blacklegs, and would not submit to union discipline. But their exclusion from the unions made it all the more likely that blacks would undercut union rates and break strikes. Later, of course, they gained admission and proved to be just as good members as whites. A bank may be perfectly solvent and adequately liquid for normal times. Yet if the belief spreads that it is not safe, people may begin to withdraw their deposits; and if the panic is not stemmed (and if the government does not prevent it) the hitherto solvent bank may rapidly become insolvent. Or, a case more familiar in the 1960s and 1970s, talk of the devaluation or revaluation of a country's currency may spark off international speculative flows of money and make it altogether more likely that the exchange rate will have to be changed. An example of a self-contradicting process is the 'paradox of thrift' (see Samuelson 1961 :270–74). In the past, thrift was considered always to be a virtue; Weber took Benjamin Franklin's homilies on thrift as the very embodiment of the spirit of capitalism. In times of depression, people were urged to save more to restore prosperity. But private prudence can be public folly. In times of unemployment, the outcome of everyone *trying* to save more and consume less can be that production falls, the depression deepens and everyone actually saves *less*. Or consider the experiment of Prohibition in the United States (Mennell 1969). Many Americans initially gave their support to Prohibition, not because they were Bible-belt fundamentalists but because they were Progressives seeking reform, and the liquor industry was intimately linked with crime and corruption. They did not allow for the tenacity of public demand for alcohol, however, and it is a familiar story that the demand continued to be met illegally, and that Prohibition immeasurably increased crime and corruption.

Self-fulfilling and self-contradicting prophecies are nevertheless only among the most melodramatic examples of unanticipated consequences of action. Imperfect knowledge is much more pervasive than are such perversities. The unanticipated consequences of people's actions only rarely return like boomerangs to hit them. Throwing stones into a pool is usually a better analogy: the consequences ripple outwards through society until we lose sight of them. This is especially true where the consequences of actions only become perceptible when carried on by numerous people independently; the link between these consequences and the actions of any single individual may remain largely unperceived. The motorist does not intend or anticipate that his own car will cause traffic congestion, higher transport costs, environmental pollution, the decline of public transport with hardship to the elderly, handicapped and other pedestrians, urban sprawl, hideous motorways across beautiful countryside, the decline of rural communities, the decline of city-centre shopping and burgeoning green-field shopping centres, or death, mutilation and hospital bills. In economic parlance, all these consequences are externalities, to him and to every one of millions of other motorists, and they will remain external until some way is found of totting up and sending every motorist a bill for his share of the cost. The benefits and convenience of private transport, on the other hand, are very much internal to the motorist's vision of his world.

The unanticipated consequences of social action are not a paradoxical footnote to sociological theory but of central significance. They demonstrate that every sociologist must be wary of the logical fallacy of composition: the outcome of an isolated individual action may be very different from the collective outcome of many such individual actions. It should now be obvious that two approaches to sociological theory often considered alternatives or even contradictory—the systemic or structural approach on the one hand, and the action or phenomenological perspective on the other—are, in fact, indispensable complements to each other. Certainly it is necessary to discover the meaning people attach to their social situations and the assumptions on which their actions are based. To quote Thomas's remark once more: if men define situations as real, they are real in their consequences. That does not mean that all their definitions are self-fulfilling. Far from it. It merely means that any sociological explanation which neglects to consider how people perceive their situations risks going sadly adrift. On the other hand, any sociology which studied *only* how people define situations would be equally deficient. Systemic analysis is necessary to explain the joint outcome of countless individual actions in aggregate. If the sociologist is to unravel social processes he must be able to spot the consequences of people's actions which they did not spot, and this involves indentifying the links missing from participants' pictures of their social environment. Indeed Murphy (1971 :147) has suggested that unintended consequences of social actions are 'the principal *raison d'être* of the social sciences; if society followed rational intent, it would be so transparent that sociologists and anthropologists would all be out of jobs'. Unanticipated consequences are among the chief sources of the unplanned and unpredictable in social life, and, in detecting them, the social scientist helps to make society more planned and predictable. That is why public and politicians often view sociology as an adjunct to policy-making, a responsibility which some sociologists assume with greater alacrity than others.

In speaking like this, there is a risk that the sociologist may be portrayed as some omniscient divinity endowed with the ability to foresee what others cannot foresee. Not at all: every man is his own sociologist, but some are privileged to be wholly engaged in the methodical study of society and others are not. Moreover, social science like any other social activity can have unforeseen and unintended consequences. The sociologist's findings become part of the social stock of knowledge and can themselves influence social processes. There is a real possibility that the diffusion of social scientific knowledge may alter the subject-matter on which it is based. An obvious example is that opinion polls may influence the result of the election they purport to predict. It is a convoluted possibility too, for sometimes public opinion polls seem to have created a bandwagon effect for the predicted winner, sometimes (perhaps by making the favourites appear over-confident to the electors) the reverse. Then again, as many writers have noted, once latent and unanticipated consequences of a person's actions are revealed to him, they become manifest and anticipated. That does not necessarily mean that his actions will change, however. There is no good reason to suppose that the Hopi ceased to perform their rain dance because Clyde Kluckhohn announced the discrepancy between its manifest purpose and latent function. Still less can many people be shown to have stopped discriminating against minorities because sociologists pointed out that their discrimination created the very facts on which their prejudice fed.

Sociology is part of the social stock of knowledge, but like other knowledge it is unevenly distributed, and it is only overweening pride which deceives its practitioners that the general public is other than totally indifferent to many of their findings. That need not detract from anyone's sense of vocation in social science. The sense of irony which gives the sociologist insight into the social process should also enable him to observe with forbearance the fate of his own findings.

Bibliography

Aberle, D. F., A. K. Cohen, A. K. Davis, M. J. Levy, Jr, and **F. X. Sutton,** 1950: The Functional Prerequisites of a Society. *Ethics,* **60,** 2, 100–11.

Adorno, T. W., E. Frenkel-Brunswik, D. J. Levinson, and **R. N. Sandford,** 1950: *The Authoritarian Personality.* Harper, New York.

Alchian, A. A., 1950: Uncertainty, Evolution and Economic Theory. *Journal of Political Economy,* **58,** 2, 211–21.

Anderson, Nels, 1923: *The Hobo.* University of Chicago Press, Chicago.

Andreski, Stanislav, 1972: *Social Sciences as Sorcery.* André Deutsch, London.

Aristotle, 1905: *Aristotle's Politics* (trans. by Benjamin Jowett). Clarendon Press, Oxford.

Arrow, Kenneth J., 1951: *Social Choice and Individual Values.* Wiley, New York.

Arrow, Kenneth J., 1967: Values and Collective Decision-Making. In *Philosophy, Politics and Society,* 3rd Series (P. Laslett and W. G. Runciman, eds.), pp. 215–32. Basil Blackwell, Oxford.

Austin, J. L., 1961: *Philosophical Papers.* Oxford University Press, London.

Bales, Robert F., 1950: *Interaction Process Analysis.* Addison-Wesley, Cambridge, Mass.

Barton, Allen H., 1969: *Communities in Disaster.* Doubleday, Garden City, N.Y.

Becker, Gary S., 1962: Irrational Behaviour and Economic Theory. *Journal of Political Economy,* **70,** 1, 1–13.

Becker, Howard S., 1963: *Outsiders.* Free Press, New York.

Benne, K. D. and **P. Sheats,** 1948: Functional Roles of Group Members. *Journal of Social Issues,* **4,** 2, 41–9.

Berelson, B., P. F. Lazarsfeld and **W. N. McPhee,** 1954: *Voting.* University of Chicago Press, Chicago.

Berger, Peter, 1973: *The Social Reality of Religion.* Penguin Books, Harmondsworth. (Published in U.S.A. under the title *The Sacred Canopy.* Doubleday, Garden City, N.Y., 1967).

Berger, Peter, and **Thomas Luckmann,** 1967: *The Social Construction of Reality.* Allen Lane, London.

Berghe, Pierre L. van den, 1963: Dialectic and Functionalism: Toward a Theoretical Synthesis. *American Sociological Review,* **28,** 5, 695–705.

Bierstedt, Robert, 1950: An Analysis of Social Power. *American Sociological Review,* **15,** 6, 730–38.

Blain, Robert R., 1971: An Alternative to Parsons's Four-Function Paradigm as a basis for Developing General Sociological Theory. *American Sociological Review,* **36,** 4, 678–92.

Blalock, Hubert M., Jr, 1964: *Causal Inferences in Non-experimental Research.* University of North Carolina Press, Chapel Hill.

Blalock, Hubert, M., Jr, 1967: *Toward a Theory of Minority Group Relations.* Wiley, New York.

Blalock, Hubert M., Jr, 1970: The Formalization of Sociological Theory. In *Theoretical Sociology* (J. C. McKinney and E. A. Tiryakian, eds.), pp. 272–300. Appleton-Century-Crofts, New York.

Blau, Peter M., 1955: *The Dynamics of Bureaucracy.* University of Chicago Press, Chicago.

Blau, Peter M., 1964: *Exchange and Power in Social Life.* Wiley, New York.

Blau, Peter M., 1968: Interaction, IV: Social Exchange. In *International Encyclopaedia of the Social Sciences* (D. L. Sills, ed.), vol. 7, pp. 452–8. The Macmillan Company and The Free Press, New York.

Blauner, Robert, 1964: *Alienation and Freedom.* University of Chicago Press, Chicago.

Blumer, Herbert, 1969: *Symbolic Interactionism: Perspective and Method.* Prentice-Hall, Englewood Cliffs, N.J.

Bott, Elizabeth, 1955: Urban Families: Conjugal Roles and Social Networks. *Human Relations,* **8,** 4, 345–84.

Bott, Elizabeth, 1957: *Family and Social Network.* Tavistock Publications, London.

Brodbeck, May, 1958: Methodological Individualisms: Definition and Reduction. *Philosophy of Science,* **25,** 1, 1–22.

Brown, A. R. Radcliffe-, 1952: *Structure and Function in Primitive Society.* Cohen & West, London.

Brown, Roger, 1965: *Social Psychology.* Free Press, New York.

Buckley, Walter, 1967: *Sociology and Modern Systems Theory.* Prentice-Hall, Englewood Cliffs, N.J.

Burgess, R. L., and **D. Bushell,** eds., 1969: *Behavioural Sociology: The Experimental Analysis of Social Behaviour.* Columbia University Press, New York.

Cancian, Francesca, 1960: Functional Analysis of Change. *American Sociological Review,* **25,** 6, 818–27.

Caplow, Theodore, 1956: A Theory of Coalitions in the Triad. *American Sociological Review,* **21,** 4, 489–93.

Caplow, Theodore, 1968: *Two Against One: Coalitions in Triads.* Prentice-Hall, Englewood Cliffs, N.J.

Catton, William R., Jr, 1964: The Development of Sociological Thought. In *Handbook of Modern Sociology* (R. E. L. Faris, ed.), pp. 912–50. Rand McNally, Chicago.

Chomsky, Noam, 1959: Review of Skinner's *Verbal Behaviour. Language,* **35,** 1, 26–58.

Chomsky, Noam, 1965: *Aspects of the Theory of Syntax.* M.I.T. Press, Cambridge, Mass.

Chomsky, Noam, 1967: The Formal Nature of Language. Appendix A to E. H. Lenneberg, *Biological Foundations of Language.* Wiley, New York.

Cicourel, Aaron V., 1964: *Method and Measurement in Sociology.* Free Press, New York.

Cicourel, Aaron V., 1968: *The Social Organization of Juvenile Justice.* Wiley, New York.

Cicourel, Aaron V., 1973: *Cognitive Sociology.* Penguin Books, Harmondsworth.

Cloward, R. A., and **L. E. Ohlin,** 1960: *Delinquency and Opportunity.* Free Press, New York.

Cohen, Percy S., 1968: *Modern Social Theory.* Heinemann, London.

Coleman, James S., 1963: Comment on 'On the Concept of Influence'. *Public Opinion Quarterly,* **27,** 1, 63–82.

Coleman, James S., 1966: Foundations for a Theory of Collective Decisions. *American Journal of Sociology,* **71,** 6, 615–27.

Coleman, James S., 1972: Collective Decisions and Collective Action. In *Philosophy, Politics and Society,* 4th Series (P. Laslett, W. G. Runciman and Q. Skinner, eds.), pp. 208–19. Basil Blackwell, Oxford.

Coleman, James S., 1973: *The Mathematics of Collective Action.* Aldine Books, Chicago.

Converse, Philip E., 1964: The Nature of Belief Systems in Mass Publics. In *Ideology and Discontent* (D. E. Apter, ed.), pp. 206–61. Free Press, Glencoe, Ill.

Cooley, C. H., 1918: *Social Process.* Scribner's, New York.

Coser, Lewis A., 1956: *The Functions of Social Conflict.* Routledge & Kegan Paul, London.

Coser, Lewis A., 1971: *Masters of Sociological Thought.* Harcourt Brace Jovanovitch, New York.

Dahl, Robert A., 1961: *Who Governs?* Yale University Press, New Haven.

Dahrendorf, Ralf, 1959: *Class and Class Conflict in Industrial Society.* Stanford University Press, Stanford, Cal.

Dahrendorf, Ralf, 1967: *Conflict after Class: New Perspectives on the Theory of Social and Political Conflict.* Longmans, Green, London.

Davis, James C., 1962: Toward a Theory of Revolution. *American Sociological Review,* **27,** 1, 5–19.

Davis, Kingsley, 1959: The Myth of Functional Analysis as a Special Method in Sociology and Anthropology. *American Sociological Review,* **24,** 6, 757–72.

Davis, Kingsley, and **Wilbert E. Moore,** 1945: Some Principles of Stratification. *American Sociological Review,* **10,** 2, 242–9.

Dawe, Alan, 1970: The Two Sociologies. *British Journal of Sociology,* **21,** 2, 207–18.

Day, Willard F., 1969a: Radical Behaviourism in Reconciliation with Phenomenology. *Journal of the Experimental Analysis of Behaviour*, **12,** 2, 315–28.

Day, Willard F., 1969b: On certain Similarities between the *Philosophical Investigations* of Ludwig Wittgenstein and the Operationism of B. F. Skinner. *Journal of the Experimental Analysis of Behaviour*, **12,** 3, 489–506.

Demerath, N. J., III, and **R. A. Petersen,** eds., 1967: *System, Change and Conflict*. Free Press, New York.

Denzin, Norman K., 1969: Symbolic Interactionism and Ethnomethodology. *American Sociological Review*, **34,** 6, 922–34.

Deutsch, Karl W., 1961: Social Mobilization and Political Development. *American Political Science Review*, **60,** 3, 493–514.

Douglas, Jack D., 1967: *The Social Meanings of Suicide*. Princeton University Press, Princeton, N.J.

Douglas, Jack D., 1970: Deviance and Order in a Pluralistic Society. In *Theoretical Sociology* (J. C. McKinney and E. A. Tiryakian, eds.), pp. 368–401. Appleton-Century-Crofts, New York.

Douglas, Jack D., ed., 1971: *Understanding Everyday Life: Toward the Reconstruction of Sociological Knowledge*. Routledge & Kegan Paul, London.

Dubin, Robert, 1960: Parsons's Actor: Continuities in Social Theory. *American Sociological Review*, **25,** 4, 457–66.

Durkheim, Emile, 1933 (orig. 1893): *The Division of Labour in Society*, translated by G. E. Simpson. Macmillan, New York.

Durkheim, Emile, 1938 (orig. 1895): *The Rules of Sociological Method*, translated by S. A. Solvay and J. H. Mueller. University of Chicago Press, Chicago.

Durkheim, Emile, 1951 (orig. 1897): *Suicide*, translated by J. A. Spaulding and G. E. Simpson. Free Press, Glencoe, Ill.

Durkheim, Emile, 1953 (orig. 1898): Individual and Collective Representations. In *Sociology and Philosophy*, translated by D. F. Pocock, pp. 1–34. Cohen & West, London.

Durkheim, Emile, 1965 (orig. 1912): *The Elementary Forms of the Religious Life*, translated by J. W. Swain. Free Press, New York.

Durkheim, Emile, and **Marcel Mauss,** 1963 (orig. 1903): *Primitive Classification*, translated by R. Needham. Cohen & West, London.

Elias, Norbert, 1969: *Über den Prozess der Zivilisation*, 2nd ed. Francke, Bern & München. (Translation by Eric Dunning forthcoming, Routledge & & Kegan Paul, London.)

Elias, Norbert, 1970: *Was ist Soziologie?* Juventa Verlag, München. (Translation by S. J. Mennell and V. G. Morrissey forthcoming, Hutchinson, London.)

Emmet, Dorothy, and **Alasdair MacIntyre,** eds., 1970: *Sociological Theory and Philosophical Analysis*. Macmillan, London.

Etzioni, Amitai, 1968: *The Active Society*, Free Press, New York.

Faris, R. E. L., 1967: *Chicago Sociology 1920–32*. Chandler, San Francisco.

Feuer, Lewis S., 1953: Sociological Aspects of the Relation between Language and Philosophy. *Philosophy of Science*, **20,** 2, 85–100.

Filmer, Paul, Michael Phillipson, David Silverman and David Walsh, 1972: *New Directions in Sociological Theory*. Collier-Macmillan, London.

Fletcher, Ronald, 1971: *The Making of Sociology*, vols. I and II. Michael Joseph, London.

Frazier, E. Franklin, 1932: *The Negro Family in Chicago*. University of Chicago Press, Chicago.

Freud, Sigmund, 1962 (orig. 1930): *Civilization and Its Discontents*, translated by J. Strachey. W. W. Norton, New York.

Friedrichs, Robert W., 1970: *A Sociology of Sociology*. Free Press, New York.

Galbraith, John Kenneth, 1952: *American Capitalism*. Hamish Hamilton, London.

Garfinkel, Harold, 1967: *Studies in Ethnomethodology*. Prentice-Hall, Englewood Cliffs, N.J.

Garfinkel, Harold, and **Harvey Sacks,** 1970: On Formal Structures of Practical Actions. In *Theoretical Sociology* (J. C. McKinney and E. A. Tiryakian, eds.), pp. 337–66. Appleton-Century-Crofts, New York.

Gellner, Ernest, 1968 (orig. 1959): *Words and Things*. Penguin Books, Harmondsworth.

Gellner, Ernest, 1970 (orig. 1962): Concepts and Society. In *Sociological Theory and Philosophical Analysis* (D. Emmet and A. MacIntyre, eds.), pp. 115–49. Macmillan, London.

Germani, Gino, 1968: Secularization, Modernization and Economic Development. In *The Protestant Ethic and Modernization* (S. N. Eisenstadt, ed.), pp. 343–66. Basic Books, New York.

Giddens, Anthony, 1968: 'Power' in the Recent Writings of Talcott Parsons. *Sociology*, **2,** 3, 257–72.

Giddens, Anthony, 1971: *Capitalism and Modern Social Theory*. Cambridge University Press, Cambridge.

Gidlow, Bob, 1972: Ethnomethodology – New Name for Old Practices. *British Journal of Sociology*, **23,** 4, 395–405.

Gluckman, Max, 1955: *Custom and Conflict in Africa*. Basil Blackwell, Oxford.

Goffman, Erving, 1955: On Face-Work. *Psychiatry*, **18,** 3, 213–31.

Goffman, Erving, 1961: *Asylums*. Doubleday, Garden City, New York.

Goldthorpe, John H., 1964: The Development of Social Policy in England, 1800–1914. In *Transactions of the 5th World Congress of Sociology*, vol. IV, pp. 41–56. International Sociological Association, Washington, D.C.

Goldthorpe, John H., 1973: A Revolution in Sociology? *Sociology*, **7,** 3, 449–62.

Goldthorpe, John H., D. Lockwood, F. Bechhofer and **J. Platt,** 1969: *The Affluent Worker in the Class Structure*. Cambridge University Press, Cambridge.

Gouldner, Alvin W., 1959: Reciprocity and Autonomy in Functional Theory. In *Symposium on Sociological Theory* (Llewellyn Gross, ed.), pp. 241–70. Harper & Row, New York.

Gouldner, Alvin W., 1960: The Norm of Reciprocity. *American Sociological Review,* **25,** 2, 161–78.

Gouldner, Alvin W., 1971: *The Coming Crisis of Western Sociology.* Heinemann, London.

Gross, N., W. S. Mason and **A. McEachern,** 1958: *Explorations in Role Analysis.* Wiley, New York.

Harris, Marvin, 1968: *The Rise of Anthropological Theory.* Routledge & Kegan Paul, London.

Heath, Anthony, 1968: Economic Theory and Sociology: A Critique of P. M. Blau's *Exchange and Power in Social Life. Sociology,* **2,** 3, 273–92.

Hinkle, Roscoe C., 1963: Antecedents of the Action Orientation in American Sociology before 1935. *American Sociological Review,* **28,** 5, 705–15.

Hobbes, Thomas, 1651: *Leviathan.* Crooke, London.

Homans, George C., 1958: Human Behaviour as Exchange. *American Journal of Sociology,* **63,** 6, 597–606.

Homans, George C., 1961: *Social Behaviour: Its Elementary Forms.* Routledge & Kegan Paul, London.

Homans, George C., 1964: Bringing Men Back In. *American Sociological Review,* **29,** 6, 809–18.

Homans, George C., 1967: *The Nature of Social Science.* Harcourt, Brace & World, New York.

Horan, Patrick M., 1971: Social Positions and Cross-Pressures: A Reexamination. *American Sociological Review,* **36,** 4, 650–60.

Horton, John, 1964: The Dehumanization of Anomie and Alienation. *British Journal of Sociology,* **15,** 4, 283–300.

Huaco, George A., 1966: The Functionalist Theory of Stratification: Two Decades of Controversy. *Inquiry,* **9,** 3, 215–40.

Kemper, Theodore D., 1972: The Division of Labour: A Post-Durkheimian Analytical View. *American Sociological Review,* **37,** 6, 739–53.

Kerr, Clark, John T. Dunlop, Frederick H. Harbison and **Charles A. Myers,** 1962: *Industrialism and Industrial Man.* Heinemann, London.

Kissin, S. F., 1972: *Communists: All Revisionists Now.* Fabian Society, London.

Koestler, Arthur, 1945: *The Yogi and the Commissar.* Jonathan Cape, London.

Kuhn, Thomas S., 1962: *The Structure of Scientific Revolutions.* University of Chicago Press, Chicago.

Laing, R. D., 1967: *The Politics of Experience and The Bird of Paradise.* Penguin Books, Harmondsworth.

Leach, Edmund R., 1961: *Rethinking Anthropology*. Athlone Press, London.
Leach, Edmund R., 1970: *Lévi-Strauss*. Fontana, London.
Lenneberg, E. H., 1967: *Biological Foundations of Language*. Wiley, New York.
Lévi-Strauss, Claude, 1963: *Structural Anthropology*. Basic Books, New York.
Lévi-Strauss, Claude, 1968a: *The Savage Mind*. Weidenfeld & Nicolson, London.
Lévi-Strauss, Claude, 1968b (orig. 1949): *The Elementary Structures of Kinship*. Eyre & Spottiswoode, London.
Lévi-Strauss, Claude, 1968c: *L'Origine des manières de table*. (*Mythologiques* III). Plon, Paris.
Lévi-Strauss, Claude, 1969 (orig. 1964): *The Raw and the Cooked* (*Mythologiques* I), trans. by J. and D. Weightman. Jonathan Cape, London.
Lévi-Strauss, Claude, 1971: *L'Homme nu* (*Mythologiques* IV). Plon, Paris.
Lévi-Strauss, Claude, 1973 (orig. 1966): *From Honey to Ashes* (*Mythologiques* II), trans. by J. and D. Weightman. Jonathan Cape, London.
Lewis, Oscar, 1951: *Life in a Mexican Village*. University of Illinois Press, Urbana, Ill.
Linton, Ralph, 1936: *The Study of Man*. Appleton, New York.
Lipset, Seymour Martin, 1960: *Political Man*. Heinemann, London.
Lipset, Seymour Martin, 1964: *The First New Nation*. Heinemann, London.
Lockwood, David, 1958: *The Blackcoated Worker*. George Allen & Unwin, London.
Lockwood, David, 1964: Social Integration and System Integration. In *Explorations in Social Change* (G. K. Zollschan and W. Hirsch, eds.), pp. 244–57. Routledge & Kegan Paul, London.
Lopreato, Joseph, 1968: Authority Relations and Class Conflict. *Social Forces*, **47**, 1, 70–79.
Lorenz, Konrad, 1966: *On Aggression*, translated by M. Latzke. Methuen, London.
Louch, A. R., 1966: *Explanation and Human Action*. Basil Blackwell, Oxford.
Luckmann, Thomas, 1967: *The Invisible Religion*. Macmillan, New York.
Lukes, Steven, 1967: Alienation and Anomie. In *Philosophy, Politics and Society*, 3rd series (P. Laslett and W. G. Runciman, eds.), pp. 134–56. Basil Blackwell, Oxford.
Lukes, Steven, 1973: *Emile Durkheim: His Life and Work*. Allen Lane, London.
Lyons, John, 1970: *Chomsky*. Fontana, London.

Macaulay, Thomas Babington, 1889: *The Miscellaneous Writings and Speeches of Lord Macaulay*. Longmans, Green, London.
McClosky, Herbert, and **John Schaar,** 1965: Psychological Dimensions of Anomy. *American Sociological Review*, **30**, 1, 14–40.
McHugh, Peter, 1968: *Defining the Situation*. Bobbs-Merrill, Indianapolis.
Machlup, Fritz, 1958: Equilibrium and Disequilibrium: Misplaced Concreteness and Disguised Politics. *Economic Journal*, **68**, 1, 1–24.

Malinowski, Bronislaw, 1922: *Argonauts of the Western Pacific.* Routledge, London.

Malinowski, Bronislaw, 1944: *A Scientific Theory of Culture.* University of North Carolina Press, Chapel Hill.

Mann, Michael, 1970: The Social Cohesion of Liberal Democracy. *American Sociological Review,* **35,** 3, 423–39.

Marcuse, Herbert, 1964: *One-Dimensional Man.* Routledge & Kegan Paul, London.

Maris, Ronald, 1970: The Logical Adequacy of Homans's Social Theory. *American Sociological Review,* **35,** 6, 1069–81.

Marshall, T. H., 1950: *Citizenship and Social Class and Other Essays.* Cambridge University Press, Cambridge.

Marx, Karl, 1947 (orig. 1846): *The German Ideology,* International Publishers Co. Inc., New York.

Marx, Karl, and **Frederick Engels,** 1968: *Selected Works* (in 1 vol.). Lawrence & Wishart, London.

Mauss, Marcel, 1954 (orig. 1924): *The Gift,* trans. by I. Cunnison. Cohen & West, London.

Mead, George Herbert, 1932: *The Philosophy of the Present.* Open Court Publishing Co., Chicago.

Mead, George Herbert, 1934: *Mind, Self and Society.* University of Chicago Press, Chicago.

Mead, George Herbert, 1936: *Movements of Thought in the Nineteenth Century.* University of Chicago Press, Chicago.

Mead, George Herbert, 1938: *The Philosophy of the Act.* University of Chicago Press, Chicago.

Mennell, Stephen J., 1969: Prohibition: A Sociological View. *Journal of American Studies,* **3,** 2, 159–75.

Merton, Robert K., 1936: The Unanticipated Consequences of Purposive Social Action. *American Sociological Review,* **1,** 6, 894–904.

Merton, Robert K., 1957: The Role-set: Problems in Sociological Theory. *British Journal of Sociology,* **8,** 2, 106–20.

Merton, Robert K., 1968: *Social Theory and Social Structure,* enlarged edition. Free Press, New York.

Mill, John Stuart, 1843: *A System of Logic.* Parker, London.

Mills, C. Wright, 1956: *The Power Elite.* Oxford University Press, New York.

Mishan, E. J., 1960: A Survey of Welfare Economics, 1939–1959. *Economic Journal,* **70,** 2, 197–265.

Murphy, Robert F., 1963: On Zen Marxism: Filiation and Alliance. *Man,* **63,** 1, 17–19.

Murphy, Robert F., 1971: *The Dialectics of Social Life: Alarms and Excursions in Anthropological Theory.* Basic Books, New York.

Nadel, S. F., 1957: *The Theory of Social Structure.* Cohen & West, London.

Nagel, Ernest, 1956: A Formalization of Functionalism. In *Logic Without Metaphysics,* pp. 247–83. Free Press, New York.

Nettler, Gwynn, 1957: A Measure of Alienation. *American Sociological Review*, **22,** 6, 670–77.

Neumann, John von, and **Oscar Morgenstern,** 1944: *Theory of Games and Economic Behaviour*. Princeton University Press, Princeton, N.J.

Nichols, Theo., 1969: *Ownership, Control and Ideology*. George Allen & Unwin, London.

Olsen, Marvin E., 1968: *The Process of Social Organization*. Holt, Rinehart & Winston, New York.

Olson, Mancur, 1965: *The Logic of Collective Action*. Harvard University Press, Cambridge, Mass.

O'Neill, John, 1970: *Perception, Expression and History: The Social Phenomenology of Maurice Merleau-Ponty*. Northwestern University Press, Evanston, Ill.

O'Neill, John, 1972: *Sociology as a Skin Trade*. Heinemann, London.

O'Neill, John, ed., 1973: *Modes of Individualism and Collectivism*. Heinemann, London.

Parsons, Talcott, 1937: *The Structure of Social Action*. McGraw-Hill, New York.

Parsons, Talcott, 1951: *The Social System*. Free Press, New York.

Parsons, Talcott, 1960: Pattern Variables Revisited: A Response to Robert Dubin. *American Sociological Review*, **25,** 4, 467–83.

Parsons, Talcott, 1961: An Outline of the Social System. In *Theories of Society* (T. Parsons, E. A. Shils, K. D. Naegele, and J. R. Pitts, eds.), pp. 30–79. Free Press, New York.

Parsons, Talcott, 1964: Evolutionary Universals in Society. *American Sociological Review*, **29,** 3, 339–57.

Parsons, Talcott, 1966: *Societies: Evolutionary and Comparative Perspectives*. Prentice-Hall, Englewood Cliffs, N.J.

Parsons, Talcott, 1969: *Politics and Social Structure*. Free Press, New York.

Parsons, Talcott, 1971: *The System of Modern Societies*. Prentice-Hall, Englewood Cliffs, N.J.

Parsons, Talcott, and **Robert F. Bales,** 1955: *Family, Socialization and Interaction Process*. Free Press, Glencoe, Ill.

Parsons, Talcott, R. F. Bales and **E. A. Shils**, 1953: *Working Papers in the Theory of Action*. Free Press, New York.

Parsons, Talcott, and **E. A. Shils,** eds., 1951: *Toward a General Theory of Action*. Harvard University Press, Cambridge, Mass.

Parsons, Talcott, and **N. J. Smelser,** 1956: *Economy and Society*, Free Press, New York.

Reddaway, W. B., 1964 (orig. 1936): Review of J. M. Keynes's *The General Theory of Employment, Interest and Money*. In *Keynes's General Theory:*

Reports of Three Decades (R. Lekachman, ed.), pp. 99–108. Macmillan, London.

Redfield, Robert, 1930: *Tepoztlán, A Mexican Village.* University of Chicago Press, Chicago.

Redfield, Robert, 1962 (orig. 1942): The Folk Society. In *Human Nature and the Study of Society* (M. P. Redfield, ed.), pp. 231–53. University of Chicago Press, Chicago.

Riesman, David, with **Nathan Glazer** and **Reuel Denney,** 1950: *The Lonely Crowd.* Yale University Press, New Haven.

Roethlisberger, F. J., and **W. J. Dickson,** 1939: *Management and the Worker.* Harvard University Press, Cambridge, Mass.

Rose, Arnold M., ed., 1962: *Human Behaviour and Social Processes.* Houghton Mifflin, Boston.

Rudner, Richard S., 1966: *Philosophy of Social Science.* Prentice-Hall, Englewood Cliffs, N.J.

Runciman, W. G., 1966: *Relative Deprivation and Social Justice.* Routledge & Kegan Paul, London.

Runciman, W. G., 1970: *Sociology in its Place and Other Essays.* Cambridge University Press, Cambridge.

Samuelson, Paul A., 1961: *Economics: An Introductory Analysis,* 5th ed. McGraw-Hill, New York.

Schacht, Richard L., 1971: *Alienation.* George Allen & Unwin, London.

Schutz, Alfred, 1962: *Collected Papers* I: *The Problem of Social Reality.* Martinus Nijhoff, The Hague.

Schutz, Alfred, 1964: *Collected Papers* II: *Studies in Social Theory.* Martinus Nijhoff, The Hague.

Schutz, Alfred, 1966: *Collected Papers* III: *Studies in Phenomenological Philosophy.* Martinus Nijhoff, The Hague.

Schutz, Alfred, 1972 (orig. 1932): *The Phenomenology of the Social World,* trans. by G. Walsh and F. Lehnert. Heinemann, London. (Published in U.S.A. by Northwestern University Press, Evanston, Ill., 1967.)

Scott, J. Finley, 1963: The Changing Foundations of the Parsonian Action Scheme. *American Sociological Review,* **28,** 5, 716–35.

Seeman, Melvin, 1959: On the Meaning of Alienation. *American Sociological Review,* **24,** 6, 783–91.

Shaw, Clifford R., 1930: *The Jack-Roller: A Delinquent Boy's Own Story.* Chicago University Press, Chicago.

Shaw, Clifford R., with the collaboration of **H. D. MacKay, F. Zorbaugh** and **L. S. Cottrell,** 1929: *Delinquency Areas.* Chicago University Press, Chicago.

Shils, Edward A., 1961: Centre and Periphery. In *The Logic of Personal Knowledge: Essays Presented to Michael Polanyi,* pp. 117–30. Routledge & Kegan Paul, London.

Simmel, Georg, 1950 (orig. 1908): *The Sociology of Georg Simmel,* trans. by K. H. Wolff. Free Press, Glencoe, Ill.

Simmel, Georg, 1955 (orig. 1908): *'Conflict' and 'The Web of Group Affiliations'*, translated by K. H. Wolff and R. Bendix. Free Press, Glencoe, Ill.
Skinner, B. F., 1953: *Science and Human Behaviour.* Macmillan, New York.
Skinner, B. F., 1957: *Verbal Behaviour.* Appleton-Century-Crofts, New York.
Skinner, B. F., 1972: *Beyond Freedom and Dignity.* Knopff, New York.
Sklair, Leslie, 1970: The Fate of the 'Functional Requisites' in Parsonian Sociology. *British Journal of Sociology,* **21,** 1, 30–42.
Smith, Adam, 1970 (orig. 1776): *An Inquiry into the Nature and Causes of the Wealth of Nations.* Penguin Books, Harmondsworth.
Smelser, Neil J., 1959: *Social Change in the Industrial Revolution.* Routledge & Kegan Paul, London.
Sombart, Werner, 1906: *Warum gibt es in den Vereinigten Staaten keinen Sozialismus?* J. C. B. Mohr, Tübingen.
Sorokin, Pitirim A., 1937: *Social and Cultural Dynamics,* vol. I. George Allen & Unwin, London.
Sperlich, Peter W., 1971: *Conflict and Harmony in Human Affairs: A Study of Cross-pressures and Political Behaviour.* Rand McNally, Chicago.
Srole, Leo, 1956: Social Integration and Certain Corollaries: An Exploratory Study. *American Sociological Review,* **21,** 6, 709–16.
Stone, Gregory, P., and **Harvey A. Farberman,** 1967: On the Edge of Rapprochement: Was Durkheim moving toward the Perspective of Symbolic Interaction? *Sociological Quarterly,* **8,** 2, 149–64.
Stouffer, Samuel A., 1949: An Analysis of Conflicting Social Norms. *American Sociological Review,* **14,** 6, 707–17.
Stouffer, Samuel A., and **Jackson, Toby,** 1951: Role Conflict and Personality. *American Journal of Sociology,* **61,** 5, 395–406.
Strauss, Anselm, 1959: *Mirrors and Masks.* Free Press, Glencoe, Ill.
Strauss, Anselm, 1964: Introduction to *George Herbert Mead on Social Psychology,* revised edition. Chicago University Press, Chicago.
Sutherland, E. H., 1947: *Principles of Criminology,* 4th edition. Lippincott, Philadelphia.
Suttles, Gerald D., 1972: *The Social Construction of Communities.* Chicago University Press, Chicago.

Thibaut, J. W., and **H. H. Kelley,** 1959: *The Social Psychology of Groups.* Wiley, New York.
Thomas, W. I., and **F. Znaniecki,** 1918–20: *The Polish Peasant in Europe and America,* 5 vols. Chicago University Press. Chicago,
Thrasher, Frederick M., 1926: *The Gang.* University of Chicago Press, Chicago.
Tiryakian, Edward A., 1965: Existential Phenomenology and the Sociological Tradition. *American Sociological Review,* **30,** 5, 674–88.
Turner, Ralph H., 1962: Role-taking: Process Versus Conformity. In *Human Behaviour and Social Processes* (A. M. Rose, ed.), pp. 20–40. Houghton Mifflin, Boston.

Vinacke, W. E., and **A. Arkoff,** 1957: An Experimental Study of Coalitions in the Triad. *American Sociological Review*, **22,** 4, 406–14.

Wagner, Helmut R., 1964: Displacement of Scope: a problem of the relationship between small-scale and large-scale sociological theories. *American Journal of Sociology*, **69,** 6, 571–84.

Weber, Max, 1930 (orig. 1904–5): *The Protestant Ethic and the Spirit of Capitalism*, trans. by Talcott Parsons. George Allen & Unwin, London.

Weber, Max, 1968 (orig. 1922): *Economy and Society*, 3 vols. Bedminster Press, New York.

Whorf, Benjamin Lee, 1956: *Language, Thought and Reality* (J. B. Carroll, ed.). Wiley, New York.

Winch, Peter, 1958: *The Idea of a Social Science*. Routledge & Kegan Paul, London.

Winch, Peter, 1964: Understanding a Primitive Society. *American Philosophical Quarterly*, **1,** 4, 307–24.

Wirth, Louis, 1938: *The Ghetto*. Chicago University Press, Chicago.

Witkin, Robert W., 1971: Social Action and Subcultural Theories: A Critique. In *Crime and Delinquency in Britain* (W. G. Carson and P. Wiles, eds.), pp. 153–63. Martin Robertson, London.

Wittgenstein, Ludwig, 1953: *Philosophical Investigations*, trans. by G. E. M. Anscombe. Basil Blackwell, Oxford.

Wolff, Kurt H., ed., 1960: *Essays on Sociology and Philosophy by Emile Durkheim et al.* Harper & Row, New York.

Woodward, Joan, 1958: *Management and Technology*. Her Majesty's Stationery Office, London.

Wrong, Dennis H., 1961: The Oversocialized Conception of Man in Modern Sociology. *American Sociological Review*, **26,** 2, 183–93.

Zorbaugh, H. W., 1929: *The Gold Coast and the Slum*. Chicago University Press, Chicago.

Index

Aberle, D. F., *et al.* 150–151, 153
Adorno, Theodor W., *et al.* 34
Affectual Action 24–25
'AGIL' Schema 151–153, 161
Alchian, A. A. 37n
Alienation 121–123
Anderson, Nels 38n
Andreski, Stanislav 3, 61
Anomie 51, 121–123
Aristotle 147
Arkoff, A. 90n
Arrow, Kenneth J. 139n
Austin, J. L. 58
Authority 104–106

Bales, Robert F. 89n, 151
Barton, Allen H. 116
'Because' Motive 24
Becker, Gary S. 37n
Becker, Howard S. 33
Behaviourism 4, 8–13, 22, 29–30, 33, 37n, 59
Behaviourism, Social *see* Symbolic Interactionism
Benne, K. D. 89n
Berger, Peter 46, 50–51, 52
Berghe, Pierre L. van den 127, 166n
Bierstedt, Robert 103
'Biographical Situation' 46
Blain, Robert R. 118
Blalock, Hubert M. Jr. 102, 114n, 143–145
Blau, Peter M. 78, 93–102, 114n, 127–128
Blauner, Robert 123
Blumer, Herbert 14
Bott, Elizabeth 87
Brodbeck, May 6n
Brown, Roger 34, 41
Buckley, Walter 161
Bureaucracy 25
Burgess, Ernest W. 32
Burgess, R. L. 9
Bushell, D. 9

Cancian, Francesca 160
Cannon, W. B. 159–160
Caplow, Theodore 90n
Catton, William R. 141
Causal Analysis 141ff.
'Chicago School' 14, 30, 31–33, 36n, 38n
Chomsky, Noam 9, 15, 36n, 53, 68n
Cicourel, Aaron V. 51ff, 68n
'Citizenship' 137
Class 107, 131ff
Cloward, Richard A. 31
Cohen, Percy S. 23, 266n
Coleman, James S. 115n, 139n
Collectivities 124–125
Colonialism 160n
'Commonsense World' 46ff
Composition, Fallacy of 170
Comte, Auguste 21, 36n
Consensus 4, 120–121, 123–128, 142, 158–159
Conflict 4, 120, 121, 128–131
Conscience collective 18, 20
Converse, Philip 127
Cooley, Charles Horton 13–14, 27, 68n, 128
Coser, Lewis A. 128ff, 139n, 142
Cross-pressures 130–131
Culture 17, 28, 30, 34
Cybernetics 30, 159–161

Dahl, Robert A. 112–114
Dahrendorf, Ralf 2, 3, 132–138, 140n
Darwin, Charles 26, 164
Davis, James C. 140n
Davis, Kingsley 142, 153–154, 157, 162
Dawe, Alan 3
Day, Willard F. 68n
Decisions, Collective 119–120
'Decomposition of Capital' 136–137

'Decomposition of Labour' 136
Demerath, N. J. III 165n
Denzin, Norman K. 52
Determinism 5, 8, 12–13, 36
Deutsch, Karl 146
Deviant behaviour 30–33
Dewey, John 13, 22
Dickson, W. J. 78, 123
Differential Association Theory 32–33
Diffusionism 147–148
Division of Labour 117–119
Douglas, Jack D. 51ff, 126
Dubin, Robert 89n
Durkheim, Emile 18–22, 27, 28, 30, 34, 40–41, 56, 62, 118, 121–123, 139n, 147, 156
Dyads 73, 81, 87
Dysfunctions 155, 169

Economic Theory 5, 24, 58
Elias, Norbert 7, 16, 29, 37n, 42, 54, 76, 82–87, 90n, 118
Elites 107–108, 158–159
'Emics' and 'Etics' 43–45
Emmet, Dorothy 57
Engels, Friedrich 143
Equilibrium assumption 146
Ethnomethodology 51–61, 62, 70, 77
Etzioni, Amitai 161
Evolutionary theory 26–27, 147–148, 161–164
Exchange theory 93–102, 120

'Free Will' problem 5, 8, 12–13, 36
Farberman, Harvey A. 22
Faris, Robert E. L. 36n
Feuer, Lewis 42–43
Filmer, Paul, *et al.* 54, 60
Fletcher, Ronald 6n, 13, 23, 37n
Freud, Sigmund 29
Franklin, Benjamin 25, 169
Frazer, Sir James 63
Frazier, E. Franklin 38n
Friedrichs, Robert W. 166n
Fromm, Erich 121
Functionalism 5, 141–165, 169
Functional Alternatives, Equivalents 156
Functional Exigencies, Imperatives, Prerequisites 149–152, 155, 163–164, 165

Galbraith, John Kenneth 80
Garfinkel, Harold 51ff
Gellner, Ernest 59–60
Gemeinschaft/Gesellschaft 74, 118–119
Generalised Other 17
Germani, Gino 26
Giddens, Anthony H. 20, 36n, 115n
Gidlow, Bob 52
Glaser, Daniel 38n
Gluckman, Max 142
Goal-directed Systems 146–147, 159–161
Goffman, Erving 38n, 52, 70–71, 93
Goldthorpe, John H. 68n, 138, 167n
Gouldner, Alvin W. 52, 126, 127, 166n
'Grand Theory' 4
Gross, Neal 79–80

Habitual Action 25–26, 127
Harris, Marvin 21, 43–44, 68n, 69n, 132, 166n
Heath, Anthony 99, 114n
Henderson, Lawrence J. 159–160
Hinkle, Roscoe C. 27, 37n
Hobbes, Thomas 7, 116
Holism 6n
Homans, George C. 4, 7, 36n, 78, 93, 99, 101, 102, 114n, 153
Horan, Patrick 131
Horton, John 122
Huaco, George A. 166n
Husserl, Edmund 45

Ideal-types 25, 47
'Indexicality' 53
'Individual' and 'Society' 1–2, 7–8
Inner Mental States, Evidence of 9, 12, 21, 22, 36
'In-order-to' motive 24
Institutionalisation 26, 30, 75, 76–78
Internalisation 29

Jakobsen, Roman 62
James, William 13, 22, 27, 45, 127

Kant, Immanuel 45
Kelley, H. H. 93
Kemper, Theodore D. 118
Kerr, Clark 156
Keynes, John Maynard 145
Kissin, S. F. 140n

Kluckhohn, Clyde 155, 171
Koestler, Arthur 129
Kuhn, Thomas S. 3

Laing, R. D. 47–48, 68n
Language 11–13, 15–16, 20, 40–45
Latent Functions 157, 169, 171
Leach, Edmund R. 61, 62, 67, 69n, 166n
Lenneberg, E. H. 36n
Lévi-Strauss, Claude 5, 61–67, 68–69n
Levy, Marion J. Jr. 142
Lewis, Oscar 63
Lipset, Seymour M. 34, 126, 137
Linton, Ralph 72–73, 76–78, 80
Lockwood, David 136, 138, 142
Lopreato, Joseph 140n
Lorenz, Konrad 167n
Louch, A.R. 58
Lowie, Robert 166
Luckmann, Thomas 46, 50–51
Lukes, Steven 21, 122
Lyons, John 36n

Macaulay, Thomas Babington 4, 101
McClosky, Herbert 123
McEachern, Alexander 79–80
McHugh, Peter 51, 52
MacIntyre, Alasdair C. 57
McKenzie, Roderick 32
Machlup, Fritz 146
Malinowski, Bronislaw 127, 147–149, 161
Manifest Functions 157
Mann, Michael 126, 127
Mao Tse-tung 104
Marcuse, Herbert 139n
Maris, Ronald 99
Marshall, Alfred 28, 37n, 101
Marshall, T. H. 137
Marx, Karl 104, 121–122, 129, 131–133, 135–138, 139–140n, 142–143
Mason, Ward S. 79–80
Mauss, Marcel 40–41, 62, 127
Mead, George Herbert 13–18, 22, 27, 28, 30, 34, 36n, 45, 72, 76–78, 159
Mechanical solidarity 118
Mennell, Stephen J. 169
Merleau-Ponty, Maurice 68n
Merton, Robert K. 2, 4, 30–31, 80, 123, 154–156, 157, 160, 168–169
Metatheory 1–2
Methodological Individualism 4, 6n
Middle-range theories 2
Mill, James 101
Mill, John Stuart 13
Mills, C. Wright 107
Mishan, E. J. 139n
Mobility, Social 138
Money 109–110
Morgenstern, Oscar 90n
Moore, Wilbert E. 142, 153–154, 157, 161
Multiple Realities 48
Murphy, Robert F. 37n, 39, 61, 63, 69n, 171

Nadel, S. F. 90n
Nagel, Ernest 160
'Natural Attitude' 46
Nettler, Gwyn 123
Networks, Social 8, 118–119
Neumann, John von 90n
Nichols, Theo. 136
Norms 123–127

Ohlin, Lloyd E. 31
Olsen, Marvin 91
Olson, Mancur 139n
O'Neill, John 6n, 68n
Organic solidarity 118

Paradigms, scientific 3
Para-theory 2
Pareto, Vilfredo 37n
Parsons, Talcott 21, 27–30, 37n, 54, 73–76, 89n, 101, 107–112, 115n, 124–128, 141–142, 151–153, 158, 160, 161, 162
Parties 107
Pattern Variables 73–74
Personality 30, 34
Petersen, R. A. 165n
Phenomenology 5, 9, 45ff
Phillipson, Michael 54 (*also see* Filmer, Paul, *et al.*)
Piaget, Jean 30, 41
Positivism 21, 36–37n
Pragmatism 13
Protestant ethic 25

Psychology, relation to sociology 1–2, 7–9, 18–20, 22, 33–34
Purposeful action 8, 12–13, 15, 22, 159

Quasi-groups 132, 136–137

Radcliffe-Brown, A. R. 147–149, 161
'Reciprocity of Perspectives' 46
Reddaway, W. B. 145–146
Redfield, Robert 63
Reference groups 2
Relative deprivation 2, 140n
Représentations collectives 18, 22
Ricardo, David 133
Riesman, David 103
Roethlisberger, F. J. 78, 123
Role Conflict 78–79
Roles 2, 71–82, 124–125
Role-sets 79–81
Rose, Arnold M. 17, 32, 38n
Runciman, W. G. 106, 140n, 160–161

Sacks, Harvey 51, 53
St Simon, Henri Comte de 21
Samuelson, Paul A. 114n, 140n, 169
Sapir, Edward 40
Sapir-Whorf Hypothesis 40–43, 55, 58, 68n
Schaar, John 123
Schacht, Richard 121, 122, 139n
Schutz, Alfred 23, 24, 45–51, 52, 56–58, 62, 68n, 158
Scott, John Finley 28
Seeman, Melvin, 123
Self 14, 15–16
Self-contradicting prophecy 169–170
Self-fulfilling prophecy 169–170
Shaw, Clifford R. 32, 33
Sheats, P. 89
Shils, Edward A. 28, 73–76, 89n, 125, 151
Silverman, David *see* Filmer, Paul, *et al.*
Simmel, Georg 71, 81, 90n, 114n, 128ff
Skinner, B. F. 9–11, 14, 33
Sklair, Leslie 166n
Smelser, Neil J. 142, 153
Smith, Adam 117
Sombart, Werner 138
Sorokin, Pitirim A. 166n
Spencer, Herbert 147, 162
Sperlich, Peter W. 131
Srole, Leo 123
Status-groups 107
Stone, Gregory P. 22
Stouffer, Samuel A. 79
Stratification, functional theory of 153–154
Strauss, Anselm 17, 38n
Structural-functionalism *see* Functionalism
Structuralism 61–67, 166n
Subconscious motivation 25
Subcultures 31–33
Super-ego 29
Sutherland, Edwin H. 31, 32–33
Suttles, Gerald D. 32
Symbolic Interactionism 9, 13–18, 28
Symbols, Significant 15, 22
Systems 141ff

Teleological Systems *see* Goal-directed Systems
Teleology 156–157, 165
Thibaut, J. W. 93
Thomas, William Isaac 13, 23, 27, 38n, 170
Thrasher, Frederick M. 32
Tiryakian, Edward A. 13, 68n
Toby, Jackson 79
Toennies, Ferdinand 74, 118
Tolman, E. C. 28
Traditional Action 24–26
Triads 81, 87
Turner, Ralph 71–72, 75
Typification 47

Uncertainty 26–27
Unintended Consequences 168–171

Values 124–128
Verstehen 23
Vinacke, W. Edgar 90n
Voluntaristic theory of action 27–30

Wagner, Helmut R. 68n
Walsh, David *see* Filmer, Paul, *et al.*
Weber, Max 22–27, 28, 30, 36n, 45, 47, 91, 102, 104–107, 133–135, 164–165

Whorf, Benjamin Lee 40, 41–42 (*see also* Sapir-Whorf Hypothesis)
Winch, Peter 58
Wirth, Louis 38n
Witkin, Robert W. 38n
Wittgensteinian philosophy 58–61
Wolff, Kurt H. 37n
Woodward, Joan 162–164
Wrong, Dennis H. 29, 54

Zero-sum conception of power 107–109
Znaniecki, Florian 38n
Zorbaugh, H. W. 38n